THE CULTIVATION OF CONFORMITY

This book explores the inter-relationship between religious groups and wider society and examines the way religious groups change in relation to societal norms, potentially to the point of undergoing processes of 'internal secularisation' within secular and secularist cultures. Received sociological wisdom suggests that over time religious groups moderate their claims. This comes with the potential loss of new adherents, for theorists of secularisation suggest unique or universal, rather than moderate, truth claims appear attractive to would-be recruits. At the same time, religious groups need to appear equivalent, in terms of harmlessness, to state-sanctioned religious expression in order to secure rights. Thus, religious organisations face a perpetual conundrum. Using British Quakers as a case study as they moved from a counter-cultural group to an accepted and accepting part of twentieth- and twenty-first-century society, the author builds on models of religion and non-religion in terms of flows and explores the consequences of religious assimilation when the process of constructing both distinctive appeal and 'harmlessness' in pursuit of rights is played out in a secular culture. A major contribution to the sociology of religion, *The Cultivation of Conformity* presents a new theory of internal secularisation as the ultimate stage of the cultivation of conformity, and a model of the way sects and society inter-relate.

'Ben' Pink Dandelion directs the work of the Centre for Research in Quaker Studies, and is Professor of Quaker Studies at the University of Birmingham and Research Fellow at Lancaster University, UK. He has published widely in Quakerism and the sociology of religion. He is the author of *A Sociological Analysis of the Theology of Quakers*; *The Liturgies of Quakerism*; *An Introduction to Quakerism*; *The Quakers: A Very Short Introduction*; and *Making our Connections: The Spirituality of Travel*, and co-author of *Heaven on Earth: Quakers and the Second Coming*; and *Towards Tragedy/Reclaiming Hope*. He is the editor of *The Creation of Quaker Theory: Insider Perspectives*, and the co-editor of *The Historical Dictionary of Friends (Quakers)*; *The A–Z of Friends (Quakers)*; *Good and Evil: Quaker Perspectives*; *The Quaker Condition: The Sociology of a Liberal Religion*; *Religion and Youth*; *The Oxford Handbook of Quaker Studies*; and *Early Quakers and their Theological Thought 1647–1723*.

THE CULTIVATION OF CONFORMITY

Towards a General Theory of Internal Secularisation

Pink Dandelion

Routledge
Taylor & Francis Group

LONDON AND NEW YORK

First published 2019
by Routledge
2 Park Square, Milton Park, Abingdon, Oxon OX14 4RN

and by Routledge
52 Vanderbilt Avenue, New York, NY 10017

Routledge is an imprint of the Taylor & Francis Group, an informa business

© 2019 Pink Dandelion

British Library Cataloguing in Publication Data
A catalogue record for this book is available from the British Library

Library of Congress Cataloging-in-Publication Data
A catalogue record has been requested for this book

ISBN: 978-1-138-74014-3 (hbk)
ISBN: 978-1-138-74019-8 (pbk)
ISBN: 978-1-315-18368-8 (ebk)

Typeset in Times New Roman
by Taylor & Francis Books
Printed by CPI Group (UK) Ltd, Croydon CR0 4YY

CONTENTS

LIST OF ILLUSTRATIONS

INTRODUCTION

This book is about the inter-relationship between religious groups and wider society and about the way religious groups change in relation to societal norms, potentially to the point of undergoing processes of 'internal secularisation' within secular and secularist cultures. This topic is of critical interest, both academically and generally, as the future role and nature of religion appears so unclear. A debate waxes in the sociology of religion about the degree to which popular religion is dying, particularly in the European north and potentially also in North America, whilst other scholars chart how the apparatus of the secularist State controls and limits what it decides is appropriate and inappropriate religious expression. Received sociological wisdom on sects and denominations suggests that over time religious groups moderate their claims. This comes with the potential loss of new adherents, for theorists of secularisation suggest religious groups require unique or universal truth claims to appear attractive to would-be recruits. At the same time, religious groups need to appear equivalent, in terms of harmlessness, to State-sanctioned religious expression in order to secure rights.

I revisit sect/denomination theories to show how the nature of this relationship is more complex than has been suggested and need not be uni-directional. I also suggest that neither 'religious groups' nor 'wider society' are single or static entities: religious groups comprise organisational and popular elements and 'wider society' can be divided into the State, and popular culture. Each of these four elements is in constant negotiation with the others to define the nature of the relationship between any given religious group and its host culture. Degrees of assimilation are dependent on the position of each of these elements.

Given this constant dynamic, the relationship between religious groups and wider culture can become turbulent at any point in time. Building on Thomas Tweed's work on religion as 'confluences and flows' and borrowing from A. K. M. Fazle Hussain's work on fluid dynamics, I develop a theory of this dynamic inter-relationship in terms of times of 'coherent motion' and 'incoherent motion' or coherent and incoherent flow between religion and non-religion.

I use the Quakers as a case study: this group is particularly interesting as after centuries of sectarian sensibility it has more recently defied easy classification in terms of sectarian or denominational form, and in its 'Liberal' form has appeared to be hybrid or 'fluid' in the ways it currently operates. Its present emphasis on continuing revelation highlights continual processes of change within the group and it has been defined as a version of a 'liquid religion'. Its non-doctrinal nature is particularly interesting in terms of assimilation within, say, secular British culture, and the book ends with a general theory of 'internal secularisation', the way in which a religious group loses an explicit religious identity. In other words, in spite of the constant dynamic negotiation between religious expression and wider culture, certain conditions lead religious groups to assimilate within a secular host environment.

I suggest further that this process is led by popular religious expression over and against more conservative and conformist organisational forms. Indeed it is 'on the street' as it were, through linguistic expression in particular, that 'internal secularisation' is nurtured and refined as religious adherents, through the desire to minimise linguistic dissimilarity with those they encounter, find non-religious language to express their spiritual insights and identities. These popular forms of expression then find their way back into the organisational environment, a process accelerated within a non-doctrinal setting such as the Quakers in Britain. At the end of the book, then, I suggest that religious groups allow the cultivation of conformity to wider society, that they accommodate their own 'internal secularisation', even if it theoretically diminishes the potential for recruitment and survival. However, in the Quaker case the non-doctrinal form masks religious truth claims so that values and social action, even when expressed in secular terms, can act as continuing points of attraction to the group. In this way, religion transmutes into new forms within, behind and beyond traditional identities.

The Quakers

The book uses British Quakers as case study. This is a fascinating group in its multiple emphases over time. It began as a highly counter-cultural and highly successful apocalyptic movement in the 1650s (during the republic) in the north-west of England. Their foundational belief was in the possibility for all of a direct and salvific encounter with God through an inward experience of 'Christ come again', an interiorised and spiritualised second coming. Everything 'outward' was cast as 'inauthentic' including outward sacraments, a separated priesthood, church buildings, and the Christian calendar. Once saved and transformed, the experience of intimacy with the divine was continual and every place and every time was equally sacred. Their universal soteriology led to a belief in the spiritual equality of all, a priesthood of all believers, and a concept of 'the free ministry' in which everyone was considered a minister (men, women and children). In turn this led to the adoption of an 'open' or 'unprogrammed' form of worship based on silence and stillness to nurture the mystical connection in which anyone might be 'given' a contribution. It was a charismatic mysticism in which absence gave its adherents a sense of 'presence'. It was a movement convinced that it represented the true church, the model of how religion as to be settled and 'the world', a pejorative term for the apostate, included all that was not Quaker. This experience of 'encounter' also led to a very particular lifestyle. Quakers refused to follow the rules of basic etiquette, refusing to doff their hats in greeting or take them off at all except when someone was in prayer. They refused to use the polite and deferential 'you' form to social superiors, rather levelling society down by using 'thee' and 'thou' to everyone. Titles were eschewed. Days of the week and months were numbered rather than names to avoid the pagan-derived nomenclature. Quakers would not pay tithes nor swear an oath following the injunction in Matthew to 'swear not at all' (5:34). They refused to support outward war but instead waged 'the Lamb's War' feeling themselves to be living at the end of the biblical timeline creating the new Jerusalem as described in the book of Revelation. They were the most successful sect of the 1650s and one which may have appeared as the most threatening, preaching as they did the equality of all.

Within a decade, the expression of Quaker faith had changed. The restoration of the monarchy and the introduction of a variety of government Acts to outlaw nonconformists and Quakers in particular encouraged a more pragmatic style, and even as early as 1658 we can find evidence of a desire to self-legitimise and to seek rights as one group equivalent to others. In 1661, following the Fifth Monarchist armed uprising in London, 4,200 Quakers were imprisoned as a preventative measure. Leading Quakers then presented a statement to Charles II declaring that they were harmless and not to be feared, claiming 'we utterly deny all outward wars'. Whilst the Quakers of today sometimes herald this statement as the corporate confirmation of the position against war, it also symbolises the end of a prophetic emphasis and the start of a more reconciliatory position between Quakers and the State.

Throughout the 1660s, 1670s and 1680s, Quakers were heavily persecuted in Britain and many left for the new world, particularly prompted by William Penn's 'Holy Experiment' in Quaker-controlled Pennsylvania after 1681. Quakers organised themselves into autonomous 'Yearly Meetings' covering distinct geographical areas: British Quakers were known as London Yearly Meeting until 1994, thereafter Britain Yearly Meeting. In Weberian terms, a rational-legal authority structure replaced a charismatic one. Relief from persecution arrived with the Act of Toleration in 1689 and the Affirmation Act in 1694. Although Quakers still appeared in court through the eighteenth century for non-payment of tithes, other Quakers acted as churchwardens, those responsible for collecting the tithes (Dixon 2007).

From 1689 then, Quakers become an acceptable part of the British religious landscape and the rights afforded them tended to mirror those given
to all nonconformists. The Marriage Act of 1753 allowed Quakers and
Jews to marry according to their own traditions but it was in 1832 that
Quakers along with all nonconformists could enter Parliament and in 1871
Quakers could work at Oxford and Cambridge, universities previously
reserved for Anglicans. In 1871, then, Quakers became full citizens. In terms
of their relations with the State, only the introduction of conscription in
March 1916 forced Quakers to have to decide between obedience to Government or Quaker tradition. Even at this point, the work of Quaker MPs
ensured a form of conscientious objection. War and the preparation for war
remained, however, the one issue most likely to provoke Quaker dissent.

In terms of wider culture, attitudes to the public, Quakers had also relaxed
their rhetoric over time. The 'peculiarities' of dress and speech, and other
forms of lifestyle (e.g. selling at fixed prices, eschewing gravestones and other
forms of vanity, avoiding the arts so as not to allow the imagination to
redirect one's piety) were maintained with vigour (in the face of increasing
dissent) throughout the eighteenth century. Quakers were only allowed to
marry other Quakers (endogamy). In the nineteenth century, however, a new
evangelical spirit and ecumenical partnerships against slavery and in Bible
societies made it increasingly difficult to continue to see all non-Quakers
purely in terms of 'the world'. By 1861, the prohibition of gravestones, marrying a non-Quaker and wearing clothes other than the Quaker uniform and
using the term 'you' had all become sanctioned options.

These changes reflect in part internal theological dispositions but they also
mark a changing relationship with wider culture and the end of successive
ideas of the world as something fallen to be replaced, and the world as
something corrupt and corrupting to be feared. A renewed interest in mission,
largely absent from Quakerism in the eighteenth century, was set alongside,
rather than in opposition to, the efforts of other Christians.

Thus at an organisational level, Quakers by 1900 were seeing themselves
and being seen as equivalent to other nonconformists and other citizens of
the State in general, a legitimate part of the religious landscape and at ease
with government and wider public in general terms. At a popular level
within the Quaker group, this position had been reached by some well ahead
of the corporate position and held by others to have gone too far. Schism in
the nineteenth century, first in 1835 by some evangelical Quakers called the
'Beaconites' and then in 1868 by conservative Quakers based at Fritchley in
Derbyshire, symbolised respectively those keen to move beyond sectarianism
and those keen to maintain it.

In the twentieth century, British Quakers adopted a new theological emphasis,
that of a liberal Quaker theology. It emphasised religious experience as primary
(over the biblical authority given greater weight in the nineteenth century) as well
as continuing revelation. Doctrine became diverse and individuated and

organisational religion became increasingly identified with form, the way in which Quakers were Quaker, rather than the particularities of theology. 'Seeking' became the dominant mode of belief and theology became an ongoing individual exercise of the interpretation of religious experience. The silent form of worship accommodates both theological change and theological diversity in the way it masked the detail of any one adherent's views. The end of endogamy spelt the end of dynastic Quakerism and by 2000, around 88% of Quakers were adult converts even whilst the mission work of the nineteenth century had been replaced by 'service' work in the twentieth.

Thus by the twenty-first century Quakers in Britain, liberal in theology and political outlook, could be seen to be part of mainstream religious expression, accepted by State and public as equivalent and, as per the 1661 declaration, 'harmless'. Overall numbers of members have fallen since 1942 and in an accelerated fashion since 1990 and yet the percentage of converts remains high. From a sociological perspective, Quakers are both declining in line with other liberal groups, as per the advocates of the secularisation thesis, and yet maintaining a distinctive worship style, attitude to theology, and position on war that continues to draw new participants. In this way, and with this rich history of change, they form the perfect case study group to try and map the way in which religious groups interact with the State and with wider culture along an axis of non-conformity and conformity over time, as well as how a popular impulse towards conformity can play out in a non-doctrinal group in a secular culture.

What we find is a dynamic relationship between church and State in which rights and freedoms are traded and contested over time, nevertheless resulting in general and slow institutional trend towards the lure that harmonious or concordant relationships with the State and wider culture brings. We also find the popular impulse towards the benefits of coherence driving institutional change (in a group without fixed hierarchies) and ultimately managing institutional religious expression in new ways.

The outline of the book

Thomas Tweed has talked of theory in terms of travel or itinerance: theory, he suggests, can be seen in terms of each of (a) a record of where we have been, (b) the journey itself, and (c) proposed new routes (2006: 11). This book represents such a situated and personal 'purposeful wandering' (Tweed 2011:13) and purposeful musing along the way, attempting to look at the surroundings in new ways, redraw maps and suggest new avenues to be explored.

This book is in three parts, matching the trichotomy that Tweed suggests. The first part maps existing theory and considers the theorisation of how religion sits within secular society and how forms of religious life routinely change over time. It maps the route. The second part is an account of the journey. It uses Quakers as a case study to show the complexity of relationships between religious groups and wider society and introduces a new model of how the two inter-relate. Part III suggests new sightings and new routes or, rather, fresh theoretical itineraries for the study of religion drawn from an exploration of the internal dynamics of the Liberal Quaker group and the suggestion of the elements and mechanics of internal secularisation.

Part I. Theoretical context: the conundrum facing religious groups

The first chapter discusses to the internal nature of religion forms and rehearses the church, sect and denomination typologies of Max Weber, Ernst Troeltsch, Richard Niebuhr and, more recently, Bryan Wilson, David Martin and others. The chapter explores the scholarship surrounding the transition from counter-cultural forms to world-accepting ones.

The second chapter moves the discussion to the scholarly discourse around the nature of religion in 'the west' and about the interplay between secularism as an ideology and the control of religious expression. Thus this chapter discusses the secularisation thesis as developed by Bryan Wilson and others from the 1960s onwards through to contemporary scholars such as Steve Bruce and David Voas. The latter half of the chapter builds on the work of Saba Mahmood, Talal Asad and Markus Dressler, amongst others, to consider the nature of the 'secular state' or, more particularly, the nature of liberal democracy in relation to religion. It identifies the conundrum faced by religious groups, to maintain unique truth claims to try and appear 'serious' and remain attractive to would-be recruits and to create 'fit' within secular State constructions of acceptable religion.

Part II. Theoretical complexities: religion and 'the world'

In the third chapter, the case study of Quaker relations with 'the world' begins. The idea of 'the hedge', after Job 1:10, is introduced as one of the ideas that Quakers used to separate themselves from 'the world' and to help police and encourage internal 'purity'. Examples of Quakers maintaining 'peculiarity' or particularity over a range of behaviours such as dress, speech, the swearing of oaths, and the opposition to war, are explored. The debates leading to the 'thinning' or lowering of the hedge in the 1850s are highlighted, as is the creation of the possibility of a 'private life' in which personal choices are given higher authority than the remnants of collective prescription and proscription, and the alternative pattern of maintaining behavioural identity codes or a Quaker 'habitus' that followed these internal reforms.

In Chapter 4, the work on Quaker 'denominationalisation' is introduced, reflecting the exploration of 'the hedge' in the previous chapter. Additionally, an overview of changing relationships between Quakers and the State is given. Using responses to war, organisational forms of Quakerism are juxtaposed with individual radicalism to highlight the way in which the two vary and also to show how patterns of sectarian and denominational outlook are not necessarily fixed over time or within either element of religious life. Similarly, the idea of 'the world' is interrogated and divided into the State and 'popular culture'. It is suggested that, whilst denominationalisation does appear to be a dominant trend, organisational and popular forms of religion each constantly interact with each of the State and popular forms of 'the world' to create a dynamic set of negotiated expressions of religion and of popular and State response. This pattern is related to the material in Chapter 1 on choices made by the State about the acceptable limits of religious expression.

Chapter 5 takes this perpetual dynamic around religious expression and State and popular response and frames it in terms of Thomas Tweed's theory of religion, presented in terms of flow and confluence. It suggests that dissonance between religious forms and societal ones creates turbulence not accounted for in Tweed's original model. Borrowing from A. K. M. Fazle Hussain's work in fluid dynamics, a model of 'coherent motion' and 'incoherent motion' is introduced and redefined to better illustrate the ways in which religious elements co-exist alongside societal ones.

Part III. New theory: a future of religiosity

Chapter 6 offers an overview of British Quaker religiosity in the twenty-first century and the way in which doctrine is marginal but form central. It considers how organisational and popular forms relate to each other and highlights the particular approach that Quakers have regarding orthodoxy and orthopraxy and orthocredence. The way in which Quakerism can be described as a sect or denomination and as 'liquid religion' is described. High levels of conversion suggest a challenge to Bruce's idea of the decline of liberal faith. However, it is suggested that the attraction may not be liberal religiosity but the very lack of any explicit religiosity. The possibility of internal secularisation becomes apparent.

Chapter 7 offers an analysis of the signs of internal secularisation in terms of subjectivisation and de-theologisation or rationalisation. It proceeds to suggest a theory of the process of internal secularisation through the minimisation of linguistic dissimilarity (and thus the maximisation of coherent motion) and through how popular expression of Quaker faith confronts and shifts organisational statements of Quaker religiosity. Linking this back to the conundrum faced by religious groups in Part I of the book, it appears that popular expression has the potential to undermine explicit religiosity and universal religious truth claims and thus, within secularisation theory, to determine the long-term recruitment potential of the group. However, as above, Quakers continue to recruit at stable levels, possibly because of, rather than in spite of, the lack of fixed or explicit religious claims, suggesting that the cultivation of conformity to wider society through popular expression may transform the nature of the religious group rather than extinguish it.

This potential for internal secularisation furthers the insights of secularisation theorists such as Steve Bruce and David Voas as well as scholars such as Paul Heelas, Linda Woodhead and Grace Davie. The cultivation of conformity within a secular society can establish a 'spiritual revolution' (Heelas and Woodhead 2005) within nominally transcendent religion. Instead of 'believing without belonging' (Davie 1994), secular Quakers can belong without believing. New forms of secular spirituality may simply hide behind traditional forms rather than in opposition to them.

Acknowledgements

To refer again to Thomas Tweed's framing of theorisation in terms of itineraries, I love travel (Dandelion, P. 2014) but this has not been an easy book to journey with. It has had the advantage of my not knowing what I wanted to say (of where I was travelling to) before writing, always a more exciting process than repeating well-rehearsed thoughts or routes, but domestic busy-ness, family bereavements and unexpected work pressures saw the first year of the project largely collapse. For a while I had no personal map, let alone a scholarly one. Like the process of 'hysteresis' mentioned in Chapter 6, incremental small changes resulted in a major or 'catastrophic' effect. However, whilst little writing took place that year (2016), the project was always in mind. Towards the end of that year, a providential meeting with Thomas Tweed himself at the American Academy of Religion re-instilled my energy for the book and I am very grateful for all Tom's support and encouragement.

Throughout I have been ably supported, both institutionally and personally. The idea for the book began in 2014 when I was asked to present at a conference in Norway marking two hundred years of their nation state. Hans Eirik Aarek, Ola Tjorheim, Richard Allen and Joan Allen all encouraged me to take initial work on citizenship and religion further. The University of Birmingham donated £1,000 in research expenses when I was given an award in 2016 for 'Excellence in Doctoral Researcher Supervision' and Woodbrooke Quaker Study Centre, my employer since 1992, kindly granted me 'staff study leave' for 2017. The participants and my co-leader, John Gray, at Writing Retreats in 2017 and 2018, all helped create a fine working environment. The Friends Historical Society gave me an opportunity to try out some of the ideas presented here in the Presidential Address in 2017 and I am also grateful for the comments of scholars at presentations at the British Sociological Association Sociology of Religion Study Group and the American Academy of Religion, both in 2016, the conference 'Jews and Quakers: on the borders of acceptability' in December 2017 and at an Anthropology of Religion seminar at the University of Durham in March 2018. Courses for the Quaker community at Glenthorne Quaker Guest House and at Woodbrooke in 2017 and 2018 also allowed me to rehearse and refine my thinking and to receive the fine insights of participants: Kersti Wagstaff needs especial mention.

Personal support has come in many forms. My colleagues at Woodbrooke are a constant model of mutual upholding, whilst editing and writing partners on other projects, such as Stephen Angell and Timothy Peat Ashworth, have offered unconditional and empathic support. Other academics I have contacted for help, such as Matthew Guest and Jennifer Hampton, have been more than generous in responding and encouraging: in addition their own scholarly industry has inspired me to carry on through those moments of self-doubt. Good friends and first-rate scholars such as Jon Kershner and Doug Gwyn have always asked after 'the writing' and have been willing to discuss my ideas, even whilst we share different disciplines. My students have been helpfully inquisitive, and patient with my absences and preoccupations. I have also greatly appreciated the huge bounty of support and encouragement from those who have no necessary interest in what I am writing but who have simply shown love and care towards someone struggling to find the time to put pen to paper: Stephen Lee, Lee Johnson, Phil Petty, Graham Sawyer, Pam Barton and George Hampton all regularly simply asked 'So, how is it going?' providing the gentle nudge of support that helped move the project along.

I am also grateful to Neil Jordan and Alice Salt at Routledge for the invitation to produce the book and their careful stewarding of the publication process. I thank Peter Stafford for his diligent and careful copy-editing.

Most of all, I am grateful to Wendy Hampton for all her huge and inspiring insights into the material and her continued interest even when the process inconvenienced our domestic life, and to Florence Hampton, for her quick thinking in response to parts of the material. They have both had to live with the process for two years, fellow travellers, and I am continually grateful for their patience and forbearing: it is wonderful to have the daily company of people wiser than you and this book is dedicated to them.

PART I

Theoretical context: the conundrum facing religious groups

1

ORGANISATIONAL TYPES AND THE INCLINATION TO CONFORM

Religious organisations continually position themselves in self-selected places in relation to the Nation State and wider culture, taking different forms at different times. In a book on religious conformity, these kinds of choices and the sensibilities that underpin them are a key part of the theoretical map we need to draw on and this chapter reviews the scholarly literature (of this part of the map), from the work of Max Weber and Ernst Troeltsch onwards on 'sect' and 'church' as 'ideal types' of religious group, also exploring David Martin's seminal work on denomination as a third form. As we shall see, church and sect types have different kinds of relationship with the Nation-State and of interest here is how and when these relationships change, when for example a group might move from a sectarian position to a church or denominational stance. As such, Richard Niebuhr's theory of the process of 'denominationalisation' is also introduced and the way in which groups move from their sectarian origins to denominational composition with the second or later generation, moderating their claims and moderating their antagonism to the host culture. Roy Wallis' work on world-rejecting and world-affirming groups is explored as well as John Walliss' idea of 'world ambivalence'. All of these typologies tend to suggest a shift over time from a counter-cultural position to a culture-accepting one.

Church and sect

Max Weber first delineated the differences between a church and a sect as different organisational types. He claimed: 'a sect is not an institution (Anstadt) like a church, but a community of the religiously qualified' (Toennies et al. 1973: 141). The mode of membership was central to Weber's distinction: he claimed that 'The "church" [operated] as a compulsory association for the administration of grace and … the sect as a voluntary association of religiously qualified persons' (Weber 2011: 139)

> Everything which arose later from sects is linked in the decisive points to the demand for purity, the ecclesia pura – a community consisting only of those members whose mode of conduct and life style do not carry public signs of heavenly disfavour, but proclaim the glory of God. The churches, in contrast, permit their light to shine on the just and the unjust alike, according to the Calvinist and the Catholic, as well as the Lutheran doctrine. According to the Calvinist doctrine of predestination, for example, it is the church's task to coerce even those who are irredeemably damned to all eternity, into external conformity to the church. The formation of the 'sect' type of community occurs first, as was said, *outside*. (Weber 2011: 142, my emphasis)

Ernst Troeltsch developed Weber's typology, shifting the focus from organisational type to behaviour. He discussed two forms of Christian organisation, sect and church, but three forms of religiosity including also 'mysticism' as a form of religious expression existing outside organisational forms.

Sects, to Troeltsch, comprised those who felt themselves outside the church and were a response to the dominant religious form expressed by the church type: 'Thus that element which could not be completely expressed within the ecclesiastical unity of civilisation and of society made a place for itself within the sects, whence it had a reflex influence upon the church itself' (1931: 330).

> The Church is that type of organisation which is overwhelmingly conservative, which to a certain extent accepts the secular order, and dominates the masses; in principle, therefore, it is universal, i.e. its desires to cover the whole of humanity. The sects on the other hand, are comparatively small groups; they aspire after personal inward perfection, and they aim at direct personal fellowship between the members of each group. From the very beginning, therefore, they are forced to organise themselves in small groups, and to renounce the idea of dominating the world. Their attitude towards the world, the State, and Society may be indifferent, tolerant, or hostile, since they have no desire to control and incorporate these forms of social life; on the contrary, they tend to avoid them; their aim is usually either to tolerate their presence alongside of their own body, or even to replace these social institutions by their own society. (Troeltsch 1931: 331)

Thus, the church type creates a universal canopy under which society operates:

> The Church relates the whole of the secular order as a means and preparation to the supernatural aim of life, and it incorporates genuine asceticism into its structure as one element in this preparation under the

very definite direction of the Church. The sects refer their members directly to the supernatural aim of life, and in them the individualistic, directly religious character of asceticism, as a means of union with God, is developed more strongly and fully. (Troeltsch 1931: 331–332)

Sects, on the other hand, accommodate the dispossessed, those outside the dominant ruling order. They emphasise spiritual capital, individual merit, and a particular stance, often one of resistance, to church and societal structures, doctrines and sensibilities. Troeltsch claimed that sectarian asceticism often involves 'renunciation of or hostility to the world … detachment from the world … expressed in the refusal to use the law, to swear in a court of justice, to own property, to exercise dominion over others, or to take part in war' (1931: 332). Sects are fuelled by the sense of purity and emphasise fundamental and original faith and do not represent the universalising tendency of mainstream Christianity (Troeltsch 1931: 334)

Troeltsch placed his theorisation within the whole history of Christian expression, using the biblical timeline of the New Testament as a way of understanding church organisational life and form. The Christian scriptures suggest that the life, death and resurrection of Jesus Christ initiated a new sense of spiritual possibility. It was the first instalment of the promise of a realignment of heaven and earth, lost at the time of creation, a time ahead that would be heralded by the second coming of Christ and the building of the new Jerusalem, as outlined in the letters of the apostle Paul and the book of Revelation. Christianity has been established in the 'meantime' between the first and second coming of Christ, helping its adherents wait faithfully for the fulfilment of the endtime (Dandelion 2005: chapter 1). As Troeltsch comments:

> the more that the eschatological horizon dimmed and the more the Church needed to construct a kingdom of its own making, 'the more was it forced to make its Divine and Christian character independent of the subjective character and service of believers; henceforth it sought to concentrate all its emphasis upon the objective possession of religious truth and religious power …'. (1931: 335)

He adds that 'Under these circumstances, however, the Church found it impossible to avoid making a compromise with the State, with the social order, and with economic conditions' (Troeltsch 1931: 335). Thus the universalising meantime establishment of a universalising organisational type found it needed to negotiate with the secular powers:

> … the radical individualism of the Gospel, with its urge towards the utmost personal achievement, its radical fellowship of love, uniting all in the most personal centre of life, with its heroic indifference towards the world, the State and civilisation, with its mistrust of the spiritual danger

of distraction and error inherent in the possession of or the desire for greater possessions, has been given a secondary place, or even given up altogether. (Troeltsch 1931: 336)

For Troeltsch, the formation of sects then becomes explicable as an organic reaction to the compromise of established religion. In this way, the ideal of primitive Christianity is preserved but moves from one group to another.

Like Weber, Troeltsch made the mode of membership a key distinction between church and sect: people are born into churches (every individual can and therefore should come under its influence), whereas the sect is voluntary community in which the adherent proves their entitlement, a gathering of the elect (1931: 338–339). Troeltsch claimed that 'the sect renounces universalism' (1931: 380), but this does not mean that sects do not make universal truth claims or see themselves as potentially universal, the new and true church.

As mentioned above, Troeltsch also identified a religiosity of mysticism or what he termed 'spiritual religion' (1931: 729) running outside ecclesiastical Christianity: 'a religious individualism which has no external organisation, and which has a very independent attitude, with widely differing views on the central truths of Christianity' (Troeltsch 1931: 381). He defined mysticism as 'simply the insistence upon a direct inward and present religious experience' (Troeltsch 1931: 730), and saw it as a reaction to 'objective practices' or a 'supplementing of traditional forms of worship'. This strand of mysticism is about the individual relationship with God rather than the community-orientation of the sect: it is ahistorical and formless. without 'a common centre of worship, history, and authority' (Troeltsch 1931: 743). Truth is inward and relative (Troeltsch 1931: 999), mysticism is non-doctrinal and may spiritualise Christ or move away from Christianity: mystical religion breaks down the separation between Christian and non-Christian (Troeltsch 1931: 750). It creates an invisible and tolerant fellowship in which liberty of conscience is preserved rather than it being a right desired by the sect type from the State. Troeltsch termed this mystical religiosity as 'the secret religion of the educated classes' (1931: 794) and, hinting at the secularisation evident in the early part of the twentieth century, commented that 'the modern educated classes understand nothing but mysticism' (1931: 798).

In summary, Troeltsch identified three types of Christian thought: (a) the church as an institution, objective rather than subjective, adaptable, oriented towards the masses, (b) the Sect as a voluntary association, its members bound to each other through experience of 'new birth', and (c) mysticism. Within the sect, '"Believers" live apart from the world, are limited to small groups, emphasise the law instead of grace, and in varying degrees within their own circle set up the Christian order, based on love; all this is done in preparation for and expectation of the coming kingdom of God' (Troeltsch 1931: 993). Mystical spirituality lies outside organised religion, an individualist popular religiosity that counters ecclesiastical form and rite.

Types of sect

Scholars since Troeltsch have worked on broadening the understanding of different types of sect or of religious organisation.

Howard Becker delineated a cult-sect-denomination-ecclesia model (1932) and later Yinger extended Becker's four types to six: cult, sect, established sect, class church/denomination, ecclesia, and universal church (1970). Yinger also developed a typology of sects that focused on relationship with the wider culture, distinguishing between a 'sect movement' and a 'charismatic sect', the former having a greater internal organisation (1970: 273–274). He also distinguished sects in terms of three responses to undesired situations: 'accepting', 'aggressive [opposition]' and 'avoiding' (Yinger 1970: 274). Yinger also used the typology of Ralph Turner and Lewis Killian to distinguish sectarian sensibilities (1957): 'power-oriented' (interested in the pursuit of power) 'value-oriented' (seeking the realisation of certain values) and 'participation-oriented' (gratifying the desires of its members).

'Accepting' groups are close to participation-oriented sects which accept the world's goals but find new means to achieve their ends: not opposed to society but to individual behaviours which need to be changed. Yinger gave the example of Christian Science (1970: 275). Aggressive sects are power-oriented movements that wish to change the world, via conversion or divine intervention, or Yinger claimed, directly: for true religion to flourish, the social order needs to change (1970: 277). Avoidance sects devalue the social order rather than accepting it or trying to change it, and these sects withdraw from the world.

The development of the typology involved particular interest in the sect type within church-sect theorising, the most substantial contribution of which was that of Bryan Wilson (1959, 1967a, 1970). The result of this scholarship was to shift the focus of church-sect theory from a tool for comparative analysis toward a classificatory system to apply sociological understandings to religious organisations. Initially influenced by Troeltsch, the theorisation of sects moved the church-sect scholarship from typology to taxonomy (Swatos 1981).

Wilson defined a sect in the following way:

> it is a voluntary association; membership is by proof to sect authorities of some claim to personal merit- such as knowledge of doctrine, affirmation of a conversion experience, or recommendation of members in good standing; exclusiveness is emphasized, and expulsion exercised against those who contravene doctrinal, moral, or organizational precepts; its self- conception is of an elect, a gathered remnant, possessing special enlightenment; personal perfection is the expected standard of aspiration, in whatever terms this is judged; it accepts, at least as an ideal, the priesthood of all believers; there is a high level of lay participation; there is opportunity for the member spontaneously to express his commitment; the sect is hostile or indifferent to the secular society and to the state. (1959: 4)

This is a more complex definition than Weber's simple focus on voluntary association, filling out the characteristics of what this kind of voluntary association implies. We see clearly here the emphasis on 'special entitlement' and the high level of separation and the high demands of participation this implies.

Wilson defined in contrast a 'denominational' type:

> it is formally a voluntary association; it accepts adherents without imposition of traditional prerequisites of entry, and employs purely formalized procedures of admission; breadth and tolerance are emphasized; since membership is laxly enrolled, expulsion is not a common device for dealing with the apathetic and the wayward; its self- conception is unclear and its doctrinal position unstressed; it is content to be one movement among others, all of which are thought to be acceptable in the sight of God; it accepts the standards and values of the pre- vailing culture and conventional morality; there is a trained professional ministry; lay participation occurs but is typically restricted to particular sections of the laity and to particular areas of activity; services are formalized and spontaneity is absent; education of the young is of greater concern than the evangelism of the outsider; additional activities are largely non-religious in character; individual commitment is not very intense; the denomination accepts the values of the secular society and the state; members are drawn from any section of the community, but within one church, or any one region, membership will tend to limit itself to those who are socially compatible (1959: 4–5)

Within the denominational form, commitment need not be high: nominal membership can bring about a voluntary degree of association and participation. Under Wilson's rubric, sect and denomination typologies are mainly played out *within* the organisational life of the group and the individual relationship to it; for example, sects demand high lay participation, denominations far less. It is primarily their attitude to the State that reveals the public sensibility of either type. The sect is hostile or indifferent to secular society: the denomination accepts the values of secular society.

Wilson initially developed four types of sect based on types of mission they were involved in: 'conversionist' (seeking to convert), 'adventist' or 'revolutionist' (seeking to change a depraved world prior to drastic change), 'introversionist' (seeking to replace worldly values with higher inner values), and 'gnostic' (promoting new and optimistic means to achieve worldly goals).

What was important to Wilson was the idea that sects differ from one another – some have very strong community allegiance and identity, others utilise a developed organisational doctrinal or authority structure. The origins of sects also differ: some are based in new charismatic leadership, others in internal schism within an existing sect, or the revitalisation of an existing group, or revivalism. Sect organisation can be minimal but needs to include the ability to call, arrange, organise and define meetings. People need to make decisions about the material culture of the group; money; hiring premises etc.; to make decisions about belief and practice; about admission into membership; to discipline transgression; to socialise the new; to handle interaction with worldly agencies (Wilson 1967a: 14–15). Some sects disappear when charismatic founders die, others continue (Wilson 1959: 7).

Wilson emphasised in particular the outward presentation of the group and its role in creating strong organisational identity:

> The relationship which a sect permits itself and its members to the external world is of vital importance to the nature of its continuance. In some measure, and by some methods, the sect is committed to keeping itself 'unspotted from the world': its distinctness must be evident both to its own members and to others. To this end there are two principal types of mechanism, *isolation* and *insulation*. (Wilson 1959: 10)

Isolation is high amongst introversionst sects, Wilson claimed, but insulation was important in all his sect types:

> Insulation consists of behavioral rules calculated to protect sect values by reducing the influence of the external world when contact necessarily occurs. Of course, insulation may be a latent function of the moral demands of sect teaching, the justification for which is biblical or revealed prescription; the sect leaders and the members themselves, however, often become aware of the real value of such precepts. Distinctive dress is such an insulating device, characteristic of some Mennonites, early Quakers, and Hutterites. Group endogamy is a more widely used method of insulation. (Wilson 1959: 11)

In a 1970 publication *Religious Sects*, Wilson extended his list of sect types and refined the criteria so that it lay in terms of the path to salvation offered by the sects (1970: 21). As a 'typical' list of sectarian attributes, Wilson listed the categories of voluntariness, exclusivity, merit, self-identification, elite status, expulsion, conscience, and legitimation (1970: 28–34). Sect membership is by voluntary confession (although children are often brought up within the sect, a point we return to below). In terms of exclusivity, Wilson claimed that commitment needs to be primary and unequivocal (1970: 29). He also suggested that an 'act of subscription' is critical but that merit can become nominal over time.

Wilson identified six types of sect: 'conversionist' with an emphasis on mission; revolutionist focused on biblical prophecy; 'introversionist' whose members withdraw into an inner life of holiness; 'manipulationist' sects which claim a special knowledge as the means to universal salvation; 'thaumaturgical' sects who emphasise spiritualist and miracle-based teachings; 'reformist' sects who try to communicate an ethic and transform the collective conscience, and; 'utopian' sects who focus on human agency to bring about a new society. Sects may change type over time as, within a typology based on soteriology, their theological emphasis changes.

Since the 1970s, the scholarship on sect types has been less prevalent. As we see below, scholars sought new ways of delineating types of religious organisation but also sociological interest turned elsewhere (mainly towards secularisation – see Chapter 2). However, another important part of church-sect scholarship has revolved around the nature of transition between types of religious organisation, in particular the shift from sect to church or denomination.

Transition

Building on Weber's organisational types of how sect membership is acquired by voluntary association, the challenge for sects appears with the second generation who inherit the tradition of their parents and are automatically seen as members albeit through *involuntary* association. Troeltsch used Methodists, Baptists, Moravians and Quakers as examples of this elasticity. It is an inevitable consequence of sectarian sensibility that membership is extended to the household in opposition to the very societal and religious culture that catalysed the sect in the first place.

Troeltsch cited the increased organisation and 'clericalism' that comes with numerical growth, a weakening of the sense of separation from, and opposition to, the world as leading to a transformation from sect to church(es) (1931: 725).

Richard Niebuhr took this aspect of how sects become church-types as his main focus (1975). His definitions of church and sect mirrored those of Weber in terms of the mode of membership and Troeltsch in terms of its relation to wider culture:

> The church emphasises the means of grace it administers and to the official administration of sacraments and teaching, the sect 'attaches primary importance to the religious experience of members … to the priesthood of all believers, to the sacraments as symbols of fellowship and pledges of allegiance … The church as an inclusive social group is closely allied with national, economic, and cultural interests; by the very nature of its constitution it is committed to the accommodation of its ethics to the ethics of civilization; it must represent the morality of the respectable majority, not of the heroic minority. The sect, however, is always a minority group, whose separatist and semi-ascetic attitude toward 'the world' is reinforced by the loyalty which persecution nurtures. It holds with tenacity to its interpretation of Christian ethics and prefers isolation to compromise. At times it refuses participation in the government, at times rejects war, at

times seeks to sever as much as possible the bonds which tie it to the common life of industry and culture. (Niebuhr 1975: 18–19)

Niebuhr saw the church as a series of denominations, and, interestingly, was highly critical of denominations as an expression of faith:

> When liberty gains a constitution, liberty is compromised; when frater-
> nity elects officers, fraternity yields some of the ideal qualities of broth-
> erhood to the necessities of government. And the gospel of Christ is
> subject to this sacrifice of character in the interest of organic embodi-
> ment ... It demands the impossible in conduct and belief; it runs coun-
> ter to the instinctive life of man and exalts the rationality of the
> irrational; in a world of relativity it calls for unyielding loyalty to
> unchangeable absolutes ... Organize its ethics – as organize them you
> must whenever two or three are gathered in the name of Christ – and
> the free spirit of forgiving love becomes a new law, requiring inter-
> pretation, commentary, and all the machinery of justice ... Place this
> society in the world, demanding that it be not of the world, and stren-
> uous as may be its efforts to transcend or to sublimate the mundane life,
> it will yet be unable to escape all taint of conspiracy and connivance
> with the worldly interests it despises. (1975: 4–5)

Culture-accepting Christianity is therefore a compromise and, Niebuhr states: 'the fact that compromise is inevitable does not make it less an evil' (1975: 5).

> Denominationalism in the Christian church is such an unacknowledged
> hypocrisy. It is a compromise, made far too lightly, between Christianity
> and the world ... It represents the accommodation of Christianity to the
> caste-system of human society. It carries over into the organization of the
> Christian principle of brotherhood the prides and prejudices, the privilege
> and prestige, as well as the humiliations and abasements, the injustices and
> inequalities of that specious order of high and low wherein men find their
> satisfaction of their craving for vainglory. The division of the churches
> closely follows the division of men into the castes of national, racial, and
> economic groups. It draws the color line in the church of God; it fosters
> the misunderstandings, the self-exaltations, the hatreds of jingoistic
> nationalism by continuing in the body of Christ the spurious differences of
> provincial loyalties; it seats the rich and poor apart at the table of the
> Lord, where the fortunate may enjoy the bounty they have provided while
> the others feed upon the crusts their poverty affords. (1975: 6)

Denominations, for Niebuhr, symbolised the corruptions of wider society with which they colluded. In this way, the sectarian impulse represented truer Christianity:

the rise of new sects to champion the uncompromising ethics of Jesus and to 'preach the gospel to the poor' has again and again been the effective means of recalling Christendom to its mission … The evil of denominationalism lies in the conditions which makes the rise of sects desirable and necessary; in the failure of the churches to transcend the social conditions which fashion them into caste organizations, to sublimate their loyalties to standards and institutions only remotely relevant if not contrary to the Christian ideal, to resist the temptation of making their own self-preservation and extension the primary object of their endeavour. (1975: 21)

Niebuhr cited the churches' support for war and its slow opposition to slavery as marks of its apostasy: 'Denominations are not religious groups with religious purposes … they are emblems … of the victory of the world over the church, of the secularization of Christianity … Denominationalism thus represents the moral failure of Christianity' (1975: 25). This is sociology wrapped in personal theological and political preference but written with all the authority typical of sociologists writing before the 1980s (see Steve Bruce's comments in his introduction to Wilson 2016.).

For Niebuhr, in spite of its purity and possibly because of it, the sectarian impulse is inevitably lost with the second generation:

by its very nature the sect is valid for only one generation. The children born to the voluntary members of the first generation begin to make the sect a church long before they have arrived at years of discretion. For with their coming the sect must take on the character of an educational and disciplinary institution with the purpose of bringing the new generation into conformity with ideals and customs which have become traditional. (1975: 19–20)

The advent of a second generation necessarily diminishes the purity and ardour of the group:

Rarely does a second generation hold the convictions it has inherited with a fervor equal to that of its fathers, who fashioned these convictions in the heat of conflict and at the risk of martyrdom. As generation succeeds generation, the isolation of the community from the world becomes more difficult. Furthermore, wealth frequently increases when the sect subjects itself to the discipline of asceticism in work and expenditure; with the increase of wealth the possibilities for culture also become more numerous and involvement in the economic life of the nation as a whole can less easily be limited. Compromise begins and the ethics of the sect approach the churchly type of morals. As with the ethics, so with the doctrine, so also with the administration of the religion. An official clergy, theologically educated and schooled in the refinements of ritual, takes the place of lay leadership; easily imparted creeds are substituted for the difficult enthusiasms of the pioneers; children are born into the group and infant baptism or dedication becomes once more a means of grace. So the sect becomes a church. (Niebuhr 1975: 20)

Thus, for Niebuhr, sects transformed into denominations axiomatically and automatically with the onset of a second generation. Organisational complexity coupled with increased wealth, the routinised authority of a leadership elite and the development of liturgical and doctrinal 'tradition' all undercut the purer impulses of the original sect.

Liston Pope in his 1942 study of mill-hands in North Carolina identified 21 indices of movement from sect to denomination that reflected some of Niebuhr's theory:

1. From membership composed chiefly of the property-less to membership composed of property owners.
2. From economic poverty to economic wealth, as disclosed especially in the value of church property and the salary paid to ministers.
3. From the cultural periphery toward the cultural center of the community.
4. From renunciation of prevailing culture and social organization, or indifference to it, to affirmation of prevailing culture and social organization.
5. From self-centered (or personal) religion to culture-centered religion, from 'experience' to a social institution.
6. From noncooperation, or positive ridicule, toward established religious institutions to cooperation with the established churches of the community.
7. From suspicion of rival sects to disdain or pity for all sects.
8. From a moral community excluding unworthy members to a social institution embracing all who are socially compatible within it.
9. From an unspecialized, unprofessionalized, part-time ministry to a specialized, professional, full-time ministry.
10. From a psychology of persecution to a psychology of success and dominance.
11. From voluntary, confessional bases of membership to ritual or social prerequisites only (such as a certificate of previous membership in another respected denomination, or training in an educational process established by the denomination itself).
12. From principal concern with adult membership to equal concern for children of members.
13. From emphasis on evangelism and conversion to emphasis on religious education.
14. From stress on a future in the next world to primary interest in a future in this world, a future for the institution, for its members, and

for their children; from emphasis on death to emphasis on successful earthly life.

15. From adherence to strict Biblical standards, such as tithing or non-resistance, to acceptance of general cultural standards as a practical definition of religious obligation.

16. From a high degree of congregational participation in the services and administration of the religious group to delegation of responsibility to a comparatively small percentage of the membership.

17. From fervor in worship services to restraint; from positive action to passive listening.

18. From a comparatively large number of special religious services to a program of regular services at stated intervals.

19. From reliance on spontaneous 'leadings of the Spirit' in religious services and administration to a fixed order of worship and of administrative procedure.

20. From the use of hymns resembling contemporary folk music to the use of slower, more stately hymns coming out of more remote liturgical tradition.

21. From emphasis on religion in the home to delegation of responsibility for religion to church officials and organizations. (1942: 122–124)

For Pope, as for Niebuhr, economic prosperity diminished sectarian sensibilities. Equally, economic marginalisation promoted and sustained sectarian religion (1942: 136). Pope also, interestingly, was clear that certain groups contained a mix of denominational and sectarian characteristics (1942: 126).

Bryan Wilson built on the work of Niebuhr, Becker, and Pope, in his understanding that sects commonly denominationalised, but, departing from Niebuhr, claimed that some sects existed over several generations (1959: 3).

> It is an oversimplification to say, however, that the second generation makes the sect into a denomination … such development depends on the standards of admission imposed by the sect, the previous rigor with which children have been kept separate from the world, and on the point at which a balance is struck between the natural desire of parents to have their children included in salvation and their awareness of the community view that any sort of salvation depends on the maintenance of doctrinal and moral standards. (Wilson 1959: 11)

For Wilson, the strength of isolation and insulation, of a separate strong identity, was the deciding factor as to how quickly a sect might become a denomination.

> If the sect is to persist as an organization it must not only separate its members from the world, but must also maintain the dissimilarity of its

own values from those of the secular society. Its members must not normally be allowed to accept the values of the status system of the external world. (Wilson 1959: 12–13)

In other words, for Wilson, as sects differ, so does their propensity to denominationalisation.

... sects with a general democratic ethic, which stress simple affirmation of intense subjective experience as a criterion of admission, which stand in the orthodox fundamentalist tradition, which emphasize evangelism and use revivalist techniques, and which seek to accommodate groups dislocated by rapid social change are particularly subject to denominationalizing tendencies. These same tendencies are likely to be intensified if the sect is unclear concerning the boundaries of the saved community and extends its rules of endogamy to include any saved person as an eligible spouse; if its moral injunctions are unclearly distinguished from conventional or traditional morality; and if it accepts simple assertion of remorse for sin as sufficient to re-admit or to retain a backslidden member. Denominationalization is all the more likely when such a sect inherits, or evolves, any type of preaching order, lay pastors, or itinerant ministers; when revivalism leads to special training for the revivalists themselves (and so leads to a class of professionals who cease to rely on love-offerings but are granted a fixed stipend); and when the members are ineffectively separated from the world, a condition enhanced by proselytizing activities. (Wilson 1959: 14)

Warren Goldstein comments: 'Wilson's dialectic of church and sect does not follow a straight line; it follows the dialectic of charisma (sect formation) and routinisation (institutionalisation of the church or religious rationalization)' (2009b: 171).

For Wilson, earlier studies of sects fell into error because the data used was related to particular kinds of sects: in his study of sects, denominationalism was not an automatic process. David Martin came to a similar conclusion from his analysis of the nature of the denomination.

Martin argued, contrary to Niebuhr's analysis of the denomination as a second-generation sect, that, firstly 'sects generally succeed in maintaining their sectarian character, and may even reinforce it, and secondly that denominations have normally possessed their denominational character from their very beginnings' (1962: 2). Sects remain sects or die and other groups start without a sectarian spirit: Martin suggested that Methodists, Baptists, and Congregationalists all had non-sectarian origins (1962: 2–3).

Martin's view of the denomination as a form of religious organisational life fitted with previous understandings:

The denomination merely claims that while there are doubtless many keys to many mansions it is at least in possession of one of them, and that anyone who thinks he has the sole means to open the heavenly door is plainly mistaken. The outlook of the denomination as an institution is therefore relatively tolerant (1962: 5)

The denomination sees itself as one church amongst many, neither exclusive (sect) nor universal (church). It is thus inclined towards co-operation and implicitly pragmatic (1962: 6). Martin drew out the distinctiveness of the denomination in comparison to both church and sect. Within denominations, a separated priestly body is rooted in collective authority, e.g. an assembly (what Martin termed 'delegated democracy' (1962: 7)) – different from a church (e.g. the singular authority of the Pope) and the sect (often with no clerical order). Denominations maintained a subjective and instrumental approach to ritual and sacraments (1962: 8) but did not dispense with them altogether as a sect might: rites, e.g. marriage, were 'potentially sacramental' as opposed to unambiguously and essentially sacramental (as per the church type).

Thus Wilson and Martin both challenged Niebuhr's polemical but influential thesis. Sects need not transition to denominations after the first generation but may become established, albeit potentially changing their sect type. Denominations are not necessarily second-generation sects but may start as denominations. Benton Johnson further suggested that some sects were as established and as accommodated as some denominations to their host culture (1971).

We return to how this sect-denomination scholarship plays out for the Quaker case study in Chapter 4. It is worth also considering, though, some of the alternative typologies developed to describe organisational life and in particular the relationship between faith organisations and 'the world'.

Other typologies

William Swatos has helpfully delineated in several places (1975, 1981) the history of the church-sect theorisation. He drew a distinction between church-sect and ascetism-mysticism typologies proposed by Weber and the way Troeltsch and subsequent scholars conflated them. Swatos further argued that they are best used to delineate different aspects of the study of religion, the first to differentiate forms of religious organisation and the latter to analyse participant orientations to wider society. Niebuhr, building on Troeltsch's conflation of these typologies, connected them to the development of religious organisational forms, which in turn, Swatos claimed, led to its own literature and a further misunderstanding around the origins of religious groups (1981: 19).

Swatos proposed a revised model of church-sect theorisation based on monopolism and pluralism, and acceptance and rejection (1975). Borrowing terms from Peter Berger's work on secularisation and types of religion-infused societies (e.g. 1967), Swatos adopted the terms 'monopolism' and 'pluralism' to represent the way in which religious groups operate either perceiving themselves as the single legitimate religious group in society or one of many legitimate forms. His other axis represents the way in which the religious group relates to its social environment. This led to four types: monopolism-acceptance (church), pluralism-acceptance (denomination), monopolism-rejection (entrenched sect), pluralism-rejection (dynamic sect) (1975: 176). Swatos posited a fifth type, an 'established sect' a less clearly defined type which would represent any group in transition between the other types (1975: 177).

The dynamic sect sits within a pluralist society that allows it to flourish whilst rejecting this very pluralism given that it believes itself to be the true church. Swatos claimed this is the kind of group which, after Niebuhr, needs to transform or perish. The entrenched sect, a nemesis of the church type and often marginalised or outlawed by it, can endure for longer, as per Wilson's observations. Thus, Swatos was able to explain differences in the existing scholarship as well as propose a more workable model.

James Beckford, when contemplating how to categorise Jehovah's Witnesses, chose to disregard sect/denomination typology as it was so confused (the muddle between typology and taxonomy) (1975: 94). He decided instead to focus on organisational attributes in order to complete a comparative analysis free of ambiguity. He developed a typology of religious organisations based on two axes, one of goal specificity and non-specificity and the second of high and low intensiveness with which the goals are pursued. Beckford proposed four types of religious organisation based on the combination of these variables: 'Totalizing', 'Activist', 'Individualist', and 'Conventional'.

The 'Totalizing' type has specific goals/high intensiveness. Examples include the Watch Tower movement and the Unification Church: 'These groups are characterized by a very assertive leadership above the level of local groupings, highly specific and narrow objectives, immense drive to achieve the goals, rigorous control over competing demands on members' time and energy, and stringent control over the quality of neophytes' (Beckford 1975: 98). We would expect the groups' ideology to dominate participants' lives and that relations with 'the world' would be strained. There would be low levels of co-operation with other religious organisations, high rates of recruitment and withdrawal and low rates of doctrinal change (Beckford 1975: 98–99).

'Activist' groups are characterised by non-specific goals coupled with high intensiveness. Examples include the Salvation Army and the Mormons. In these cases, high levels of activism are diffused over a wide range of goals. The laity has a mild form of control over the leadership and there is a low level of influence over the lives of members. Groups are mildly co-operative with the secular authorities and other religious groups. There are low rates of recruitment and of membership turn-over (Beckford 1975: 99).

The 'Individualist' type has specific goals but low levels of intensiveness with which to pursue them. Leadership is weakly articulated and there is a low degree of collective action. There is a weak ideological hold over members, a fluid concept of membership, conformity with societal values and peaceful relations with the secular authorities. Indifference to other religious groups, and high rates of membership recruitment and disaffiliation, are typical of this type. Beckford gives Christian Science as an example (1975: 99).

The 'Conventional Type' has non-specific goals and low levels of intensiveness. This type, Beckford claims, includes most British denominations and churches. The groups are highly differentiated between different roles and factions, between clergy and laity, there is a low selectivity of members, low ideological influence on members' lives, a close correlation with dominant societal values, a willingness to co-operate with other religious groups, and low rates of recruitment and turn-over (Beckford 1975: 99–100).

'Totalizing' groups have strong short-term stability but are prone to major disruption. Conventional groups rarely suffer disruption but also integrate their members less well (Beckford 1975: 100). The types of groups differ in their ability to recruit and retain members and in the way they interact with political issues: conventionalists and activists interact more openly and fully whilst 'Totalizing' groups may find their own internal means to discuss the same material. Beckford drew correlations between organisational types and the class base of their membership (conventionalist groups are typically middle class, activist groups lower-middle and working class). Significantly, Beckford claimed that the mode of membership (obligatory or voluntary as in church/sect typology) is not a variable (1975: 101).

Roy Wallis (1984) proposed a threefold typology of religious movements in terms of their attitudes towards 'the world': world-rejecting, world-affirming, world-accommodating (1984: 6). He claimed that any mapping should be time-specific as 'a movement may shift around considerably during the course of its development' (ibid.), although Wallis did not suggest that this would *necessarily* occur as in, say, Niebuhr's analysis of second generation denominationalisation of sects (1975 [1929]). Indeed, rather, he was suggesting the possibility of ongoing movement between types.

Wallis' definition of 'world-rejecting religions' incorporated movements that view 'the prevailing social order as having departed substantially from God's prescriptions and plan' (1984: 9–10). An adherent is involved in a life of service and suppress their 'own desires and goals in expression of his commitment to the greater good of the movement, or love of God and his [sic] agent' (1984: 11). According to Wallis, such movements expect that the end of the world will shortly come or that the movement will 'sweep the world' and that a new world order will then begin – one that is more humane, more spiritual, utopian. Groups that fall under this umbrella collapse distinctions between secular and religious (Wallis 1984: 12). Adherent lifestyle may appear deviant but is also highly organised and controlled (Wallis 1984: 14). Individual will is subjugated to collective solidarity, the former self completely repudiated (Wallis 1984: 18). Communal clothing or shared and uniform dress codes may be one representation of this (Wallis 1984: 20).

In contrast, Wallis claimed that world-affirming groups may have no collective ritual of worship nor a developed theology or ethics. The prevailing social order is seen largely as desirable (Wallis 1984: 21) but with the caveat that humanity has not yet realised its potential. These groups claim they have the means to unlock this puzzle (Wallis 1984: 22). Rather than challenge the world, however, such movements are about benefiting more easily from all the world has to offer (Wallis 1984: 23).

Wallis described world-accommodating groups in far less detail than he does the other two and Finnish scholar Kaj Björkqvist claims that the multi-dimensionality of Wallis' typology created by the addition of an ill-defined 'world accommodating' category, is problematic (1990). Instead, Björkqvist utilises only the world-rejecting and world-affirming parts of Wallis' schema and proposes a unidimensional axis. Björkqvist incorporates Gross and Etzioni's theory of goal displacement (1985) in which new goals (goals that are either more attractive, more attainable, or better able to allow the organisation to survive) replace old goals and create new organisational emphasis. Using this framework, Björkqvist suggests how groups move back and forth between world-rejecting and world-affirming predispositions (1990).

John Walliss in his study of the Brahma Kumaris adds another predisposition to Wallis' work, that of 'world-ambivalence' (2007). He suggests 'world ambivalence' is present when an organisation 'appears to entail two distinct and unresolved orientations toward the world' (2007: 45). In the case of the Brahma Kumaris, there is both the clear belief that the world is headed towards apocalyptic destruction and frenetic activity to ameliorate the ills of the world. World-rejection and millenarianism sit alongside world affirmation, reformism and utopianism (2007: 46). (We return to this idea of parallel orientations in Chapter 4 when we explore an understanding of religious groups maintaining organisational and popular stances and identities.)

It is this focus on the predisposition of religious adherents to wider culture that obviously most interests us here. In this way, Wallis' and Walliss' frameworks are relevant and interesting. They mirror the stance of the group towards other churches and 'the world' found in sect/ denomination theory (see Pope's 21-point list for example). In general, sects are 'world-rejecting' in broad terms and denominations 'world-accepting'. Both terms reflect the organisational disposition rather than the popular religious sensibilities within any group.

Thus, the received sociological wisdom is that religious groups that begin as sects typically 'denominationalise'. They hold more diffuse and less universal truth claims and make lower demands on their members. Membership is not by voluntary association and may be nominal. These groups accept other religious groups as potentially equivalent and they present themselves as potentially equivalent. This is a critical step in the negotiation of rights within their host Nation-States.

Chapter summary

Thus, we have been able to delineate the beginnings and deviations of church-sect theorisation and, with the help of Swatos, unpick the two streams of thought that have become confused and conflated. We can understand sects in terms of their voluntary association from Weber, but also classify them in terms of their relationship to wider society as well as the nature of their internal dynamics. From Niebuhr, Wilson and Martin, we can locate the influential idea of sect development and denominationalisation. This idea of a sect becoming a denomination is portrayed as normative.

Whilst we can see that this is a deviation from Weber's original model, it is one that has been applied widely and which this volume continues to use and interrogate. Thus, Niebuhr's work is important, as is Wilson's model of sect development. We return to how the Quakers fit into this theorisation in Chapter 4. The lack of clear fit between the more elaborate typologies and social reality has led to continuing work in this area and the invention of alternative models such as those by Swatos, Beckford, Wallis and Walliss. What is clear, however, is the dynamic nature of religious organisation, and, from Troeltsch, how different religious dispositions in relation to mainstream Christianity drive people towards sectarian or individualist mystical religion.

2

SECULARISATION, SECULARISM, RIGHTS AND RECRUITMENT

As mentioned above, the sociology of religion in the past decades has been captivated by theories of secularisation and religious organisational change and this chapter offers an overview of 'secularisation theory' and the expected plight of liberal religion and how, as theorists have claimed, its permissiveness undermines its ability to transmit its beliefs clearly and recruit. Groups with distinctive belief systems and which oppose dominant value systems are expected to survive longer. A broader view is given by the theorists of secularism who challenge the tendency within secularisation theory to separate religion and non-religion in terms of a binary. The chapter concludes with sections on religious recruitment and the conundrum faced by religious groups as they balance public appeal through universal truth claims with public acceptability based on the perception of equivalence with other religious groups.

Secularisation

Given the marginalisation of religion within the global north or 'higher-income countries', and the constant interplay between the processual nature of the Nation-State and of religions themselves, much has been made of the sociological processes surrounding the nature and future of religious life. The differentiation of religion from other aspects of political and social life, its diminishing importance and role within the political sphere, and the reduction in individual membership and participation has led in the last decades to a focus on 'secularisation theory' and the attempt to chart the processes of change affecting religious life.

Such was the proliferation of theories about secularisation in the 1960s, 1970s and 1980s that in 1991, Olivier Tschannen constructively analysed the similarities between seven different approaches to secularisation: those of Luckmann,

Berger, Wilson, Martin, Fenn, Parsons, and Bellah (Tschannen 1991). Whilst Tschannen found that different theories did not cohere into a single unified theory, he found that there was a commonality at a paradigmatic level between the major theorists in that they used similar and shared examples. The three areas of commonality he located were 'differentiation', 'rationalisation', and 'worldliness'.

> In the course of history, religion becomes progressively differentiated from other domains of social life, eventually emerging as a very specific institutional domain within a new type of social structure made up of several such institutions (education, politics, economy, etc.). For example, the Church and the State become clearly differentiated (*differentiation*). At the same time, the different non-religious institutions born from this process of differentiation start working on the basis of criteria that are rationally related to their specific social functions, independently from any religious control or guidance. Thus, for example, the economy starts to work in a rational way dictated by its own inherent logic (*rationalization*). The impact of these processes on the religious sphere itself causes it to lose some of its specificity and to become more worldly. Religious organizations start to cater to the psychological needs of their members (*worldliness*). (Tschannen 1991: 400–401)

Within the process of differentiation, religion loses control over the other domains it becomes separated from. Education, for example, becomes autonomous (*autonomisation*). Religion, as a consequence, alters its mode: it becomes one competing institutional narrative for understanding the world from which the individual needs to construct their own version of religion (*privatisation*). Further, according to Tschannen's analysis of the different theories, religion become generalised, reappearing in new and non-specific forms such as civil religion (*generalisation*). Given the loss of social control, religious affiliation and practice decline. (*decline in practice*).

Rationalisation entails the emergence of science as a worldview (*scientisation*) and the emergence of rational scientific approach to societal questions (*sociologisation*). Traditional religious explanations, for example connected with theodicy, lose their plausibility both within religious groups (*collapse of world view*) and for individuals generally leading to unbelief (*unbelief*). The whole process sits within two broad assumptions: (a) that secularisation has its roots in religion itself, and (b) that religion will never disappear (Tschannen 1991: 402).

Tschannen's work of course did not curtail the debate over the nuances of the theory and its applicability in a changing social world. The main recent proponent of the secularisation thesis has been Steve Bruce, and his output on the topic has been prolific (2001, 2002, 2003, 2011 amongst many others). Bruce follows in Bryan Wilson's theoretical footsteps and Bruce edited the reissue of Wilson's seminal 1966 publication *Religion in Secular Society* (Wilson 2016). For

Wilson and Bruce, secularisation is 'the process whereby religious thinking, practice and institutions lose social significance' (Wilson 2016 [1966]: xiv), what Tschannen refers to in terms of autonomisation, the development of separate institutions to look after different aspects of social life in which religion becomes only one institution amongst many and in which the others become autonomous with their own narratives. Religious institutions decay, religious rules and principles about behaviour become displaced, and religious agencies lose their property and control of a variety of social activities and functions. Wilson claimed:

> As the institutions of society grew apart, and as religious institutions and functionaries lost, first their control of, and later much of their access to, various social activities – diplomacy, education, the regulation of trade, etc. – so the civil authority gained in power, and, having less need for the good offices of the Church, was less disposed to protect its ancient privileges. The emergence of new classes with new skills and resources, who were unaccommodated in the Church, but whose social importance sometimes won for them the protection of princes, created a pluralism which became the first properly instituted invasion (there had been many unlegitimated invasions before) of the Church's claim to spiritual monopoly as far as the temporal sovereign's writ could run. (2016: 203)

Some of the debate here then is about the roots and timing of the processes leading to the dominance of the secular. For Wilson and Bruce, religion loses both its spiritual monopoly and its social significance as competing institutions offer both faith options and alternative political and social agency. Further, at a popular level, people devote less time, energy and resources to supernatural concerns and a specifically religious consciousness is replaced by a more rational orientation (Bruce 2011: 2).

Following Wilson, Bruce has created a comprehensive model of the secularisation paradigm. It includes factors concerned with rationalisation, the nature of religious organisation, economy, society, polity and cognitive style.

Bruce emphasises rationalisation and the effects of increased human agency within religion and, through science and technology, in all aspects of society. Science and technology offer different explanatory systems but also different solutions to societal suffering. Bruce compares the religious response to the Black Death in the fourteenth century, when the church called for weeks of fasting and prayer, with the Church of England's response to AIDS in the 1980s when it called for increased government funding for medical research (2011: 44). For Bruce, the Protestant Reformation fed this sense of human agency as well as emphasising an individual work ethic, and encouraging industrial capitalism and economic growth.

As societies grew larger, they became more internally varied and specialized ... social life fragments as specialized roles and institutions are created
to handle specific features or functions previously embodied in one role or
institution ... Increased specialization directly secularized many social
functions that were once dominated by the church: education, health care,
welfare, and social control. (Bruce 2011: 29–30)

This structural differentiation is accompanied, in Bruce's model, by social
differentiation. Patterns of housing and lifestyle start to differentiate and
Bruce argues that in more fluid social structures, the idea of single moral
universe starts to lose its salience (2011: 310).

This, he argues, affected the nature of religious organisation as different
classes and groups of people sought different religious solutions. Bruce argues
that, unlike Catholicism with its clarity over religious authority and control,
Protestantism with its emphasis on voluntary association (and indeed on
protest) encourages and accommodates theological deviation and innovation.
The Reformation did not create a single equivalent of the Roman Catholic
Church but a number of competing groups (2011: 32). The Protestant tendency to ideas of spiritual equality encouraged the increase of the potential
for human agency, whilst increased wealth and education made choices real
rather than simply notional. Alternative models of religious organisation, e.g.
the advent of lay preachers or the abolition of a separated clergy, also
affirmed alternative models of social organisation (Bruce 2011: 35).

Bruce talks of a technological consciousness as a cognitive style in which
humanity has come to understand activity as made up of repeatable elements,
what he terms 'componentiality', leaving little space for the 'eruption of the
divine' (2011: 46).

The fragmentation of an overarching singular religious tradition for the
nation, the increase of democratic control (e.g. an elected parliament running
the nation instead of a divinely appointed monarch) and the increased sense of
someone as an individual with rights as well as responsibilities all contributed
to the formation of modern liberal democracy: a lack of integrated national
culture leads, Bruce claims, to the growth of a secular State (2011: 34). (here
secularism is seen as a consequence rather than an ideology – see below for an
alternative view).

With religious fragmentation and decline within secular States, privatisation
becomes one of the responses religions can make in the face of secularism. Religion
as an optional and potentially unfashionable activity becomes a private affair,
paraded only before co-religionists or household members. Privatisation may lead
to ongoing personal interpretation of any one tradition or a high degree of
syncretism, what has been termed 'pick and mix' religion (Punshon 1990: 23).

Bruce claims that the fragmentation of national religious culture also
diminished the plausibility of any one set of religious truth claims, the more so,
as sects co-operated to secure rights, or, as denominations, began to self-present

as one option amongst many. A multiplicity of competing but equivalent theological articulation diminishes the authority of all of them, especially if they are presented as equivalent in their difference. Mixed-marriages, in faith terms, offer the children the same challenge within the home. If both parents see the other's faith as acceptable or equivalent, why should the offspring take either any more seriously than the other or, indeed, feel the need to choose either (Voas 2003)? This relativism of belief is, for Bruce, the bottom line of the secularisation paradigm. Liberal or permissive religions, then, are particularly susceptible to the decrease in the perceived plausibility of their theological claims, a key point in the framing of this volume and one we return to in Chapter 6.

Bryan Wilson did not see the end of religion as inevitable but rather was attempting to account for the decline to date. Warren Goldstein argues that secularisation theorists such as Wilson, David Martin and Richard Fenn were not proposing a unilinear model of secularisation but one that is dialectical in which secularisation and sacralisation can occur at the same time (2009b: 159).

More recent proponents of the secularisation thesis, such as Bruce and David Voas, appear to predict the end of organised religion (Bruce 2011: 56; Voas 2009: 167). In 2003, Bruce predicted that Britain would be a secular society by 2030 (Bruce 2003, 60). Other theorists have suggested adjustments to the thesis, mainly to show that the theory cannot be applied universally, or that whilst organised religion is in decline, 'spirituality' is being expressed in new ways.

David Martin was clear that context affected levels of secularisation and theorised different styles of secularisation depending upon geographical and cultural setting (1978). Grace Davie has noted that the theory is at its strongest in northern Europe, that there is a European exceptionalism, and that, in other words, the secularisation thesis can only apply to particular geographies (1994). Rodney Stark, Laurence Iannaccone and Roger Finke are amongst those who suggest that countries with a State-sponsored 'established' Protestant church have secularised most because the 'supply' of religious provision has been too impoverished, thus suppressing demand (e.g. Stark and Iannaccone 1994; Finke 1997). It is not that demand has reduced but that the supply of religious variety has not been enticing enough: secularisation occurs most in countries where a religious mono- poly has existed, e.g. an established church. Steve Bruce claims only sta- tistical sleight of hand has supported this kind of theory (2011: 145). Jose Casanova identified three aspects of secularisation: a decline of religious belief and practices; the privatisation of religion and the marginalisation of religion from public life; the differentiation of various aspects of life (law, welfare, education etc.) and separation from the religious domain. Casanova argued that these three aspects are often conflated whereas they need to be studied separately (1994).

Other theorists have looked at how religious participation may be changing rather than disappearing. Grace Davie talked of 'believing without belonging' to represent the large numbers of unchurched who nevertheless claimed they believed in God (1994). She has also emphasised the place of 'vicarious religion' and how there is still a demand for the existence of religious institutions, if not active participation: she argues that people express their religious values and involvement vicariously through the institutional expression of faith (Davie 2007). Non-belonging believing (the statistical basis of which has been challenged by Voas and Crockett (2005)) and vicarious religious are highly privatised and neither phenomenon slows numerical decline of church attendance and membership or explicit religious practice and yet does not equate to popular secularisation.

Paul Heelas and Linda Woodhead conducted a study of faith practice in Kendal comparing rates of church attendance and membership (religion with its transcendent reference point) with interest in what they termed the 'holistic milieu' (spirituality with its subjective reference point, such as Reiki, Taizé singing, yoga, etc.) (2005). They were looking for evidence of what they termed the 'spiritual revolution', the point at which rates of participation in subjectivised spirituality outstripped that of religion, suggesting that interest in the non-material was not declining but changing its terms of engagement. However, their evidence for decline in regular church attendance supported the idea of secularisation and the levels of engagement in the holistic milieu were very small, just 1.6% of the population (Heelas and Woodhead 2005: 48). John Knox's follow-up study in McMinville, Oregon, showed less evidence of decline in levels of church participation (but also virtually no evidence at all of engagement with organised 'spirituality') but did illustrate the changed nature of religious authority underpinning church-going (2016). People still went to church but on their own terms, choosing services and pastors whose message supported their own privatised beliefs. Knox suggested a move away from more traditional authority systems such as sacro-theism, sacro-clericalism and sacro-communalism towards 'sacro-egoism' (2016, see Chapter 7 of this volume for a fuller description of this research). Voas and Chaves have more recently suggested that religious participation in the USA is following a pattern similar to that of northern Europe, just two decades behind (2016).

Robert Putnam has argued that the reduction in church participation is part of wider societal phenomenon in which fewer people join voluntary associations, whether they are trade unions, churches or the Women's Institute, and in which more and more we do engage in a privatised form of social life, even going out bowling, alone (2000). In Britain, pubs as well as churches are closing: in 2014, the Campaign for Real Ale claimed two pubs closed every week.

Grace Davie in the second edition of *Religion in Britain* (2015) reformulates her 'believing and not belonging' in Putnam's terms and talks of 'believing and not *bonding*'. Where religious participation is growing, such as in cathedrals, the fluid nature of the large congregation and the consequent anonymity of the setting may be one of the attractions (Davie 2015: 138). Karen Leth-Nissen recently described this phenomenon as 'churching alone' (2018).

Many of these alternative theorisations contest the teleological nature of Bruce's theorisation but also emphasise the way in which these theorists believe that individual spirituality will outrun collectivised religious participation and practice or create new modes of expression. None of these theories bodes well for sustained religious recruitment in northern Europe and possibly North America.

Popular and institutional religion, popular and institutional secularisation

Most secularisation theory is concerned with corporate expression but also those individual acts that create an expression of the corporate in the minds of outsiders.

Karel Dobbelaere posited three levels of secularisation: societal (macro), within religion (meso) and individual (micro):

> I sought to differentiate these three dimensions, by using the terms 'laici-sation' for the societal or macro level, 'religious change' for the organi-sational or meso level, and 'religious involvement' for the individual or micro level. The concept of secularisation should be used only if one referred to all three levels at the same time. (2002: 13)

There is a dialectical interaction between these levels, each feeding the other. This volume takes as read that religion and thus secularisation operates on these different organisational and popular levels.

Secularism and the nation-state

Whilst theorists of secularisation focus on the nature of the change of religious influence and agency, theorists of secularism focus on the nature of the liberal-secular nation-state and the way in which religion is controlled and constrained. In this way they view the nature of a secularisation of the State in term of political ideology, State involvement, and individual rights. Some contest the kind of binary divide between religion and wider society that secularisation theorists tend towards in its emphasis on the binary differentiation of church and State (see for example Mandair and Dressler 2011: 19). This 'differentiation', so prominent in Tschannen's analysis, may be understood as the decline of established religion in the public realm but, as we see below, secularism presupposes the continuing connection of State and religion.

A key focus in this scholarship on secularism has been on religious freedom and the rights of minority groups. This plays out in different ways in different contexts. As Grace Davie has commented using the contrasting example of

France, with its laicist or secular constitution, and Britain with a State-accepted established (but marginalised) church, democracy does not equate to toleration (2015: 193). Further, as we shall see below, religious toleration does not equate to religious liberty. In laicist regimes such as France, it is legal to practise Islam but not legal to wear a burka and there have been ongoing court cases in France and Switzerland about the wearing of headscarves, or hijabs.

As Saba Mahmood comments:

> The right to religious freedom is widely regarded as a crowning achievement of secular-liberal democracies, one that guarantees the peaceful coexistence of religiously diverse populations. Enshrined in national constitutions and international laws and treaties, the right to religious liberty promises to ensure two stable goods: (1) the ability to choose one's religion freely without coercion by the state, church, or other institutions; and (2) the creation of a polity in which one's economic, civil, legal, or political status is unaffected by one's religious beliefs. (2012: 418)

For Mahmood and scholars such as Talal Asad (2003), societal secularisation (Dobbelaere 2002) is best described as political secularism, 'the modern state's sovereign power to reorganise substantive features of religious life, stipulating what religion is or ought to be, assigning its proper content, and disseminating concomitant subjectivities, ethical frameworks, and quotidian practices'. (Mahmood 2016: 3). The Nation-State comes to define the role and content of religion right down to its everyday practices.

Thus, whilst religious toleration may at first appear positive in terms of religious practice, it is actually intertwined with the State's role in determining what is acceptable religious belief and practice. Secularism is not about 'state neutrality toward religion but the sovereign prerogative of the state to regulate religious life through a variety of disciplinary practices that are political as well as ethical' (Mahmood 2010: 293).

> Secularism, in this understanding, is not simply the organizing structure for what are regularly taken to be *a priori* elements of social organisation – public, private, political, religious – but a discursive operation of power that generates these very spheres, establishes their boundaries, and suffuses them with content, such that they come to acquire a natural quality for those living within its terms. (Mahmood 2016: 3)

Asad defines secularism as a political doctrine based on the separation of religion from secular institutions of government. In terms of religious liberty it seeks to find the lowest common denominator amongst conflicting sects, and also seeks to 'define a political ethic independent of religious convictions' (Asad 2003: 2). It asserts the centrality of the public sphere (with the right of all to discuss affairs of the State), an extension of market principles with all citizens as legal equals and the development of ideas of citizenship (accompanying individualism) within the modern Nation-State (Asad 2003: 2) The concept of time is crucial too. Time in the secular State is secular homogeneous time with no external mediators, or imagined extensions (such as an after-life). Asad comments that '"the secular" should not be thought of as the space in which *real* human life gradually emancipates itself from the controlling power of "religion" and thus achieves the latter's relocation' (2003: 191). Religion is not relocated 'out' of the social. Rather 'From the point of view of secularism, religion has the option either of confining itself to private belief and worship or of engaging in public talk that makes no demands on life' (Asad 2003: 199).

Charles Taylor connects secularisation theory with his understanding of secularism. The secular age does not entail a lack of religion but rather the differentiation of the religious from the Nation-State. There is a falling off of religious belief and practice and the conditions of belief have changed whereby residual religious belief is seen as one option amongst many, rather than being dominant and unchallenged (Taylor 2007: 2–3).

Thus, the secular is not the negation of religion but the condition within which religion is now constructed. Arvind Mandair and Markus Dressler discuss this construction of religious life in terms of the 'politics of religion-making', state constructions of the religious and the secular (2011: 3). They comment:

> Broadly conceived the term *religion-making* refers to the way in which religion(s) is conceptualized and institutionalized within a matrix of globalized world-religions discourse in which ideas, social formations, and social/cultural practices are discursively reified as 'religious' ones. (Mandair and Dressler 2011: 21)

Mandair and Dressler suggest there is both 'religion-making from above' and 'religion-making from below'. Religion-making from above includes the State regulation of the political activities of religions (2011: 22), e.g. when 'religion becomes an instrument of governmentality, a means to legitimise certain politics and positions of power' (2011: 21). Using the USA as a case study, they claim that 'U.S. religion builders are less concerned with keeping religion out of politics than with regulating its political manifestations' (Mandair and Dressler 2011: 22).

'Religion-making from below' is described as 'a politics where particular social groups in a subordinate position draw on a religionist discourse to re-establish their identities as legitimate social formations distinguishable from other social formations through tropes of religious difference and/or claims for certain rights'. In other words, religion-making from below is the way in which religious groups negotiate their religious identities as distinctive but equivalent in their desire for rights. To undertake this task, they need to work within the language and semantics of the Nation-State to which they are responding (Mandair and Dressler 2011: 22).[1]

For Mandair and Dressler, secularism is not about one way State separation and regulation of religion but the control of the spaces of negotiation between these two forms of religion-making. Religion is processual but so are the regulatory mechanism of the State, a point we return to in Chapter 4. In this negotiation, religion is not essential or universal and is defined in terms to fit the State's cultural preferences. Hindusim, Sikhism and Buddhism became incorporated as world religions in the nineteenth century. These are not separated out as 'religion' in India, e.g. as there is no need for a religion/secular binary (Mandair and Dressler 2011: 17) In particular, Mandair and Dressler challenge the idea that the differentiation of church and State, religious and political, is necessary for religious freedom. Jürgen Habermas has called for post-secularity, in which the religious and the secular dialogue as equal partners transcending their differences (2006). For Mandair and Dressler, it is not about the end of the binary but the end of the construction of the binary (2011: 19). This analysis makes secularisation theory more complex (Asad 2003: 201).

The regulation of religion

Religion-making from above can be clearly seen in terms of the construction of religious minorities.

For Mahmood, a State which tolerates religious expressions equally increasingly stands outside them all and one of the paradoxes of the secular State is the degree to which it is concerned with the regulation of religion (Mahmood 2016: 2). Mahmood suggests too that secular States whilst notionally advocating religious freedom often perpetuate and intensify pre-existing interfaith (and inter-church)inequalities (2016: 2). In those nations which claim a clear separation between church and State, the very notion of separation is contradicted by the State intervention to try and sustain that separation.

> The establishment of the nation-state as the dominant political form put into play a new rationale of governance that divided up the governed differently from the logic of empires: instead of recognizing parallel and contiguous communities distinct by virtue of their confessional, denominational, or tribal/ ethnic affiliation, the nation-state sought to represent 'the people,' united by a shared history, culture, and territory, wherein each individual qua citizen was tied to the state through a legal system of rights and obligations. The terms 'majority' and 'minority' came to serve as a constitutional device for resolving differences that the ideology of nationalism sought to eradicate, eliminate, or assimilate. (Mahmood 2012: 424)

Mahmood here introduces the ideas of majority and minority to replace the ideas of equivalent communities. Instead the nation is about 'the people' with those who are not part of 'the people' cast as a minority. However, as Mahmood comments, there is a tension in the idea of a 'national minority':

> The concept of 'national minority' is built, however, on a fundamental tension: on one hand, it signifies the membership of a minority group in a national polity; on the other, the minority group by virtue of its cultural, racial, religious, ethnic, or linguistic difference from the majoritarian culture also represents an incipient threat to national unity. (2012: 424)

This tension between sub-groups and groups representing the dominant ideology predates the language of 'minority' (some 'dissenters' can become 'minorities'), and this tension between who is and who is not an automatic part of 'the nation' has repeatedly been enshrined in law to create categories of citizens, part-citizens or conditional citizens, and outlaws or non-citizens. Secularism is not anti-religion or non-religion but rather represents the latest version of the State operating to distinguish good religion from bad religion: as Dressler states, it is about the 'making of religion in the context of the nation-state' (2011: 187).

Dressler writes about the plight of the Alevis within Turkish laicism to show how the State regulates acceptable religiosity. Alevis constitute 15% of the Turkish population who self-identify as distinct from Sunni Muslims through different historical experiences and separate formational influences and practices (Dressler 2011: 203). Regarding Turkish laïcité, Dressler comments:

> as for the organization of political space, endorses not only the primacy of the political over the religious, as is common in Western forms of secularism, but also the control of the religion in the public [arena]. Both French and Turkish laicist discourses are rhetorically directed against a previous, now othered, political order, in which religion had a central role in the organization of the state and public life. (2011: 188)

Echoing Mahmood's comments above on the centrality if the control of religion within secularist States, Dressler is clear that laicist discourse continually centres on religion, thus, paradoxically, normalising particular notions of religion and thee secular: 'laicism disciplines the religious by subordinating it to a modernist/secularist framework' (2011: 188).

> The discourse on Turkish laicism is dominated by principles of separation of religion and politics and control and administration of religion by the state. While the former justifies repression of religious activism in politics, the latter secures the superiority of the state over religious institutions. (Dressler 2011: 189)

A 'Directorate for Religious Affairs' (DRA) is:

> the sole institution authorized to represent Islam in the Turkish Republic ...
> Located *within* the state organization, the DRA represents theological
> authority combined with secular-political legitimacy. The laicist Turkish
> state thus formally divides and brings together within its structure theologi-
> cal and structural authoritries ... Turkish secularism from this perspective is
> less about policing the boundaries between religious and secular spheres and
> more about asserting state hegemony over the definition and signification of
> what are legitimate practices in the public sphere. (Dressler 2011: 189–191)

The DRA defines, represents and organises and regulates the public forms
of Islam. For the Alevis, they need to choose between presenting as a sub-set
of permissible Islam and Islamic practices (described by a former DRA
President as 'the common-share of Islam' – Dressler 2011: 191) or being
regulated as 'other' and thus as publicly 'cultural' rather than religious.

Alevis are not protected by the 1923 Lausanne Peace Treaty (which regulated
the reconstruction of the former Ottoman Empire) which only guaranteed rights
for non-Muslim minorities, and Alevis cannot claim to be a 'minority' a term
only used to refer to non-Muslims outside the Turkish Muslim nation: 'In other
words, non-recognition of their socio-religious and ethno-cultural difference has
been the price they had to pay for being integrated into the national project'
(Dressler 2011: 190). The non-recognition of difference equates to the possibility
of rights. The Alevis then are forced to assimilate in public and privatise distinctive religious expression.

'Alevis are forced to position themselves theologically within an Islamic
system of reference' (Dressler 2011: 202–203) either as a sub-group or as an
alternative religion. The mode of negotiation is shaped by the secularist State
and is not a neutral space. We return to the kind of challenge this poses to
religious groups within secularist democracies at the end of this chapter.

Section summary

As Talal Asad comments, the secular is 'neither continuous with the religious
that supposedly preceded it (that is, it is not the latest phase of a scared
origin) nor a simple break from it (that is, it is not the opposite, an essence
that excludes the sacred)' (2003: 25). Rather the secular State is a particular
mode of regulation, offerings rights in return for assimilation. It is not free
from religion but is centred on its constraint.

More forcefully, Wendy Brown suggests, 'The secular state is not non-
theological or neutral ... politics is laced with religious debate and the
regulation of the social based on religious preferences: 'the secular
state ... is a distinctive kind of theological state, never "free" of religion'
(2015: 332–333).

Western secular practices feature constant leakages from the private to the public, the individual to the collective, the free mind to the bowed head – leakages that contour everything from the veil debates to judicial decisions to inaugurations of heads of state that begin and end with invocations of God. (Brown 2015: 326)

Courtney Bender, building on this kind of analysis, suggests that: '... secularism shapes and is shaped by the coordination and regulation of religious difference and, likewise, co-ordination of narratives of religious pluralism and religious freedom' (2013: 153).

Religious toleration has been highly specified and race-specific for centuries. The language of religious tolerance within a Protestant plurality accommodated a critique of nineteenth-century Catholic immigration and the 'problems' that accompanied it, and allowed it to be categorised as 'other'.

In the colonial period, 'pluralism' reinforced and established certain kinds of Protestant religiosity as uniquely able to participate in American secularism and, increasingly, to pose as a more authentic kind of general religiosity that other religions could emulate. (Bender 2013: 153)

Bender argues that democracy has been regulated and citizenship limited to those who appear to fit the implicit religiosity of the State. Within the USA, questions about Chinese or Indian religions followed questions about Catholic immigrants, and now there are questions of how far Muslims can 'secularise' (2013: 153), i.e. fit. As Mahmood comments: 'The political solution that secularism proffers ... lies not so much in tolerating difference and diversity, but in remaking certain kinds of religious subjectivities (even if this requires the use of violence) so as to render them compliant with liberal political rule' (Mahmood 2006: 328).

In short, secularism has informed the dominant mode of liberal democracy at least throughout Europe and North America. It revolves around the Nation-State's desire to accommodate religious difference through the regulation of the role of religious organisations in the political and public life of the nation. It is rooted in an ideology of common citizenship rather than religious difference. In places such as Britain this has involved the constraint of the established church and the management of dissent. In France and other laicist nations, the State is created to be free from all religious influence and public life is constructed and regulated as secular. Within these tropes of secularism, we can identify processes of secularisation, the falling away of the social and public significance of religion in everyday life. In part these processes are supported by secularism, but they also depend in part on new rationalist and scientific ways of thinking about the world as well as personal choices over church membership and participation.

Thus within the secular Nation-State, religions need to constantly negotiate their place as collectives seeking rights to practise their faith in the terms of State regulatory control. Taking Britain as a secular Nation-State for all intents and purposes (Taylor 2007: 2), this book uses the Quakers as a case study to reflect on these processes of negotiation and expression. However, first, let us consider recruitment and the conundrum facing religious groups within this dynamic relationship between religion and non-religion.

Religious recruitment

Dean Kelley argued in the 1970s that growth in the membership of any particular church relied on the perception of its seriousness from the world-be converts. Typically conservative churches which made more resolute universal claims fared better than those which were more permissive (1972, 1978). Liberal groups might pick up recruits from those previously unchurched but could also lose them again as their commitment to the religious life increased and they felt the need to move on to a setting which appeared 'more serious'. Reginal Bibby and Merlin Brinkerhoff argued that most church growth occurred in terms of recruitment from other churches, what they termed the 'circulation of the saints hypothesis' (1973), thus reinforcing the idea that liberal or permissive groups would ultimately lose out as people transferred to more 'serious' settings.

Steve Bruce in his work on secularisation is clear that liberal religion is declining more quickly than conservative forms (2003: 56). Bruce suggests that ideological diffuseness is more difficult to sustain and reproduce: 'Lack of obedience to a central authority ... makes consensus on the detail of belief impossible, it weakens individual commitment, and it reduces the ability and the need to evangelise' (2003: 57). In other words, pluralistic faith groups offer little to adherents to commit to and make faith transmission difficult. He continues: 'the individual's right to choose what to believe is so elevated that the idea of discipline is largely absent from liberal religion. The result has been a gradual loss of cohesion and identity' (Bruce 2003: 58).

Tolerance, then, is unhelpful for levels of sustained participation. Bruce argues:

> the willingness to embody a certain ideology depends on maintaining negative evaluations of alternatives ... such evaluations must entail some degree of sacrifice (if only the sacrifice of positive social relationships with those from whom we differ), they are most likely sustained when there is a strong community of like-minded believers to provide alternative rewards to those available elsewhere and to stiffen the resolve of the believer in the face of subtle pressure to abandon anything that is distinctive in belief or behaviour. (Bruce 2003: 58)

Even a liberal or diffuse religious group will maintain a distinct identity in order to maintain internal cohesion which, Bruce claims, entails a constructed sense of difference. This can be doctrinal or behavioural but necessarily sets up a sense of difference between adherent and outsider. The weaker the sense of difference and the sacrifice required to sustain it, the less strong and cohesive is the identity of the group and thus its resistance to low levels of commitment.

The lack of zeal required to sustain participation in turn affects religious transmission to children and wider society, as, as above, does the lack of a single agreed message. If liberty of conscience is a hallmark of liberal religion, why join to gain something you can have and enjoy anyway (Bruce 2003: 59)? Thus, attempts to maximise the plausibility of religion in a rationalistic world may have a short-term positive effect but be ultimately unhelpful to the long-term success of the group.

The conundrum facing religious group in liberal democracies

From these first two chapters we can see that sects compete with each other and State regulation for cultural control but also aim, ultimately, for rights. Within liberal democracies, secularism underpins the idea of religious freedom and rights are given to groups that conform to the preferences of the State. However, this comes at a cost to the vibrancy of religious expression in three ways: (a) the secularisation of religious fervour and universal truth claims that accompanies mass denominationalisation, (b) the ceding of public and political religious expression within the preferences of secularism, (c) the internal group management of the presentation of religious expression in order to secure rights from the State. The first of these, according to Steve Bruce, undermines the plausibility of religious truth claims, the second two limit the ability of the group to make stronger universal truth claims over and against other religions that may appear attractive to would-be converts.

Armand Mauss, building on the work on commitment mechanisms by Rosabeth Moss Kanter (1972), is clear about the value of strong sacrificial mechanisms to enhance commitment to the group:

> ... people tend to commit themselves to causes for which they are required to sacrifice to some degree ... A religion that achieves greater comfort or respectability in a society, therefore, does not necessarily enhance thereby the commitment of its members at the individual level ... The more 'costly' such products, in terms of member sacrifice, investment, and stigmatization, the more 'valuable' they become. (Mauss 1994: 6, 10)

From secularisation theory too, we can see that pluralisation of religious expression undermines religiosity. Wilson made this point in 1966: 'once tolerance was extended to organised dissenters, the Church was reduced to the status of a denomination, albeit for a very long time a dominant and privileged one' (2016: 203–204). Thus, in a secular society there are, strictly speaking, no churches, just denominations (2016: 205). Yet denominations in their conformity to the world are an aspect of secularisation:

> Denominational diversity, however, has in itself promoted a process of secularization, in providing for the uncommitted a diversity of religious choice, in creating institutionalized expression of social differences and divisions ... the divergence of belief systems and ethical codes in society ... is likely to reduce the effectiveness of the religious agencies of social control. (Wilson 2016: 39)

Peter Berger also argued that pluralism and secularisation are intertwined (1967: 151, 155; 1971: 15).

In turn, secularisation may involve a secular response from religious groups. We can see the scaling down of demands made on believers by churches in the face of numerical decline. In the twentieth century, the popularity of books such as John Robinson's *Honest to God* (1963) with its liberal or permissive understanding of Christianity has been accommodated by the Church of England eager to hold on to participants as traditional theodicies failed to satisfy those who had lived through the traumatic events of the first half of the century.

At the same time, when religious freedom becomes a constituent part of the modern liberal Nation-State, religious affiliation becomes irrelevant to one's rights in society. Saba Mahmood confirms that religious toleration does not equate to an absence of regulation but also suggests that it is the focus on individual rights, within liberal-secular States, that drives religious freedom, not a religious acceptance of diversity. In this, the established churches are dethroned from their role as arbiters of religious truth and judges of religious probity. It is not that Nation-States have turned an ecumenical corner, as it were, but that the State has prioritised individual rights above the exclusive truth claims of any one religious group.

> Despite claims to religious neutrality, liberal secular states frequently regulate religious affairs but they do so in accord with a strong concern for protecting the individual's right to practice his or her religion freely, without coercion or state intervention. (Mahmood 2012: 418)

Mahmood gives the example of the Bahá'ís in Egypt who are allowed to believe privately but not allowed to manifest beliefs in public, because of 'public order' (2016: 162). Within laïcité in Switzerland, there is the notional freedom of all to believe, but not the freedom to influence and so no headscarves are allowed for school teachers (Mahmood 2016: 169–172). Markus Dressler concurs in his study of laïcité in Turkey:

The privatization of religion has been a key feature of secularist projects worldwide, which were both predicting and claiming for the public to be a space untainted by religious claims. Demanding privatization as a must for the establishment of secularity, the … laicist discourse is organized by private-public distinctions correlated with ideas about legitimate and illegitimate religion. (2011: 190–191)

Dressler usefully argues that the provision of rights involves the 'non-recognition of difference' (2011: 190).

The legal right to practise is the end point of the dissenting groups' claim for the freedom to worship and creates for them a version of citizenship, a type of equivalence, to which further rights may be added over time. The State grants and governs toleration nationally and internationally through allegiances with those States which maintain similar constitutions. Governments choose who and how to tolerate, and on what terms. The right to worship is often conditional or checked by other laws that constrain aspects of religious practice or freedom. Protestant nonconformists could worship freely in Britain after 1689 but only enter Parliament after 1832. Even the 1689 Act was conditional upon an Oath of Supremacy and excluded Catholics, non-Trinitarians and atheists, whose equivalent rights would only come one hundred years or more later.

This does not make erstwhile nonconformists 'conformists' (they may still oppose the status quo and the teachings of other religious groups in a number of ways) but it represents the recognition that these groups manifest sufficient conformity with the values of the State. In this, the location of 'conformity' has shifted from the original definition of not conforming to the teachings and practices of the church, as regulated by the State, to position in which the State is now defining for itself what is and is not non-conformity. Further it is from within religious groups themselves that conformity is cultivated.

Thus, thirdly, religious groups need to manage the public expression of their faith. Todd Endelman, talking about attitudes to Jewish communities claims that what is at stake 'is the price to be paid for inclusion rather than the right to be included' (2015: 2) Citizenship cannot be taken for granted. Assimilation privatises faith and faith expression, a process termed by Zionist leader Arthur Ruppin in 1911 as 'the undermining impact of assimilation' (Endelman 2015: 1). Integration may be unrewarded.

At the same time, stigma may not be not rubbed off by assimilation (Endelman 2015: 4–5), the 'otherness' of Jews for example so embedded in the Christian imagination and popular culture that even 'radical assimilation' – ceasing to identify as Jews and cutting their ties to Judaism and the Jewish community – did not work for some, e.g. Disraeli who was lampooned for his ethnicity in spite of having converted to Christianity (Endelman 2015: 12). As Endelman states: 'the conditions that encouraged defection in the first place were the same as those that later frustrated the hopes of those who chose this path' (2015: 12).

The conundrum then is this: if we agree on the idea that relativism diminishes the plausibility of truth claims, the more groups present themselves as equivalent or harmless, the more they run the risk of losing their public appeal in terms of recruitment based on strong universal claims. Thus, religious democracies offering religious freedom are bad for religious recruitment, or sustained recruitment mechanisms are bad for the continued provision of rights to religious groups. Religious groups are thus continually needing to manage the balance of their presentation between acceptability and plausibility.

Chapter summary

This chapter has briefly surveyed some of the scholarship on secularisation, secularism and ideas of recruitment within liberal religion. It offers us a map, a picture of diminished religious participation within a changed and changing relationship between religion and the State. The loss of the social significance of religious capital, particularly amongst liberal or diffuse groups, makes sustained recruitment less likely. More importantly, from Steve Bruce's analysis of the challenge of recruitment for liberal religious groups, we can see a tension for religious groups who have the choice between the desire to maintain universal truth claims that might appear attractive to would-be recruits and the lure of rights offered by the Nation-State in exchange for political harmlessness and religious equivalence. Sectarian groups may appear more salient to religious seekers but maintain their counter-worldliness at the potential cost of rights to worship freely. It is this dynamic we focus on in Part II of this volume.

Note

1 Mandair and Dressler also suggest there is 'religion-making from a (pretended) outside', such as 'scholarly discourses on religion that provide legitimacy to the first two processes of religion-making by systematising and thus normalizing the religious/secular binary and its derivatives' (2011: 21).

PART II

Theoretical complexities: religion and 'the world'

3

THE HISTORY OF THE HEDGE

This part of the book is the account of 'the journey' in terms of Thomas Tweed's idea of theory (see 'Introduction'). It uses a case study of British Quakers to reflect on the territory marked out in Chapters 1 and 2 about religion's relationship with non-religion. This chapter presents an overview of the varying dynamic between the Quaker group and what they have perceived as 'the world'. The Quaker idea of 'the hedge', separating pure from impure, is introduced and explored, and the different attitudes across time to both 'world' and 'hedge' outlined. We can begin to locate the material used by scholars to examine the Quaker case in terms of the sect/denomination typology, explored in Chapter 4, and in Chapter 5 explore the dynamics of the relationship between religion and non-religion in terms of flow.

Sectarian separatism

From the work of Weber, Troeltsch, Wilson and Martin we can deduce that all sectarian groups construct and maintain mechanisms of separation between themselves and wider society that in turn support and reflect distinctive faith understandings and identities. We can think of the Amish, for example, with their distinctive patterns of language and dress, the refusal to be connected to the national grid, and the use of horse and buggies rather than automobiles.

We can see the sect form as prophetic, less inclined to assimilation, 'serious' rather than permissive, offering universal truth claims rather than diffuse ones. Sects do not necessarily want to appear as 'harmless' but rather as faithful and may take up the stance of holy outlaw rather than citizen mystic. A commitment to recruitment may take precedence over the desire for rights. Involvement requires high levels of participation.

For Christian groups, the New Testament provides plenty of support for a distinction between faith and worldly conformity. Romans 12:1–2 requests and instructs adherents to inhabit a counter-cultural position.

> I beseech you therefore, brethren, by the mercies of God, that ye present your bodies a living sacrifice, holy, acceptable unto God, which is your reasonable service.[2] And be not conformed to this world: but be ye transformed by the renewing of your mind, that ye may prove what is that good, and acceptable, and perfect, will of God. (KJV)

The contrast between the temporary nature of '*this* world' and the promise of eschatological hope, prefigured by personal transformation, is clear. 2 Corinthians 6:14–17 is more strident on the need for separation:

> [14] Be ye not unequally yoked together with unbelievers: for what fellowship hath righteousness with unrighteousness? and what communion hath light with darkness? [15] And what concord hath Christ with Belial? or what part hath he that believeth with an infidel? [16] And what agreement hath the temple of God with idols? for ye are the temple of the living God; as God hath said, I will dwell in them, and walk in them; and I will be their God, and they shall be my people. [17] Wherefore come out from among them, and be ye separate, saith the Lord, and touch not the unclean thing; and I will receive you. (KJV)

Here Paul echoes the sentiments of parts of the Hebrew Scriptures but to his new broader audience of a mix of Jews and gentiles. The dualism between believers and unbelievers is clear. Separation and purity are necessary in order for the faithful, God's people, to be received by God. The Amish talk of non-Amish as 'the English' and Exclusive Brethren limit company at mealtimes to co-religionists as part of their 'principle of separation' (Plymouth Brethren 2015). Groups may be wary of worldly schooling or company more generally, and marrying only within the group (endogamy) is a common practice in sectarian groups. Whilst many of these groups may claim to be 'the true church', that claim only holds for those within any one group. All else, including other 'true churches', are portrayed as wrong. In the case of the Quakers, the intimacy with God claimed by the earliest adherents gave them a sense of co-agency which cast anything and anyone that was not 'of the faith' as apostate and as part of 'the world'.

Quaker converts Francis Howgill and his preaching companion Edward Burrough, were both highly critical of groups who claimed to be with God but were essentially of the world. Howgill wrote in 1659: 'the Whore's cup is Drunk of, and the Dragon hath Power, which sought to destroy the man-Child, and made war with the Remnant of the Seed of the Woman, who was Clothed with the Sun; you all stick yet in *Babylon*, and the best of you all, are but yet in the

Suburbs thereof' (Howgill 1676: 210). Even the most faithful remain within the suburbs of Babylon whilst they continue to resist the full power of God's message. In 1665, Howgill returned to the theme of Babylon, who he argues has claimed Christ as her husband and lured the nations to drink of her golden cup:

> Then all the nations becoming water, and unstable, being drunk with fornication, staggered up and down, and reeled up and down, and stood in nothing, being out of the power which should have stabilised them; and then a great beast arose out of these waters, with seven heads and ten horns; and these apostatized ministers, who preached for filthy lucre, and those who believed them, sheltered them under the beast, and cryed: "who is able to make war with the beast?" And the kings of the earth gave their strength to the beast ... and the false church gets upon him ... and rides upon the beast, and he carries her, and hath done this many years; and she has travailed in the greatness of his *strength; Then laws began to be made about religion; then began compelling|: we heard of none in primitive times or in the true church* ... Now Rome look to your beginning and read thy original and view your antiquity ... If nations, and kindreds, and tongues, and people have drunk the whore's cup *since John's days* ... then what cause have thou Rome to boast of antiquity and universality? For that doth the sooner prove thee to be a harlot than the true Church. (1676: 412–413)

The church has been, and is, corrupt. Its claim of tradition is meaningless given its apostasy. Burrough, nine years earlier in *A Trumpet Sounded Forth out of Sion* (1656) targeted 23 different groups and individuals who had fallen short and who needed to repent. Even his own erstwhile affiliation, the Seekers, were not spared the clarity that only the Quakers, or the saints, were right in their theological witness.

Quaker founder George Fox encouraged his fellow 'saints' to 'trample all that is contrary under' (Nickalls 1952: 263) as he established a counter-cultural sect in which the idea of spiritual equality was taken to liturgical limits whereby men and women and children were all ministers. Quaker baptism and communion were inward after Revelation 3:20 and worship was in stillness and silence, after Revelation 8:1, to allow God to break into the hearts of believers. As Francis Howgill wrote:

> [We] were reckoned, in the north part of England, even as the outcasts of Israel, and as men destitute of the great knowledge, which some seemed to enjoy; yet there was more sincerity and true love amongst us and desires after the living powerful presence of God than was among many in that day who ran into heaps and forms but left the cross behind them. God out of his everlasting love did appear unto us, according to the desire of our hearts, who longed after him; when we had turned aside

from hireling-shepherds' tents, we found him whom our souls loved; and God, out of his great love and great mercy, sent one unto us, a man of God, one of ten thousand, to instruct us in the way of God more perfectly; which testimony reached unto all our consciences and entered into the inmost part of our hearts, which drove us to a narrow search, and to a diligent inquisition concerning our state, through the Light of Christ Jesus. The Lord of Heaven and earth we found to be near at hand, and, as we waited upon him in pure silence, our minds out of all things, his heavenly presence appeared in our assemblies, when there was no language, tongue nor speech from any creature. The Kingdom of Heaven did gather us and catch us all, as in a net, and his heavenly power at one time drew many hundreds to land. We came to know a place to stand in and what to wait in; and the Lord appeared daily to us, to our astonishment, amazement and great admiration, insomuch that we often said one unto another with great joy of heart: 'What, is the Kingdom of God come to be with men? And will he take up his tabernacle among the sons of men, as he did of old? Shall we, that were reckoned as the outcasts of Israel, have this honour of glory communicated amongst us, which were but men of small parts and of little abilities, in respect of many others, as amongst men?' And from that day forward, our hearts were knit unto the Lord and one unto another in true and fervent love, in the covenant of Life with God; and that was a strong obligation or bond upon all our spirits, which united us one unto another. We met together in the unity of the Spirit, and of the bond of peace, treading down under our feet all reasoning about religion. And holy resolutions were kindled in our hearts as a fire which the Life kindled in us to serve the Lord while we had a being, and mightily did the Word of God grow amongst us, and the desires of many were after the Name of the Lord. O happy day! O blessed day! the memorial of which can never pass out of my mind. And thus the Lord, in short, did form us to be a people for his praise in our generation.

(*Quaker Faith and Practice* 1995: 19.08)

These were people 'destitute of the great knowledge' that some 'seemed' to enjoy but which ultimately led them astray. In the place of outward notions, 'The Lord appeared daily' to these Quakers, without any need for external rite or even speech, galvanising the commitment of the group to a life of mission as part of the new covenant promised in Jeremiah 31:31–34 and Hebrews 8:8–14. The 'law' was written on their hearts and all 'reasoning' about religion was suppressed. Early Quaker convert Thomas Ellwood personally discovered that he was led to lead a new life:

And now I saw that, although I had been in a great degree preserved from the common immoralities and gross pollutions of the world, yet the spirit of the world had hitherto ruled in me and led me into pride, flattery, vanity and superfluity, all which was naught. I found there were many plants growing in me which were not of the Heavenly Father's planting, and that all these, of whatever sort or kind they were or how specious soever they might appear, must be plucked up. (Crump 1900: 16)

A whole range of behaviours and practices quickly became part of the corporate Quaker identity, part of a priestly code delineating pure from impure in which all adherents were part of the priesthood. Paying tithes to the church would be to give money to the 'world' and swearing an oath contravened the instruction found in Matthew 5:34, 'swear not at all'. Quakers refused to 'bow or scrape' before social superiors and they would not use the deferential form 'you', preferring 'thee' and 'thou' and eschewed titles similarly as they levelled society. Hats were kept on except when someone was in prayer, contravening the everyday etiquette expected when meeting someone you knew. Ellwood wrote of an encounter soon after his conversion:

A knot of my old acquaintance [at Oxford], espying me, came to me. One of these was a scholar in his gown, another a surgeon of that city ... When they were come up to me, they all saluted me, after the usual manner, putting off their hats and bowing, and saying, 'Your humble Servant, Sir', expecting no doubt the same from me. But when they saw me stand still, not moving my cap, nor bowing my knee, in way of congee to them, they were amazed, and looked first one upon another, then upon me, and then one upon another again for a while, without a word speaking. At length, the surgeon ... clapping his hand in a familiar way upon my shoulder and smiling on me said, 'What, Tom, a Quaker!' To which I readily, and cheerfully answered, 'Yes, a Quaker.' And as the words passed out of my mouth I felt joy spring in my heart, for I rejoiced that I had not been drawn out by them into a compliance with them, and that I had strength and boldness given me to confess myself to be one of that despised people. (Crump 1900: 23–24)

For Ellwood, it was crucial that he align himself with the 'despised people' and not be drawn into 'compliance' with the world's people and worldly ways.

Quakers refused to use the names of days and months given their pagan origins, and used a numbering system instead. Thus Sunday became first day, Monday second day, etc. Until 1752, March was the beginning of the year and was named as first month by the Quakers. Quite early on, Fox advised on a plainer form of dress with lapels that are not too wide and with no unnecessary buttons (Braithwaite 1912: 511), in an attempt to curb the temptations of vanity and pride. Quakers in the eighteenth century prohibited the use of gravestones for similar reasons. Individualism could be dangerous for a group reliant on direct revelation.

Adrian Davies found evidence of talk of a Quaker gait or way of walking (2000: 58–60), distinct from a more worldly carriage. One way of men displaying wealth in the seventeenth century was to wrap themselves in yards of material, requiring a swinging of the limbs in order to walk, possibly with the aid of a cane. Those of a more puritanical disposition, however, might use the barest amount of material to construct their apparel and be physically constrained by its paucity. Rather than an exaggerated swagger, perhaps these Quakers took short straight steps with a reduced movement of the arms, as the amount of material afforded.

Quakers also established a witness against outward fighting. Fox refused release from jail in return for a captaincy in the battle against Charles 1's son, claiming that Quaker Christianity excluded killing: 'I told [the Commonwealth Commissioners] I lived in the virtue of that life and power that took away the occasion of all wars ... I told them I was come into the covenant of peace which was before wars and strife were' (Nickalls 1952: 65).

Throughout the 1650s, Quakers maintained this position collectively as part of their understanding of a perfected life realised through their salvation experience.

The Quaker experience of God was framed in these soteriological terms but also eschatological ones. Quakers understood the inward light of Christ as an interiorised experience of the second coming of Christ, as foretold in Matthew, the letters of Paul and the book of Revelation. Thus, these first Quakers felt themselves to be living in the end times, at the end of the biblical timeline, helping usher in the kingdom for the rest of humanity (Dandelion 2007: 30–34). The church in all its forms (themselves designed to be temporary until the time of the second coming of Christ) was holding humanity back as long as it continued to insist on 'meantime' practices that, to the Quakers, were now anachronistic. In 1 Corinthians 11:26, the suggestion is to 'break the bread' until the Lord comes again. For Quakers, the Lord had come again and there was thus no need to continue the practice of outward communion. Similarly, in this new sense of time, the Christian calendar based on remembrance of the first coming and anticipation of the second, becomes redundant. For Quakers, all places and all times become equally sacramental. Fox preached up a tree in Sedbergh church-yard for he claimed it was equal to the church building (Nickalls 1952: 107).

The hedge

The separation inherent in the sense of dualism between Quaker and 'world' encouraged by George Fox and the other Quaker leaders was framed in some tracts in terms of 'the hedge' and in the 1850s the value of the 'hedge' was explicitly debated amongst the Quakers.

Sociologically, we can cast the hedge as a boundary-marker between 'pure' and 'impure' defined by the faith group with its concomitant actions and behaviours. In pastoral and rural societies, the hedge protected plants from animals; it enclosed that which was to be nurtured. The biblical roots of the idea of the hedge are found in Job 1:10. Here Satan complains to God that Job has been particularly cared for by God: 'Hast not thou made an hedge about him, and about his house, and about all that he hath on every side? thou hast blessed the work of his hands, and his substance is increased in the land' (KJV).

The hedge represents a barrier against worldly constraint or contamination. In Job 3:23, Job himself admits that he is 'hedged in' by God, although the sense is less positive here, perhaps even suggesting being trapped in his dreadful state by God: 'Why is light given to a man whose way is hid, and whom God hath hedged in?' (KJV) The passage in Lamentations 3:7 echoes this sense of being trapped by the hedge.

Common to both passages, however, is the sense that worldliness lies on the other side of the hedge. In Psalm 80, verse 12, the vine that God has brought out of Egypt is referred to as growing hedges which protect those behind it from the heathen. In Psalm 89, verse 40, the hedge is again portrayed as the protection against ruin. In Isaiah 5, the vine or hedge is associated with the house of Israel and its ability to resist worldly contamination, so again there is the connection between the chosen people and God's hedge, and the way in which God is clear that the hedge will be removed if the faithful fall short. In Ezekiel 13:5 and 22: 30, God hopes that a hedge will be built to help Israel face the battle ahead in the Day of the Lord but God cannot find anyone to make up the hedge and stand before him and argue against the impending destruction. The hedge, then, in these passages, is synonymous with conditional protection and/or divinely ordained constraint.

William Laud in dedicating his tract against Jesuit influence in 1639 to Charles I wrote: 'the external worship of God in his church is the heart witness to the world, that our heart stands right in that service of God'; ceremonial 'is the hedge that fences the substance of religion from all the indignities which profaneness and sacrilege too commonly puts upon it' (Laud 1839 [1639]: xxxi).

In 1676, Fox reflected on the early days of mission work, commenting:

> And thus the Lord's power hath carried us through all, and over all, to his everlasting glory and praise! For God's power, which was before the devil's was, hath been **our** hedge [Job 1:10, Isa 5:5], our wall, and our keeper, and the preserver of his plants and vineyard, who have not had the magistrates sword and staff to help them, nor ever trusted in the arm of flesh [Jer 17:5]. (1831a: 13)

Here 'hedge' is equated to 'wall' and 'keeper' and 'preserver'. In the same year, dated 17 June from Swarthmoor, Fox wrote an epistle to Quakers at Dantzic (Danzig). It began:

> Dear Friends, – In the love of God, and the Lord Jesus Christ, look above all your outward sufferings, and him that is out of truth, that makes you to suffer; and let nothing separate you from the love of God which you have in Christ Jesus, by whom all things were made: I say, let

not the birth of the flesh, with all his carnal weapons, jails, and prisons, threats, or reproaches, move you, nor separate you from the love of God, nor from your foundation, the rock of ages, Christ Jesus: but feel the well of life springing up in you, to nourish the plant that God has planted in you, of his renown, that that may grow up within his hedge, his power, which will keep out the devil and all the venomous beasts, from entering into God's garden, or kingdom. And therefore let your faith stand in the Lord's power, which is your hedge and defense, and which is your keeper, and will keep you safe, that you need not be afraid of your enemy, your adversary; for the Lord's power is over his head, and you within his power, then nothing can get betwixt you and God; and in the power of the Lord is the city set upon his hill, where the light shines, and the heavenly salt is, and the lamps burning, and trumpets sounding forth the praise of God, of the eternal joy, in his eternal word of life, that lives, and abides, and endure forever. And so to the praise and glory of God you may bring forth fresh and green fruit, being grafted into the green tree that never withers. (Fox 1831b: 127)

In this passage, Quakers are encouraged to mature spiritually within God's hedge which will protect them from the devil and any other enemies who might threaten that space of connection with the divine. The hedge is equated to the Lord's power, a defence and safeguard, so that there is no need to be frightened of any enemy. Reference to the book of Revelation with the city set upon the hill completes this opening part of the epistle. In a style typical of when Fox is writing to other Quakers it is an encouraging exhortation, suggesting utopian outcomes to counter present-day suffering and tribulations.

Compared to themes of purity and impurity in other epistles of his, it seems Fox favoured the hedge metaphor particularly in 1676. Given the condition of the Quaker movement in the 1670s, when Fox was dictating a longer version of his journal, it is perhaps unsurprising that Fox uses passages from Job. The Quakers who, it appeared, were securing the nation for God in the 1650s, had lost so much momentum, as well as key leaders, by the 1670s. Fox may have felt like Job, favoured by God but then bereft of so many of the earlier fruits of that co-agency. In his journal, he wrote of time before his convincement when, like Job, he wished for night when it was day, and day when it was night (1952: 7).

Also in the journal, he talks of the time of his release from Scarborough Castle, 1666, reflecting on the persecutions Quakers endured under the laws of the Restoration parliament: 'But Oh, the body of darkness that rose up against the Truth, who made lies their refuge. But the Lord swept them away, and in his power and truth, light and life, hedged his lambs about and did preserve them as on eagles' wings' (Nickalls 1952: 504).

Here again we have the sense of divine protection of 'his lambs' behind the hedge. The reference to 'eagles' wings' comes from Exodus 19:4–6.

[4]Ye have seen what I did unto the Egyptians, and how I bare you on eagles' wings, and brought you unto myself. [5]Now therefore, if ye will obey my voice indeed, and keep my covenant, then ye shall be a peculiar treasure unto me above all people: for all the earth is mine: [6]And ye shall be unto me a kingdom of priests, and an holy nation. These are the words which thou shalt speak unto the children of Israel. (KJV)

This passage from Exodus connects to the "peculiar people" language of 1 Peter 2:9: 'But ye are a chosen generation, a royal priesthood, an holy nation, a peculiar people; that ye should shew forth the praises of him who hath called you out of darkness into his marvellous light' (KJV).

In his journal, then, George Fox is drawing out a picture of Quakers as the holy nation, the kingdom of priests, the children of Israel, ideas that inform Quaker ecclesiology as well as the sense of consequent separation from 'the world'. Quakers, in this reading, are the 'peculiar treasure'. They are called to be the particular people of God. We return to eighteenth-century conceptions of Quakers as 'holy nation' below.

When in 1676 Robert Barclay, a highly educated gentry convert to Quakerism, published his *Apology for the True Christian Divinity*, a publication which was to set a tone for the Quakerism of the next century (2002), the title page highlighted the passage in the Letter to Titus about being purified as a 'peculiar people'.

[11]For the grace of God that bringeth salvation hath appeared to all men,[12] Teaching us that, denying ungodliness and worldly lusts, we should live soberly, righteously, and godly, in this present world;[13] Looking for that blessed hope, and the glorious appearing of the great God and our Saviour Jesus Christ;[14] Who gave himself for us, that he might redeem us from all iniquity, and purify unto himself a peculiar people, zealous of good works. (Titus 2:11–14, KJV)

Douglas Gwyn expounds the nature of 'peculiar' in its biblical meaning (2016). Whereas modern translations talk of the chosen people as God's 'treasured possession' (Deut 14:2), the KJV translation renders 'treasured' as 'peculiar', related to the idea of personal possession. The chosen people belong to God in as much as they are selected by God and in this sense 'particular' (Gwyn 2016: 28). They are to act for God in a particular way, to enact God's plan in God's way and to communicate it to the wider world. This way of acting will not fit with human culture, but is part of a wider eschatological drama being played out between God and humanity (Gwyn 2016: 32). God's people are necessarily peculiar or chosen/particular, called to live in chosen ways (Gwyn 2016: 36). For Gwyn, a commitment to peace is a hallmark of being God's treasured people.

Early Quakers stood in this place, experiencing themselves as God's peculiar possession, called to the Lamb's war, a spiritual warfare waged through the inward experience of Christ rather than outward weapons.

> The church in God, is not an imitation, gathered from the letter, nor is high flown people in their imaginations, but are they who are born again of the immortal seed, by the word of God ... which the world knows not ... For the church is the pillar and ground of truth, gathered by the eternal power that was before [the] letter was. (Fox 1653)

For Fox, the church is the community of believers gathered by God quite separate from any formal institutions or textual injunction. The church is particular in that it is selected. Fox retained a sense of peculiarity and his reference to Exodus ('carried on eagles wings') next to his sense of being hedged in by God in his *Journal* gives a clear sense of Quakers as a chosen people being borne towards the promised land. The kingdom of God did not appear as quickly as they first imagined and, as with the Apostle Paul, they needed to eventually develop a *meantime* strategy to accommodate the delay of the end-time drama that they had rooted their liturgy and ecclesiology in.

Kristianna Polder describes how William Penn and other seventeenth-century Quakers saw themselves as part of the true church coming out of the wilderness to which the false church had banished true Christianity (2015: 124–126). To mark this distinction, all the forms and outward signs of the false church were shunned, including its liturgical form. William Dewsbury wrote:

> Come out of Babylon, all forms, and observations, and traditions, which are set up by the will of man ... examine your hearts, and mind the Light in your conscience ... for it is the heart the Lord requires: He will no longer be worshipped in words, forms and observations, but in spirit and in truth and in sincerity in the inward parts ... for the Lord will make the Earth as the garden of Eden, and hath begun his great and strange works in this nation. (1655: 11)

Margaret Fell wrote in a similar fashion:

> Friends, whom the Lord God hath called unto the Light which is Eternal, which the Lord God hath sent, to bring his Seed out of Bondage, and out of the House of Darkness ... the Lord God of Life and Power hath visited you, and sent his servants to awaken you, and to raise you from the Dead, that Christ might give you Life, who is now come, and coming to redeem Israel. (1655)

Fell maintained that the true church was coming out of bondage as Israel had been delivered from slavery. (Polder 2015: 129–130). Polder (2015: 133) notes that William Erbery, father of Dorcas Erbery who became a Quaker, wrote of being 'be-wildernessed' out of the postasy (Erbery 1658). The true church needed to be extracted from the apostate structures and forms in order to emerge from the wilderness into its rightful place in the spiritual landscape.

Polder suggests that the discipline around endogamous marriage and its right ordering was particularly indicative of the desire of the Quakers to manifest their claim of being the true church, being renewed into the Paradise of God, directly by Christ, the second Adam (2015: 142–143). In no other realm did Quakers so clearly delineate pure people (the Quakers) from the impure ('the world'): Polder compellingly relates the refusal of Margaret Fell the younger to marry Colonel West, a non-Quaker, on theological grounds (2015: 155–161). Nevertheless, it is possible and plausible to extend this claim about specific delineation of true church and unbelievers to the whole of Quaker peculiarity. All Quaker practices delineated the separation of saint and sinner.

The challenge of the second generation

The challenge for sectarian religion comes, as Niebuhr suggested (see Chapter 2 above), with the advent of the second and third generations. Many of the first Quakers came into the movement as a result of personal transformation experiences, or 'convincement' (the often painful conviction of former beliefs coupled with a regenerative sense of personal salvation and a renewed life.) The children of Quaker converts were then necessarily schooled in the way of the true church and brought up to follow the peculiar lifestyle ordained by God. However, they were in a sense 'in waiting', a group of people following Quaker ways but awaiting their own convincement experience. Robert Barclay's *Apology* became the theological handbook for navigating this spiritual and temporal delay, both corporately as Quakers stepped back from the sense of a rapidly unfolding second coming of Christ and individually as young and new Quakers awaited their convincement. It is as if human agency had taken over from divine. It is the Quakers now who need to make intentional effort rather than receive God's protection.

Barclay's *Apology* is divided into 15 propositions. By the time of its publication in 1676, Quakerism had an increasingly formalised set of structures including the Second Day Morning Meeting which acted a publications committee. The book was approved by the Meeting and appeared in Latin in 1676 and in English in 1678. Its function was to systematise Quaker thinking during a period of persecution and attack, to try and make the enthusiasm of the first period make theological sense. Largely it follows the teaching of Fox, albeit in a more scholarly tone. It maintained the emphasis on direct spiritual experience as the primary religious authority and the idea of universal convincement, salvation and perfection as a single process initiated by God. However, to account for the unregenerate who died, Barclay introduced the idea of a 'singular day of visitation', a singular moment when God would invite each of the elect (2002: 132). This was available to all, but if ignored meant that people could outlive the possibility of salvation. This created high stakes for those in waiting. The sense of agency created anxiety and tension.

Barclay's final proposition was not concerned with eschatology as might have been expected in a 1660 version but with 'salutations and recreations', how to live in 'the world' (Barclay 2002: 429). The Quaker mindset lost its spiritual confidence during the years of the Restoration (Tousley 2008) and Quakers no longer imagined themselves as co-agents with God or benefactors of the divine realm. Rather they became both God-fearing and worried about worldly contamination. Their salvation lay more in their own actions. Instead of the hedge being a consequence of intimacy with God, their hedge was of their own planting in order to secure intimacy with God. They felt themselves to be on the natural plane aspiring to the supernatural one whilst resisting the world's ways. Anything which excited the emotion might lower the spiritual guard or diminish the diligence required to respond to one's personal day of visitation. Music, theatre and fiction were all proscribed, especially as the last were also not 'true'. Dress was codified into a plain style in spite of Margaret Fell's protestation that it was a 'silly poor gospel' (*Quaker Faith and Practice* 1995: 20.31). Consequence became turned into simplified codification. Peter Collins has described these shifts as an exercise in 'plaining' (1996, 2001), a process central to the construction of a peculiar Quaker identity. Until the 1860s, Quakers would be audibly and visibly distinct, a paradoxically outward expression of an inward spirituality set against forms and rite. Quakers operated behind God's hedge but performed their faith in public. This hedge was not so much a barrier between the world and the faithful (although it did operate as such) but a means of protecting and preserving the spiritual purity of the group. The hedge was primarily to create a space in which Quaker spirituality could flourish and in which Quakers could guard against the dangers of their own humanity.

Throughout the eighteenth century, as Jack Marietta has shown in his work on Pennsylvania Quakerism (1984), Quakers collectively policed each other's lives and the purity of the Meeting community. Those whose behaviour took them beyond the hedge and who failed to see the error of their deviation were disowned, losing their right to participate in the business affairs of the Society and losing their recourse to Quaker funds. (They could still attend worship as this was public and some disowned Quakers came back into membership as the community realised that they had rejoined the narrow path of Quaker spirituality.) According to Marietta, nearly one half of all offences were concerned with marrying before a priest (Marietta 1984: 6), either because a Quaker had married a non-Quaker or because a Quaker couple had married without the permission of their parents and thus of the Meeting. If the couple lived as Quakers and came to the Meeting, they were often readmitted.

Contrition, and following Meeting processes, was important for a sense of solidarity with the Quaker community. Processes had to be followed legalistically and undertaken seriously and sincerely.

Quaker worship was legalised in Britain in 1689, and the focus on the internal mechanism within the hedge may have replaced the energy required to campaign for rights or to organise emigration to William Penn's colony in the new world. Both Richard Vann (1969) and Barry Levy (1988) emphasise the centrality of the household in eighteenth-century Quakerism. Kathryn Damiano too has emphasised the role that family played in reinforcing peculiar Quaker spirituality (1988) and the way in which 'familied monasticism' or a 'guarded domesticity' operated to maintain the hedge.

Quaker mission receded and the emphasis on the internal preservation of peculiarity increased. The Irish Friend Richard Shackleton wrote to his daughter:

> Mayst thou, dear child, be preserved in simplicity and nothingness of self; in humility and lowliness of mind, seeking diligently after, and waiting steadily for, the inward experience of that which is *unmixedly good*. This is the way to be helped along from day to day, through one difficulty and proving after another, to the end of our wearisome pilgrimage. (Jones 1921: 65)

The 'unmixedly good' is God, the 'wearisome pilgrimage' the necessary attitude to life prior to salvation. The second generation were waiting for the kind of transformation their parents had experienced. Jones claims that this spirituality of anxiety led to an introspection but also the need to separate the human and natural from the supernatural. Sarah Lynes Grubb wrote in 1780:

> I am often afraid lest by indulging my own ideal of what is good, and not labouring after total resignation of mind ... I should frustrate the divine intention, which may be to humble and reduce self more than flesh and blood would point out. (Jones 1921: 68)

Catherine Phillips waited 23 years before being sure that her intended was truly God's choice and not just her own. She even considered other men but finally in 1766, she recounted: 'I had an intimation in my mind, which seemed to point to revival of our intimacy.' She married aged 46 (Damiano 1988: 183) When John Conran met Louisa Strongman:

> I felt in silence, a strong draft of love more than natural, and a secret intimation impressed my mind that she would be my wife; this I hid in my heart, and it was nearly two years before I felt at liberty to disclose it to any one, waiting as I apprehend the Lord's time to communicate it ... and when I felt the way open to proceed in it at that time, it was nearly six years after this before we were married. (Damiano 1988: 184)

The phrase 'more than natural' signals the spiritual authenticity of the experience.

The tendency to personal introspection was mirrored by an inclination to corporate self-examination. This gathered pace in the middle of the century and Jack Marietta dates a 'Quaker reformation' as beginning in 1748 when perceptions of lax standards prompted the introduction of greater internal discipline (1984). The reformers most heavily policed the life within Meeting and the life at home. Marietta shows an increasing number of offences deemed spiritual delinquency as the century wore on, matched by an increased number of those offending (Marietta 1984: 6–7).

Those deemed to offend were required to prepare a confession and appear before their Monthly Meeting (Marietta 1984: 7). The confession or the notice of disownment would also be posted outside the Meeting House to inform the world's people of the confession, or of the disownment where the Friend had refused to admit wrong. If the offence had taken place in a particular location, the paper would be read out there. If the offence was widely known, the paper would be widely circulated, as in the case of Edward Shippen in 1706, who had been a very public political figure and whose offence of marrying his third wife before a priest was well known (Marietta 1984: 9). This process accommodated the continued cloistering of the peculiar people but also preserved the nature of the true church and the presentation of its purity. Personal purity was to be matched by collective purity and collective purity was to be matched by the individual diligence and obedience. Here we see the personal pitted against the corporate: many did not take disownment lightly or without protest. The value of parts of the hedge has been constantly under negotiation.

This emphasis on getting the meantime right and on faithful waiting was made explicit in the 1789 Epistle from London Yearly Meeting, part of which ran:

> Wait in humble reverence for spiritual ability to worship acceptably the Lord of heaven and earth. Wait humbly and diligently in the spirit of your minds for the (inward) coming of Him who told His disciples, 'Without me ye can do nothing'; that ye may happily experience the influence of His Spirit to enlighten and quicken the soul to a true sight and sense of it condition; that feeling the spirit of supplication ye may approach the throne of grace. (Jones 1921: 102)

Frederick Tolles wrote about the tension between life 'in the world' and spiritual integrity:

> There was a conflict implicit in the Quaker ethic insofar as it applied to economic life. On the one hand, Quakers were encouraged to be industrious in their callings by the promise that God would add his blessing in the form of prosperity; on the other hand they were warned against allowing the fruits of their honest labours to accumulate lest they be tempted into luxury and pride. (1948: 82)

James Walvin, in his study of Quakers and business, juxtaposes 'plainness' and 'plenty' and shows how, in spite of increasing group discipline, Quakers adapted and thrived in the mercantile culture of the eighteenth century (Walvin 1997: 59). The Meetings regulated and policed business failure (bankruptcy or business failure or extravagance was prosecuted by the Meeting) and the expression of success (Walvin 1997: 72–79). It is not possible to divorce Quaker business life or worldly activity from Meeting life but it is important to establish the nature of the relationship between the two.

J. William Frost is clear that Pennsylvania Quakers were of no single class but that they were disproportionately represented amongst the richest in Philadelphia (1973: 206). Quakers were not levellers but lived modestly, whatever that might mean given their station. In Philadelphia particularly, political power and Meeting influence might be combined. The Reformation which Marietta charts was to try and place these two spheres of Quaker life in right relationship.

In sum, the eighteenth-century Quaker Meeting wanted no compromise of God-given commandments. Endogamy, plain dress, plain speech, the avoidance of the arts, literature and anything which was fictional or might excite the (natural) emotions, a separated and (only) basic education for Quaker children and the testimony, or witness, against the world's ways, (for example resistance to gravestones and 'times and seasons' and war), all acted as a collective mutually reinforced reminder of group identity and function. Marcia Pointon suggests that there was a keen Quaker sense of public representation of purity, thus managing the relationship between signifier and signified (1997: 423). As Polder suggested for the seventeenth century, the public visibility of endogamy in particular was hugely symbolic of the distance placed by Quakers between themselves and non-Quakers (Frost 1973: 210–211).

At the same time, joint work with non-Quakers on social justice issues such as slavery, and later collaboration within Bible societies meant that Quakers not only lived alongside and traded with non-Quakers but that some also campaigned with them. This was by no means universally accepted and well into the nineteenth century some Quakers refused to join with non-Quakers in work on a common cause. However, some did and the example of anti-slavery campaigner Anthony Benezet is helpful in exploring the way in which attitudes to the world's people changed from one of active disregard to one of ambivalent ecumenism.

Philadelphia Quaker Anthony Benezet has been credited by Irv Brendlinger as the single most influential Quaker campaigner against slavery (Brendlinger 2007). We see too that this commitment outweighed his sense that some of his fellow campaigners were of different religious persuasions. Benezet wrote of Granville Sharp, an Anglican anti-slavery campaigner:

> I am not insensible of his attachment to the outward practices of the Church, in the support of which, in opposition to our simple mode of worship &c he is rather more positive [*sic*], & somewhat tart, than I

should have expected from one of so much sense and charity. I have avoid [*sic*] any altercation on these points; sensible that neither circumcision nor uncircumcision; neither forms, nor the omission of them will avail, but a change from the natural corruption of the heart, the selfishness, revenge &c to a frame of humility and love. (Brendlinger 2007: 26)

Benezet here decided against challenging Granville Sharp as even the debate would focus on the outward rather than the inward. Benezet wrote to the Countess of Huntingdon in 1774: 'Among the many Snares and Temptations, which are peculiar to this part of the World, there are none that more sensibly impedes the growth of Truth, and has a greater tendency to hinder the heart, against the impressions of grace, than the practice of Slavery' (Brendlinger 2007: 93). In a second letter to her, he concluded; 'where the lives & natural as well as religious welfare of so vast a number of our Fellow Creatures is concerned, to be Silent, where we apprehend it a duty to speak our sense of that which causes us to go mourning on our way, would be criminal' (Brendlinger 2007: 104). The focus here is on slavery, their common and paramount concern. In letters to Wesley, the shared campaign against the slave trade superseded any theological differences (Brendlinger 2007: 76).

At the same time, Benezet was clearly a Quaker committed to the inward spirituality of his religious culture. Benezet desired 'that a truly humble, self-denying state of mind may prevail in me. I earnestly wish for myself & all those I love & indeed all mankind; that we may sensibly see & feel the benign influence, the true peace & happiness & indeed the nobility and strength of such a state' (Brendlinger 2007: 58). He was concerned 'lest we should mistake the activity of our minds for the putting forth of the divine hand' (Brendlinger 2007: 101) as ''tis God alone, by his Almighty power, who can & will in his own time bring outward, as well as spiritual deliverance to his afflicted & oppressed creatures' (Brendlinger 2007: 100) It is clear that he was committed to following the inward promptings of God in eighteenth-century Quaker tradition.

Tolles claimed he never spared the feelings of his wealthier co-religionists (Tolles 1948: 237), and indeed, when writing to fellow Quakers, Benezet is less concessionary than in his letters to Sharp and Wesley. In one letter to John Smith, who at the time was deciding upon membership in the Governor's Council, Benezet writes:

Remember, human nature is apt to deceive itself, especially when her propensities are flattered. I fear the snares consequent upon such a station will exceed the good thou can do in it. The common conversation and the very breath of most politicians is earthly and sensual, and too often devilish, not to mention the weakness of flesh and blood, which in spite of all our good resolution, if too much exposed to danger, will, like some combustible matter, catch fire, when only approached near the flame. Our Saviour's

Kingdom was not of this world. One thing is necessary, which I am more and more convinced is most likely to strike the deepest root, in as much as possible withdrawing from the spirit of the world. (Tolles 1948: 237)

This direct talk to co-religionists as opposed to the gentler tone afforded 'fellow pilgrims' denotes the dichotomy between guarded Quakerism and worldly piety. Benezet, I suggest, was tender (denominational) with those in wider ecumenical circles who were helping him achieve his politico-spiritual ends because his correspondents were *not* part of the true church. In this way, they and their sensibilities mattered less in terms of his spiritual counsel. They mattered rather as means to an end consequent to his true-church spirituality. At the same time, this moderation of anti-worldly sentiment is noteworthy and would pave the way in the nineteenth century for a greater degree of co-operation and in turn, a reflection on why Quaker spirituality needed to be so different from other forms of Christianity.

In these terms, we can talk about separate spheres of Quaker life, that eighteenth-century Quaker spirituality employed a dualistic attitude different from the seventeenth century in its sectarian approach to the 'unalloyed' and a denominational approach to 'the World'. Frost, like Vann and Levy, places the Meeting, school, and family at the centre of Quaker life (Frost 1973) and he charts, as does Marietta, the way in which Meetings focused on the behaviour of their members, holding all of their lives accountable. 'Friends had to cultivate an indifference towards the world and a deference before the Meeting' (Frost 1973: 60). As Frost claims: 'the family symbolized not only the bonds of unity and love amongst members but also the subordination of the individual to the group' (Frost 1973: 64). Thus, eighteenth-century Quakerism was caught between the ideal of reforming the world and the desire to escape from the world to build a holy community (Frost 1973: 188). (See Chapter 4 for Sarah Crabtree's theorisation of Quakers and the concept of 'holy nation'.)

Quakers never attempted monastic separation. Their ideal was to live that contemplative life within the worldly setting. William Penn wrote that Quakers could achieve 'the mortification and abstraction from the love and cares of this world, who daily are conversing in the world (but inwardly redeemed out of it) both in wedlock, and in their lawful employments, which was judged could only be obtained by such as were shut up in cloisters and monasteries' (1825: 295–296.) What was critical was that the faithful married the faithful and conducted life behind the 'hedge' with the spiritual protection afforded by a guarded life.

The idea of the 'hedge' has been characterised as a mechanism designed to protect the faithful from an apostate and corrupt world. However, as we have seen, the 'peculiarities' it entailed were also used to police purity within the group. The organisational mores potentially conflict (when disownment was at stake) with personal interpretations of the faith. The hedge divides the organisational sense of the pure from the less-pure within and outside the group.

Nineteenth-century reforms

The emphasis on the hedge faded in the nineteenth century as fewer activities were proscribed. Isichei argues that theatre and music gained acceptance between 1840 and 1880: whilst the Yearly Meeting epistle of 1881 condemned theatre and dancing, an article soon after in the *Friends Quarterly Examiner* claimed that music and novel reading were commonplace in one form or another in most Quaker families (1967: 165). Elizabeth Fry and her sisters had stated how they adored music as early as the end of the eighteenth century (Jones 1921: 494). In 1850, British Quakers agreed to the use of gravestones as long as they were all the same size and height as each other and carried no more words than name and dates.

The use of hedge was debated in the 1850s and explicitly mentioned both by its advocates who feared what might happen to an unguarded society, and its reformers who wished to end the constraint policed upon themselves and would-be converts. How far were the Quakers still a particular or peculiar people and how necessary was peculiarity to faith? How far were Quakers part of wider Christianity which had fewer proscriptions, prescriptions and prohibitions?

At Yearly Meeting 1856, the matter of whether or not to abolish the latter part of the fourth query, on the necessity of plain dress and plain speech was discussed. *The Friend* reported:

> John Pease spoke at considerable length upon the value of the peculia-rities to our Society. He regarded them as a hedge and a safeguard and called to mind is own experience: when a young commercial traveller in the traveller's room, he was saved from many temptations by appearing as a consistent Friend. (*The Friend* 13 (1856): 98)

Pease felt his on career had prospered because of the expectations of others of his sectarian identity, knew that others who had foregone Quaker garb had 'made a shipwreck of faith', and 'knew scarcely of any cases where parties had thrown off the plain dress and at the same time evinced in other matters an increase of devotedness in the service of their Lord' (*The Friend* 13 (1856): 98). Those opposing Pease advocated simplicity but not the necessity of peculiarity and argued about how essential the peculiarities were.

In 1859 an anonymous donor, concerned about the low and falling numbers of Quakers in Britain (around 13,000 – Chadkirk 2015: 57), sponsored an essay competition. The two winning entries from John Stephenson Rowntree and Thomas Hancock both criticised the practice of endogamy for leading to so many disownments and resignations. Whilst not wishing to entertain a worldly practice of marriage, centuries of trading and campaigning with non-Quakers and campaigning had diminished concerns about religious contamination. Within a new evangelical sensibility within British Quakerism, many Quakers began to see the Quaker faith as part of the true church rather than as *the* true church. Thus the need for endogamy appeared anachronistic and potentially threatening to the ongoing life of the group. In 1859, just shortly after the publication of the essays, British Friends agreed to drop endogamy, allowing Quakers to marry other Christians in Quaker weddings.

Isichei charts the tension over the place of theological learning and whether the nineteenth-century focus on Bible societies and adult schools was undermining the free ministry advocated by the Quakers (1967: 167–169). Theological education eventually became encouraged, finding its foundation in the interest of Liberal Quakers in Quaker history and discouraging the shifts that had taken place in parts of the USA towards a professional ministry. Isichei suggests that this renewal of the free ministry of all impeded denominationalisation (1967: 169).

In 1861, the latter part of the fourth query was dropped, the need for 'simplicity' being emphasised above 'peculiarity'. After 1861, a Quaker could be invisible and inaudible as a Quaker in the street, and head home to a non-Quaker spouse. The spiritual journey for the Quaker or Quaker convert now no longer needed to start in the tailor's shop. Membership immediately rose and reached around 20,000 by 1900 (Chadkirk 2015: 57). For the traditionalist Quakers, these reforms were not light matters. One Quaker at the time commented: 'I would rather die as a dog in a ditch than say "you" to a single person' (Isichei 1967: 171).

John Sargeant spoke up against the dropping of the latter part of the fourth query in 1856 and Daniel Pickard, one of the leading conservatives of the British Quakerism in the nineteenth century, saw the reforms as dangerous and ill-founded. He was part of the movement that held annual conferences from 1861 for those opposed to the new 'book of discipline', some of whom seceded in 1868 and joined John Sargeant's schismatic group at Fritchley in Derbyshire in 1868. In 1864, Pickard published a detailed comparison between the old and new disciplines. Part one of the volume compared the old and new queries and part two new minutes and advices. The changes to the fourth query were of particular concern (Pickard 1864: 24–31) as was how Quakers were increasingly closing their shops at Christmas (Pickard 1864: 29). He was concerned about content as well as process. Whereas the old queries had been answered at Preparative, Monthly and General Meeting level, the new advices were simply to be read (Pickard 1864:36.) The 1850 reform over the matter of gravestones, permitting them over and against the instruction of 1717, following a concern of Norfolk Quakers, had been the start of the malaise. Pickard claimed the reform had been rushed through with 'extraordinary haste, almost wilfulness … laying a worm at the root' (1864: 1). The term 'wilfulness' spoke of human agency rather than diligent discernment: 'It was pressed on the meeting's acceptance … in contravention of the wholesome usage of waiting on the Lord for a *united sense* in His peaceable kingdom' (Pickard 1864: 1). Pickard claimed that this same hasty process had been repeated over the marriage reform initiated by Yorkshire Friends.

Explicit evangelical theology required no external reminders as to the nature of salvific faith. Indeed, in the USA the evangelical branch, the Gurneyites, stopped wearing plain dress as, given it was worn by a rival branches, the Hicksites and Wilburites, and could therefore be considered 'worldly' (Hamm 1988: 85).

Many in Britain continued to exercise the option of plain dress but, as Hannah Rumball has shown, Quakers might adorn it with removable trim or with flourishes of haberdashery (2016). Quakers became more ecumenical in theology and more accepting of societal norms, reflecting an increased spiritual confidence around 'the worldly'.

The extent to which Quakers might be cast as 'citizens' is an ongoing dynamic for each Quaker group and can lead to contested negotiations within the group. When the British King Edward VII died in 1910, the date of Yearly Meeting coincided with his funeral. There had already been correspondence in *The Friend* over how large hats worn at Yearly Meeting should be. Now there was a division about whether Friends should wear mourning dress for the monarch. The question was over the extent to which Friends were part of 'the nation united in grief'.

In 1997, these questions of how far British Quakers were part of the nation were rehearsed after the death of Diana, Princess of Wales. Two articles appeared in *The Friend* offering sympathy to her two sons and the Clerk of Meeting Sufferings, the national executive, independently wrote to the princes offering them the condolences of the Religious Society. As one Friend responded, in part:

> We Quakers, who look back on a long tradition of dissent and 'swimming against the tide', have we lost our ability to examine popular movements, and to resist pressure to conform to a mass emotion, even idolatry? Have we exchanged our traditional moral rigour for a more modern and conventional easy sentimentality? We have a testimony to equality: the death of a celebrity is not more important than any other. (Letter to *The Friend* 19 September, 1997)

Are Quakers to be cast as citizens or spiritual purists, word-affirming or world-rejecting, reconcilers or prophets? In summary, it is more useful to understand the operation of this tension between world rejection and world affirmation, as framed by Wallis' typology and Björkqvist's axis, as an ongoing dynamic rather than try to agree upon particular dates as to when or if Quakers evolved from one type of group to another. Changes in perception of goals and strategy lead to innovations in expression. The desire for citizenship and religious toleration belong to one end of this axis and as such, may itself be contested within the group when pressures mount to achieve new goals using alternative strategies, or when notions of exclusivist religious claims regain popularity. The Quaker Member of Parliament T. Edmund Harvey wrote in 1937:

> We have ... in our Quaker history a lesson for our own lives of the meaning of Christian citizenship. You can see there a two-fold strand constantly interwoven: one, respect for the state as representing authority in the community: and the other, desire to serve the community through the state and in other ways, but along with that, the desire above all to serve the Kingdom of God: this means that we must be willing, when loyalty to the Kingdom of God demands it to refuse the demands of the state and show the highest loyalty to the state and the best citizenship by refusing demands that are wrong, because it is only in that way that the conscience of our fellow citizens can be reached, and in the end a better law come into being. (*Quaker Faith and Practice* 1995: 23.88)

The emphasis here on reaching the conscience of 'fellow citizens' readily fits Bryan Wilson's typology of 'reformist sect' (see Chapter 1).

From the reforms of the nineteenth century, the Quaker group experienced the development and realisation of the possibility of a private life, in other words a life beyond the disciplinary reach of the Meeting. Unannounced home visits by Elders to police domestic life dropped away as the number of prohibitions diminished. Whilst Birmingham Quaker Joseph Edward Southall presented his artistic career in terms of craft and tempura revival (Homan 2006a), the visual became more and more acceptable amongst British Quakers. The distrust of emotion disappeared and signalled a greater confidence amongst participants in their ability to embed a spiritual life within worldly practices. By the end of the twentieth century little remained inadmissible. Alcohol in moderation was acceptable, dancing had been allowed whilst Quakers were at the forefront of reform of legislation outlawing male homosexuality, and later same-sex marriage. Helena Chambers' work on Quaker attitudes to drugs and alcohol reveals a higher percentage of personal drug use than the general population (2006). In 1978, a Quaker Youth theatre was established. Music was celebrated if not often incorporated into worship. Whilst nationally Quakers have opposed the lottery, some Quakers admit to buying lottery tickets. Advertisements for Christmas presents appeared in *The Friend*, the Quaker weekly, from the early twentieth century with a section for Quakers to send Christmas greetings to each other being introduced in 1961.

In addition to the reduction of proscription, shifts in Quaker understanding from plainness to simplicity, for example, entailed a more diffuse interpretation of practice. It had been straightforward to understand what was plain and what was not. Quakers had removed anything that was too fine from their houses (Homan 2006b) or masked the real value of their possessions: Quaker wills or letters obscured the value of particular domestic items and often the finest possessions were kept hidden, whilst lower quality 'plain' items were restrained by bailiffs for non-payment of tithes (Pointon 1997: 424). The concept of simplicity was more difficult to pin down and its interpretation became individualistic. For some it might mean cycling everywhere or refusing to use private transport, for others buying a reliable car.

Values and virtue ethics replaced set rules: Scully found that British Quakers in the 1990s operated a collage of moral decision-making tools in their search for moral and just outcomes (2008). The latest British Quaker 'book of discipline' (the key authoritative text for British Quakers, last revised in 1994) did not contain *one* entry on the morality of abortion as might be expected in other church settings, but a range of experiences included to help personal discernment.

Significantly most personal moral decision-making moved to the private sphere, with individual Quakers required to self-construct a Quaker moral practice. If they needed help they would have to ask increasingly unpractised Meetings for it. Meetings focused on what took place within the Meeting House, what could now be counted as the legitimate arena of their moral authority (Dandelion 1996: foreword). Those Quakers who have felt unsupported during personal crises may have experienced not a lack of care but an uncertainty about how far Meetings could comment or intervene in what was now outside routine Meeting decision-making. The dramatic twentieth-century increase in the number of Quakers joining as adults brings with it the need to incorporate pre-Quaker habits and preferences into the new affiliation. Concern about falling numbers tends to support greater permissiveness around personal practice, especially when those habits are privatised.

Twice in the twentieth century, organisational aspiration went beyond the popular will. In 1918, the True Foundations of a Social Order were adopted by Yearly Meeting, and they are retained in the most recent book of discipline. They read:

1 The Fatherhood of God, as revealed by Jesus Christ, should lead us toward a brotherhood which knows no restriction of race, sex or social class.

2 This brotherhood should express itself in a social order which is directed, beyond all material ends, to the growth of personality truly related to God and man.

3 The opportunity of full development, physical, moral and spiritual, should be assured to every member of the community, man, woman and child. The development of man's full personality should not be hampered by unjust conditions nor crushed by economic pressure.

4 We should seek for a way of living that will free us from the bondage of material things and mere conventions, that will raise no barrier between man and man, and will put no excessive burden of labour upon any by reason of our superfluous demands.

5 The spiritual force of righteousness, loving-kindness and trust is mighty because of the appeal it makes to the best in every man, and when applied to industrial relations achieves great things.

6 Our rejection of the methods of outward domination, and of the appeal to force, applies not only to international affairs, but to the whole problem of industrial control. Not through antagonism but

through co-operation and goodwill can the best be obtained for each and all.

7   Mutual service should be the principle upon which life is organised. Service, not private gain, should be the motive of all work.

8   The ownership of material things, such as land and capital, should be so regulated as best to minister to the need and development of man.

(*Quaker Faith and Practice* 1995: 23.16)

Thomas Kennedy argued that this combination was not far removed from the 'four pillars' adopted by the Labour Party (2001: 384). The references to the bondage of material things, the problem of industrial control, and the regulation of the ownership of land and capital, are particularly interesting in this regard, as is the fact that they remain in the book of discipline.

In 1996 and 1997, British Quakers embarked on an exercise entitled 'Rediscovering our Social Testimony' and at the Yearly Meeting sessions in 1997, a minute relating to a draft document 'Reaffirming the Spiritual Basis of our Testimony' was accepted which asserted in part: 'it calls us to a style of living and a generosity of giving that perhaps we cannot all yet attain, but we feel called to recognise the principles expressed in this document. Small steps, taken in faith, make a joyful journey' (Minute 37, Britain Yearly Meeting 1997).

In both cases, the declarations represented a moral aspiration rather than a concerted political programme. By the time of the General Strike in 1926, some Friends were saying that the 1918 Yearly Meeting may have gone further than they ought to (Wood 1927: 288) and in the session that adopted the 1997 statement, some Friends declared that whilst the sentiment was admirable, it would not change their lifestyle choices.

Thus the popular articulation of the hedge is sometimes lower than the organisational one. In terms of personal behaviour, the choices, and the means to reach them, are left to the individual, thus displaying a denominational outlook rather than a sectarian one.

Chapter summary

In summary, we have explored the idea of the hedge as a boundary between pure and impure but also as a mechanism for maintaining internal purity, drawing on its biblical roots of being protected by God. Since the nineteenth century, the value of hedge has been increasingly questioned and most outward and explicit manifestations of it have been dropped by the Quaker group. Universal truth claims are not to be found amongst British Quakers in behavioural prescriptions and interpretations of moral integrity vary between the organisational and personal. The next chapter looks at how sociologists have worked with changing Quaker self-perceptions and accompanying political stances in their use of sect/denomination theory and how relationships between religious groups and wider culture are more complex than being just being a religious organisation and the state apparatus.

4

QUAKERS AS CITIZENS AND OUTLAWS

This chapter reviews the numerous theories put forward by a variety of scholars as how best to categorise the way in which Quakers began as a counter-cultural sect but now represent a respected denomination. Deliberately set apart from the exploration in the last chapter of the self-construction of the hedge internal to the Quaker group, an overview is given here of the changing external relationship between Quakers and the State and wider society. The continuing case study of Quaker experience illustrates that sectarian sensibilities can emerge at any point in the lifespan of a religious group. Further, it is argued that notions of 'Quaker' and 'world' are oversimplified. Rather, a more complex set of relationships exist which need to be taken into account when modelling church and sect organisational types.

In *Early Quakers and their Theology*, Michael Birkel and Stephen Angell write about Richard Farnworth, seventeenth-century Yorkshire Quaker and key architect of Quaker ecclesiology. Farnworth also wrote pamphlets seeking religious toleration to allow Quakers the benefits of being treated as equal citizens. Birkel and Angell conclude:

> Ultimately, Farnworth's efforts did not convince non-Quakers. His works did not anticipate the more persuasive tactics of William Penn who argued for toleration not only for Quakers but for other dissenters as well. Even at the end of his writing career, Farnworth adhered to the first generation's conviction that Quakers alone had the truth, and therefore he could not in good conscience argue for toleration as a right equally due to non-Quakers. (2013: 94)

Birkel and Angell identify here the tension between the idea of 'true church' and the bid for toleration, which, by default, needs also to apply to those beyond

Quakerism. In Farnworth's case, he held more to the first idea (of Quakers representing the one true church) and was unconvinced and unconvincing with regard to the latter (that all religionists might be treated equally). It is this tension between the self-perception of a religious group, in this case the Quakers, as uniquely correct in its religious proclamations and one which sees itself as equally relevant as other groups, which I explore in this paper. One path leads to a rejection of any organisation or law which hinders spiritual self-expression, the other seeks assimilation within the nation in an attempt to be treated as citizens in spite of an alternative spiritual persuasion. Is 'the world' a place described in pejorative terms to be opposed or overcome or does wider society represent a viable context in which to express a spirituality to be regarded as equivalent? Is the group to adopt a sectarian or denominational outlook, a world-rejecting or world-accepting one?

Quaker historiography, and as we shall see below the sociology of religion in general, has tended to try to identify a single key moment when the originating sectarian tendency gives way to the denominational. Thus, for example, historians of Quakerism tend to portray the first ten years of Quakerism as an expression of essential Quaker spirituality, in which the 'world' is used as a pejorative term denoting all that is not of God, which is then overlaid by a subsequent period characterised by an increased codification and formalisation of what it meant to be Quaker. This 'second period' of Quakerism has been variously marked by scholars as 1656, 1660, 1666 and 1678. Richard Allen's and Rosemary Moore's volume on the second period starts in 1656 with the caution shown by Quakers following the James Nayler incident (2018).[1] Barry Reay suggests the term 'restoration Quakerism' to denote the new form of Quakerism which emerged under the Restoration of the British monarchy in 1660 (1985). Rosemary Moore suggests that the 'Testimony of the Brethren' of 1666, written by Richard Farnworth, which laid out a discipline for British Quakerism and clarified the nature of authority within the group, marked the end of the first period of Quakerism (2000: 225). Richard Bailey (1992) and Michele Lise Tarter (2001) have both claimed that Second Day Morning Meeting, established in 1673 to review Quaker publications, operated as a censorship committee which separated original enthusiasm from a more regulated second period, and Daniel Zemaitis claims the first period finally ended with the establishment of the Yearly Meeting of Ministers and Elders as the centralised authority for British Friends, in 1678 (2012). Historians of Quakerism are very keen at debating periodisation.

The 1661 declaration to King Charles II extolling the peaceful nature of the Quakers is another example of a change in religious expression. This declaration came in the wake of the Fifth Monarchist uprising and their occupation of the City of London. As the most numerous and outspoken of the other sects, 4,200 Quakers were placed in preventative detention (Braithwaite 1919: 13). The declaration made it explicit in its opening lines that Quakers would not plot or take up arms against the Crown. It is an unequivocal declaration of harmlessness. The declaration highlighted the move towards greater negotiation with the State, born out of the need to survive and the related self-realisation amongst the group that England was not turning to God at the rate that had earlier been predicted: global transformation was not unfolding at the pace that had been thought likely less than a decade before. Such statements fit with a parallel campaign for religious toleration and, as the 1660s unfolded with an increasing set of prohibitions on the Quakers including a specific Quaker Act of 1662, for the freedom to worship.

The campaign by Quakers seeking to be treated as citizens is part of a move away from the enthusiasms of the first decade to an alternative expression and self-understanding of what it was to be Quaker. Indeed, in wider terms, citizenship' and 'religious freedom' are concepts that denote the aspiration of a new social movement to be assimilated within dominant culture. Citizenship is a concept which by definition is embedded and distributed within hegemonic culture. However, I also want to suggest that the dynamic between resistance and assimilation is an ongoing one and that any debate therefore about watershed dates marking irreversible change is misleading.

Quakers as sect and denomination

Interestingly, many of the key sect/denomination theorists have used the Quakers as an example of the transition from one to the other. As per Chapter 2, Max Weber developed a church/sect typology where a church was defined as a 'compulsory association for the administration of grace' and a sect 'a voluntary association of religiously qualified persons' (Gerth and Mills 1946: 314). Weber also talked of 'the idea of the purity of the sacramental communion as decisive' at the time of origin Weber 2011: 139) 'or, as among Quakers, the interest in the purity of the community of prayer' (Weber 2011: 142). For Weber, the discipline of the asceticist sect was, in fact, far more rigorous than the discipline of any church and he presented the Quakers as an example of voluntarist inner-worldly asceticism (2011: 139).

When Ernst Troeltsch added further characteristics to sect typology such as different perceptions of priesthood, the sacraments, and 'the world', he did not use the Quakers as an example of a sect, but rather of his third organisational form, 'mystical religion' (1931: 780). Quakers offered a counter-example of his own claim that mysticism supplanted traditional forms of worship, for whilst that was true for the Quakers historically, the Quakers had built a new tradition upon their practice of nurturing the mystical.

> Mysticism means that the world of ideas which had hardened into formal worship and doctrine is transformed into a purely personal and inward experience; this leads to the formation of groups on a purely personal basis, with no permanent form, which also tends to weaken the significance of forms of worship. doctrine, and the historical element (Troeltsch 1931: 993)

Contrary to Troeltsch's insights here, mystical religion and holiness revivalism had powered renewal within the Quaker movement at regular intervals as a collective experience. Troeltsch, it seems, chose to disregard this understanding of Quaker spirituality and instead framed Quakerism as the 'final expression of the purest form of the Anabaptist movement' (1931: 781) which became bourgeois:

> They found it impossible to continue to live in their original detachment from the world; more and more they combined the Calvinist ethic of the 'calling' with their ascetic way of life. Then God 'blessed their business' with those economic results which this ascetic Protestant idea of the 'calling' usually brings with it. Thus a religious body which sprang into existence out of an entirely unworldly spiritual movement, developed into a community with an entirely different ideal; in its ultimate form it exhibited the following characteristic traits; a high sense of the duty of labour; the limitation of the kind of work which may be undertaken to useful and practical understandings in trade, industry, manual labour, and agriculture; strict personal economy and a minimum amount of luxury, with a maximum amount of effort for the welfare of the community; supervision by the Society of the business honesty and solvency of its members, of family life, of the education of the children; in short, it is the same ideal as that of Geneva in the days of early Calvinism, the only difference being that this community is founded upon a voluntary basis. (1931: 781)

In this way, Troeltsch also regarded Quakers as a sect and in one passage calls them a 'passive persecuted sect' (1931: 805). Other scholars have been less ambiguous about the sectarian nature of early Quakerism.

Richard Niebuhr (1975 [1929]) and David Martin (1962) introduced the concept of a denomination. Niebuhr's claim was that sects denominationalised in the second generation (1929) (see Chapter 1). Niebuhr, like Weber and Troeltsch, used the Quakers as an example:

> The Quakers, no less than their predecessors among the churches of the poor, soon settled down to an 'equable respectability.' They accommodated themselves to the social situation and confined their efforts toward social reformation to the work of gaining converts to their faith, to the works of charity and to occasional efforts to influence public opinion on social questions. (1975: 54)

For Niebuhr, there was a reduction in persecution, the advent of the second generation, and the consequences of economic success. All were present in the Quaker case according to Niebuhr (he ignored the fact that persecution worsened at the time of the second generation).

In the second and third generations, with the aid of the prosperity prevailing in the days of good Queen Anne, this church of the disinherited became a more or less respectable middle-class church that left the popular movement from which it originated far behind. It continued to hold the tenet of its social program but now as the doctrines of a denomination rather than as the principles of inclusive social reconstruction ... The Millenarian hopes which had fired the popular movement of the seventeenth century with enthusiasm were definitely left behind. (1975: 55–56)

Martin used the example of the Quakers to challenge Niebuhr's work:

The Friends began in a chiliastic atmosphere with a stern rejection of the world and all its ways; with the course of time they came to distinguish themselves in business and in scientific pursuits and so eventually modified their position. But even as applied to the Society of Friends the conventional view of sectarian development is only partially accurate. Although Friends believed in a doctrine of the inner light which was peculiarly favourable to change, the process of becoming a denomination was slow and partial, partly on account of the complementary doctrine of unanimity. The traditionalist element was always strong, while the contemporary pacifism of the large majority of Friends indicates that sectarian perfectionism has largely succeeded in maintaining itself in spite of the wealth and intellectual sophistication of some members. Moreover such denominational tendencies as have appeared were in fact present in some degree from the beginning. (1962: 1–2)

Martin argued that some groups began life as denominations and used the sectarian approach to eschatology as one way of highlighting this:

The sect having members who are largely alienated and rejected, frequently expects a Divine reversal of its secular position or a total destruction of the corrupt material world in which members will be a select remnant miraculously transported to the New Jerusalem. As regards these eschatological events sectarians either wait passively, or actively prepare to engage in Armageddon when the trumpet shall sound. Meanwhile they refuse to consider any attempts to merely ameliorate present conditions and refuse to participate in wars for secular purposes. When the Divine Advent does not occur or when the holy war of Armageddon has failed in its object, the concept of the New Jerusalem is sometimes spiritualized and regarded as realized within the religious community, in which eventuality the idealism bound up inside the Adventist myth may realize itself in radical reforms on the secular plane. The Society of Friends is the most obvious example. By contrast the denomination, which has a genuine stake in the present social order, retains the traditional eschatology of heaven and hell. This single fact places a sociological gulf between denomination and sect. With this criterion in mind it is quite clear that neither the Methodists, nor the Congregationalists nor the General Baptists (except momentarily and partially in one unique historical situation) were ever sectarian. In the modern situation even the traditional eschatology has largely given way to a form of universalism or to more subtle conceptions. (1962: 9)

Bryan Wilson used the Quakers as an example of his 'introversionist' type of sectarian sensibility suggesting that the Quakers claimed an inward illumination that encouraged an indifference to other religious groups as well as a separated ministry (1959: 6). Later, Wilson mirrored Martin's approach in his work on Quakerism labelling Quakers an introversionist sect in its eighteenth-century expressions and a reformist sect, achieving salvation through the reformation of conscience, in the twentieth century (1970).

Wilson also challenged Niebuhr's view of second generation denomi-nationalisation and used the Quakers as an example:

> The Quakers undoubtedly began with a strong sense of separateness and of the need for real worthiness in recruits. Separateness persisted, but eighteenth- and early nineteenth-century English Quakers were often admitted virtually on the strength of birth-right. The sect came near to being a set-apart, self-recruiting people, a type of descent group. (Wilson 1970: 30)

For Wilson, Quakers in the twentieth century remained a sect although the group placed 'less and less emphasis on tests of merit for admission' (1970: 30). Wilson claimed that modern Quakers represent about the only thoroughly developed form of a reformist sect (1970: 46).

> The reformist sect is a rarity and arises only in advanced societies. Even then, it arises only among groups which, by a long process of intensive socialisation, have acquired a very strong and perhaps partly collective conscience towards the wider world. (1970: 177)

Wilson emphasised the role of conscience as a driving force in Quaker thought and practice, prompting philanthropy, political involvement, integrity as employers, relief work, and penal reform: 'Quakers have thus taken upon themselves the task of being society's self-appointed conscience ... social reform has arisen as a primary orientation. Quakers in the twentieth-century may be regarded as a reformist sect' (1970: 180–181).

Milton Yinger labelled Quakers an 'avoidance sect' (1970: 277), a type that devalued the social order rather than accepting it or trying to change it and which withdrew from the world. Yinger mistakenly placed early Quakers in this category, presumably thinking of eighteenth-century Quakers. The Amish might have been a better example.

Wilson and Yinger apart, scholars working within Quaker studies have tended not to focus on types of sect but rather the timing of when the change from sect to denomination, 'denominationalisation', occurred.

Richard Vann (1969) and Richard Bauman (1983) suggest Quakerism began life as a movement and became a sect in the second period, the point at which Niebuhr claimed Quakers became a denomination. Michael Mullett investigated the appropriateness of the sect-denomination model applied to eighteenth-century Quakers. He examined the following characteristics:

> cultural integration/isolation; relations with other churches; group behavioural rules; endogamy/exogamy; use of excommunication; political outlook; prevalence or absence of millenarianism; acceptance of the obligations of mission; attitude to education and scholarship; emergence of a formal ministry. (Mullett 1984: 171)

He related these characteristics to use of the ale house, popular entertainment, celebration of weddings, etc., middle-class culture, relation to other churches, dress and language, marriage and disownment, respect for the law, etc., and found that Quakers had some of these features in common with other nonconformists, while others were unique to Quakers. Mullett concluded:

> As far as eighteenth-century Quakerism was concerned, the Society retained too many features of the primitive sect to be described as a denomination, and too many embryonic features of the denomination to be satisfactorily described as a sect. In this complex mix, though, one inclines to see Hanoverian [period 1714–1901] Quakerism rather more in terms of the sect than of the denomination. (1984: 191)

Elizabeth Isichei argued that British Quakers were 'profoundly sectarian' until the middle of the nineteenth century (1967: 162) when the State ceded them the rights to become MPs, attend university and join the professions (in other words when they established the right to full citizenship). However, she also questioned the idea of a linear development from sect to denomination:

> Clearly no theory of linear progression from sect to denomination fits this pattern; instead of a steady progression from sect to denomination we have recurrent phases of conversion and withdrawal, which must be explained in terms of social and ideological change, rather than through the simple passage of time ... A sociological analysis of the group suggest strongly that a sect does not evolve automatically or even typically into a denomination, that these terms represent attitudes which may well co-exist, and that a sect is likely to move through successive phases of outward and inward orientation, which makes difficult the formulation of a single generalisation about the typical development of sects. (Isichei 1967: 176, 181)

Isichei concluded that 'Quaker experience suggests that the sectarian and denominational outlooks may well exist in the same movement at the same time' (1967: 180). Indeed, at the very point that Quakerism was becoming more ecumenical in outlook, Isichei was also able to claim that in some ways: 'English Quakerism was remodelled in sectarian terms, with the abolition of the custom of recording of ministers, and of birthright membership' (1967: 181).

In Chapter 6, I suggest that modern Quakers behave both as a sect and a denomination in terms of the demands made upon participants depending on which aspect of collective religious life is being examined. Suffice to say here that the very debate about the timing and extent of transition suggests a difficulty of 'fit' between theory and reality.

Framing Quakerism in other typologies

Douglas Gwyn charted a shift from a covenantal understanding of faith to a more secular contractual model within the Quaker group (1995). This connects with his later work, with Timothy Peat and myself, on the movement within Quakerism from an apocalyptic end-time spirituality to a 'meantime' one (Dandelion et al. 1998).

Gay Pilgrim has used Foucault's concept of 'heterotopia', of social settings being juxtaposed in unexpected ways, to argue that Quakers were heterotopic in the way they turned courtrooms into pulpits and undermined the existing social order with their patterns of behaviour (2003, 2008), a theorisation that fits with Wallis' world-rejecting characteristics. Pilgrim asserts that this tendency to 'alternate ordering' acts as an historical thread throughout Quaker history as well as offering present-day Quakers unity and identity (2003: 147). The term 'heterotopia' was originally used to refer to body parts that were out of place or dislocated. Foucault used it to refer to places that unsettle or disturb and he uses the example of fairground within a prison exercise yard. Foucault contrasted heterotopia with utopia: whilst both subvert or invert existing relationships, Foucault claimed that utopias were 'fundamentally unreal spaces', heterotopias were a 'kind of effectively enacted utopia' (1986: 24), a counter-cultural site which creates confusion by highlighting structures of power. Pilgrim build on Foucault and also the work of Kevin Hetherington who defines heterotopias as 'Spaces of alternate ordering [which] organise a bit of the social world in a way different to that which surrounds them' (1996: 2). Early Quakers created heterotopic space, turning courtrooms into pulpits for example. In her analysis of the present day, the heterotopic become internalised, manifest only through the moments of exposure of the diversity of popular doctrine and personal understanding about the nature of Quakerism. In outward forms, the group appears to cohere through its adherence to a set form or worship. In Pilgrim's analysis, Quakers become less concerned with the corporate and the group's relations with wider culture than with their own journeys.

Juxtaposition is a central concept in Hetherington's description of modernisation. It is connected with Foucault's two principles of ordering, 'resemblance' and 'similitude'. While resemblance is finding likenesses which coincide, 'Similitude, however, is all about an ordering that takes place through a juxtaposition of signs that culturally are seen as not going together, either because their relationship is new or because it is unexpected' (Hetherington 1997: 9). My idea of the 'absolute perhaps' is an example of this: the same can be said of 'double culture' theory and the concept of 'behavioural creed' (Dandelion 2007: 151; 138; 1996: 100ff.; 131, see Chapter 6 of this volume below).

Hetherington's conclusion on heterotopia is that:

> no space can be described as fixed as a heterotopia … heterotopia always have multiple and shifting meanings for agents … heterotopia are always defined relationally to other sites or within a spatialization process, and never exists in and of themselves, heterotopia must have something distinct about them … being an obligatory point of passage, heterotopia is about both resistance and order. (1997: 51)

This means that heterotopias are defined from outside, from the relationship to contrasting social spaces: 'It is how such a relationship is seen from outside, from the standpoint of another perspective, that allows a space to be seen as heterotopic' (Hetherington 1997: 43).

Helen Meads critiques Pilgrim's understanding of heterotopia, in particular her shift from Foucault's and Kevin Hetherington's understanding of heterotopic 'sites' towards a collective activity or mode of action rooted in 'visibility', and in particular that heterotopias may involve 'intention' (2011: 117–118). Meads uses heterotopia as a way of explaining the internal processes of Quakers involved in a particular form of guided Quaker reflection called 'Experiment with Light' and how 'Experimenters' are located in terms of their relations with Quaker Meetings generally (2011). The concept of 'heterotopia' is also used by Simon Best in his study of adolescent Quakerism in relation to the rest of the Quakers (2008: 210). More recently, Hans Eeirk Aarek has argued that Norwegian Quakers are best described as a 'heterotopic denomination' (forthcoming), creatively combining Pilgrim's theorisation into sect/denomination typology.

In more theo-sociological terms, Wolf Mendl argued that religious-based activism pulls in two directions, one of prophecy, and the other of reconciliation (1974). Prophecy is seen in term of obedience to the supernatural, regardless of consequence, whereas reconciliation is clearly rooted in a desired outcome, the fulfilment of which may involve compromise. We can understand, theologically, all of the early Quaker 'peculiarities' such as plain dress, plain speech, the refusal to swear an oath or pay a tithe, Quaker testimony (the enactment of the faith), in terms of not simply individual eccentricity but as holy imperatives (heterotopic) prophetic end-time acts ordained by God.

We can see the prioritising of denominational negotiation with the State over religious freedom as reconciliatory.

Jane Calvert has described Quaker political navigation in terms of the nautical term 'trimming'. Trimming is the process by which the ballast or cargo was positioned to keep the vessel afloat (Calvert 2009: 13) with those responsible keeping their eye on the horizon of desired direction, even if in the immediate locality a severe turn was required. Calvert uses this analogy to make sense of Quaker political expediency in eighteenth-century Pennsylvania where the Quakers shifted the balance of their positions to make political headway as the 'world' accrued around the Holy Experiment. Used in a laudatory sense, as opposed to castigate those who trimmed their sails to steer the ship with the prevailing winds, it referred to those who managed the ballast and cargo on the ship to keep it afloat.

> Trimmers such as these acted on principle, espousing moderation and eschewing self-interest. The story of a principled trimmer – as opposed to an opportunistic one – is complicated. This sort of trimmer functions both relative to his immediate environment and apart from it. His job is to keep the state of the ship from listing right or left on a straight and true course to the desired destination. Because of this, something of an optical illusion occurs: The trimmer is fixed in relation to the destination, which gives him the appearance of sometimes-drastic movement in relation to his immediate surroundings. It is true that he adjusts his position slightly, but only for the sake of staying straight and balanced. He is not static; but neither is he changeable. He does not ally himself too closely with one side or another to protect his own interests as an opportunistic trimmer would. Rather, he remains independently in the middle with a view to the object beyond himself. Those short-sighted people on either extreme who do not understand the trimmer accuse him of cowardice or rashness, indecision or haste, and, invariably, duplicity and self-interest. If he is weighty, they resent the fact that he does not side with them ... (Calvert 2009: 13)

Calvert characterises Quaker relations to the polity of colonial Pennsylvania. It is a positive characterisation and not one that would fit all Quakers, but it highlights the other-worldly emphasis that was maintained from the seventeenth and into the eighteenth century within Quaker political ideals, even when faced with running the government.

Thus, the use of Quakers to enhance theorisation about the categorisation of religious groups and the categorisation of Quakers themselves has been a regular preoccupation with sociologists of religion and those within Quaker studies. The second half of this chapter offers a brief overview of the changing relationship between Quakers and the 'world'.

Quaker organisational life and citizenship

What shifts over time is the balance between the prophetic and the reconcilia-tory, between world rejection and world affirmation. An analysis of the writings of early Quaker minister Edward Burrough (Dandelion and Martin 2013) reveals how Burrough changes his mode of discourse between 1657 and 1658.

In *All ye Inhabitants of the Earth in all Nations through the World*, Burrough begins with:

> ALL ye Kings, and Princes, and Rulers through the whole World; the Lord is coming up with his mighty Host against you all; he, who will fan you, and sift you, and try you, and search you out; for his Fan is in his Hand, and he will throughly purge you ... all your Glory shall fade away, all your Majesty, and Honour, and Dignities, and Dominions shall come to an end; all your strength is but as a Straw, all your treasure as a Thing of nought, all your glory as a fading Leaf in the Presence of the Lord God ... all Nations upon Earth are but as the drop of a Bucket before him, and the hearts of all men are in his Hand, and by him Kings rule. (1657)

Worldly power is nothing compared to the glory and majesty of God and indeed, it is only through God's will that Kings rule. There is a strong dualism here between the worldly and the heavenly, between those who know the way to the Lord and those who do not.

After 1658, Burrough writes to those in authority in a more measured tone. He is interested in negotiating with authority, persuading them to understand the Quaker position and how it does not threaten law and order. For example, in 1658, he writes to magistrates on religious toleration signing the tract as 'a real Friend to the Common-wealth' (1658).

In the late 1650s, Quakers were already feeling the effects of national instability as well as the consequences of a blasphemy trail surrounding key leader James Nayler. In 1659, in a tract to the 'broken nation', Burrough emphasises the peaceful nature of the Quaker position (1659a). They claimed that the Quaker motive was to save the rest of humanity and that the means would always be peaceful. In the same year, he wrote to the Pope (1659b), also to Friars and Nuns in Dunkirk (1659c), perhaps signalling a more ecumenical temperament.

After the restoration of the monarchy, Burrough addressed the King on a number of occasions. In *The Case of Free Liberty of Conscience* (1661), Bur-rough presented 15 reasons as to why religious conscience should be upheld by government. Given that it is God's right to judge the spiritual life of humanity, it would be wrong for government to do that. If government did take on this unlawful aspect of rule, it would undermine its own legitimacy as well as oppose God. If force was involved, that attitude of persecution would infect the whole nation. This would be a poor legacy to be remembered by.

Equally, using force would never achieve the goal anyway as that is not how Christ works. Force itself is considered a sin and the perpetrators would need to face the charge of sin. Breaking the holy law in this way would allow others to break it against you. Using violence would contradict the golden rule. Enforcing conformity effectively means creating a nation of hypocrites, forced to say one thing but believe another: who could be trusted? Enforced conformity would destroy people's souls, and, additionally, would lose the rulers any sense of moral high ground over 'heathenish' or papist groups. Limiting toleration would affect trade and merchandise as trade depends on those prepared to travel and accept difference. Such constraint, given all the above, could even lead to war. The wrong people and groups could be constrained and heretics may be allowed to rise in prominence. Finally, constraining the religious freedoms of the wrong people will damage the reputation of the government. In this pattern of argument, ending with the threat of rebellion by God-less folk, Burrough was not only using a purely theological argument but also ones that appealed to reason, pride, Scripture and justice. It built systematically on his opening point that it was not up to humans to determine the spiritual liberty of others. It was the argument of a citizen faithful to an established order, trying to work within the system to secure religious freedom. It was reconciliatory compared to his 1657 work.

As stated above, we can see the 1661 Quaker declaration to Charles II, in similar terms. It is entitled 'A Declaration from the harmless and innocent people of God, called Quakers, against all plotters and fighters in the world …' and one of its most oft-quoted passages reads: 'All bloody principles and practices, we, as to our own particulars, do utterly deny, with all outward wars and strife and fightings with outward weapons, for any end or under any pretence whatsoever. And this is our testimony to the whole world' (Weddle 2001: 234). Plotting and fighting belonged to 'the world', whereas Quaker weapons were spiritual rather than carnal and Quakers 'desire and wait' for everyone to come to a place where 'nation shall not lift sword against nation, neither shall they learn war any more' (Isa 2: 4, Mic 4:3): 'This is given forth from the people called Quakers to satisfy the King and his Council, and all those that have any jealousy concerning us, that all occasion of suspicion may be taken away and our innocency cleared' (Weddle 2001: 237) This is a reconciliatory document, not a prophetic one. Nowhere do Quakers claim the Crown is wrong or should repent but rather it presents the sufferings of the innocent and harmless people and explains their spiritual understandings in order to clear their name and seek toleration and freedom. It may well, as Weddle argues (2001), reflect the general position of Quakers but its tone and style is world-affirming. It marks a negotiation with 'the world' even whilst criticising the world's treatment of Quakers. It is not the keystone of a prophetic Quaker witness for peace but a mark of the increasing marginalisation of that prophecy. In its separation of a single issue, it also signifies a breakdown of the heterotopic impulse which placed a unified sense of Quaker prophecy into each situation, however inappropriately in the world's eyes. This is not a heterotopic document. It does a particular job in terms that reflect the nature of the task.

At those historical points when Quakers have decided that they wished to be treated as citizens to secure the State-given right to religious freedoms and toleration, instead of self-representing purely as God's children who assert religious practice regardless of the consequences, they have moved from acting as prophets to acting as reconcilers.

Anne Helier has charted the regular manner in which Quakers appealed to the State (2017) and N. Crowther-Hunt has argued that Quakers very quickly adopted the reconciliatory practice of petitioning government for legal change (1979).

Throughout the 1660s and 1670s, British Quakers suffered persecution under Conventicle Acts outlawing dissenter gatherings, and the Quaker Act forcing Quakers to swear an oath of allegiance. Only in 1689 with the Act of Toleration were Quakers and other nonconformists offered the right to worship. In the American colonies, Quakers had a great number of options and in Pennsylvania controlled the Assembly ensuring religious freedom for the Quaker settlers (Frost 1990). However, the tension between renewal within the Quaker movement, what Jack Marietta has termed a 'reformation' (1984), and the compromise inherent in political power led Quakers to abandon the Assembly in 1756.

Peter Brock characterises the withdrawal from the Assembly in 1756 as the result of an awakening to tenets of the Quaker faith that gathered pace, encouraged by British Quakers who advised that Pennsylvania Friends should retire from provincial politics. British Friends who had never enjoyed direct political control may have misunderstood the reluctance of Philadelphia Quakers to withdraw from their Assembly but on 7 June, six of the leading Quakers resigned. This moment, Brock states, symbolised the end of the 'Holy Experiment', even whilst other Quakers maintained their seats and the 'Quaker party' swept to power the following October. (Brock 2015: 128–129, also Calvert 2009: 184–185). Quakers became subjects or citizens and not rulers.

Sarah Crabtree has argued that Quakers replaced the political influence they had relinquished in some of the American colonies such as Rhode Island and Pennsylvania with a conception of a trans-national Quaker identity rooted in the concept of a 'Holy Nation' (2015). As the British surrendered to the American Forces in the American Revolutionary War, Anthony Benezet wrote the following:

> As a people, we are called to dwell alone, not to be numbered with the Nations, content with the comfortable necessities of life; as pilgrims and strangers, to avoid all incumbrances, as well as proposed to Israel of old, to be as a Kingdom of Priests, an holy Nation, a peculiar people to shew forth the praise of him that hath called us. (Crabtree 2015: 1)

This was a renewed call to form a peculiar people and royal priesthood set against worldliness (see Chapter 3) but, Crabtree argues, it was also part of a new Quaker spiritual self-conceptualisation that could transcend national politics. The creation of a Quaker holy nation allowed Quakers to see themselves above any State and to act as a unified trans-national spiritual force, freed from State constraint and the kind of political compromise that had forced, for example, Quakers in Pennsylvania, for example, to leave the Assembly rather than vote through further war taxes for the Crown. As subjects became citizens in the new 'United States', Quakers could transcend citizenship and retain their political and spiritual integrity. This formulation (a) renewed their sense of themselves as a chosen people, (b) articulated their history of persecution in framing their relationship to government, (c) democratised geographical location by unifying scattered communities, and (d) re-instilled the requirement to prophecy (Crabtree 2015: 33). Taken together, Crabtree identifies these four factors in terms of a Quaker interpretation of the Zion tradition (2015: 33). It also fitted with the early Quaker tradition of being set apart to create and control heaven on earth, 'a kingdom of priests and a holy nation' (Crabtree 2015: 35).

The holy nation conceptualisation inspired a particular approach to education and a generalised desire to remain apart from the world and the world's revolutionary democracies. It would falter as a younger generation of Friends felt more comfortable with direct political involvement and as the Society itself begin to fragment along theological and sociological lines prior to the 'Great Separation' of 1827, when the Society divided into Hicksites and Orthodox parties, a division which consumed not only Quaker energies for decades but also the desire for a geographical spiritual unity that had underpinned and established holy nation theology.

The French Revolution, for example, was not an easy time for British Friends. Whilst American Friends' pacifism had brought them disrepute during the American Revolutionary War, Quaker radicals upset the British Quaker desire to maintain a perception of 'harmlessness' on the part of an anxious British government: Rob Alexander argues that the disownment of Hannah Barnard in 1801 was less for her theological views, the presenting issue in her case, but because of her political radicalism and her republicanism (2006: 56) and claims that the growth of evangelicalism in the first half of the nineteenth century was 'engineered in reaction against political radicalism' (2006: 62). Quakers, if we take on board Crabtree's and Alexander's conclusions, moved from transcending national politics to becoming part of the Christian establishment. In some ways the Great Separation was as much about the degree to which traditional Quaker distinctives should be emphasised as about theological content, although Quakers on both sides of the divide maintained a sense of the hedge as crucial. Rachel Seaman Hicks deplored Hicksite involvement with women's rights and abolitionist movements (Eisenstadt 2005: 714) because of the potential contamination from the 'hireling ministry' who were also involved.

The Evangelical Quakerism which grew in the Orthodox wing saw itself as part of true Christianity rather than as the sole true church and Quakers in the nineteenth century more and more joined with other Christians in social justice campaigning, such as anti-slavery, social witness work, such as the adult school movement, and in Bible societies and eventually overseas mission: Rachel Metcalfe was the first overseas Quaker missionary when she travelled to India in 1866. Alongside this, Quakers and other nonconformists sought to eradicate the discriminations they faced in legislation.

Quakers had the unusual privilege along with Jews of being able to marry their own members after the 1755 Hardwicke Act but in other ways Quakers, like other Dissenters, were not given the same rights as those in the Established Church until the nineteenth century. The Test and Corporation Acts, prohibiting nonconformists from holding office, were abolished in 1828, and in 1832 Joseph Pease became the first Quaker Member of Parliament (he was allowed to take his seat after it was decided he could affirm rather than swear the oath of office and was noted for never removing his hat in Parliament). In 1868, church rates were made voluntary under the Compulsory Church Rate Abolition Act. After 1854, nonconformists could attend Oxford and Cambridge and from 1871 they had full access to degrees and fellowships. Thus by 1871, Quakers in Britain could count themselves as full citizens.

Brian Philllips suggests this new sense of citizenship led to an idealistic self-construction of Quaker agency. Quakers saw themselves as 'the nonconformists of the nonconformists' (Phillips 1989: 53), a civilising influence on the world alongside empire. Editorials in *The Friend*, the London-based Quaker weekly, reminded Quakers how Elizabeth Fry had had the King of Prussia to tea or reported on any notable Quaker achievement in the world. Any positive statement made by others about the Quakers was rehearsed in the journals' pages. When one Methodist minister asked 'Where would the world be without the Quakers?', it was reported by *The Friend*. Another had stated that Jesus was essentially a Quaker, a comment affirmed and discussed in the editorial (Phillips 1989: 55).

Whereas John Bright, Quaker MP for Birmingham, had declined appointment as Quaker Elder saying his political and spiritual lives were incompatible, the move to Liberal Quakerism at the end of the twentieth century harnessed its reconceptualization of Quakerism to a strong sense of citizenship. There were nine Quaker MPs elected in the 1906 Liberal landslide. There was not a Quaker line and Philip Ashton has shown how Quakers voted in different ways over Irish Home Rule (2000) and Pam Lunn has detailed the mix of attitudes Quaker women and men held on the issue of suffrage (1997), but the Quaker involvement in the heart of national politics marked a new civic and political spirit. Phillips explores what he terms the hubris of Quaker peace-making initiatives leading up to the First World War as Quakers repeatedly felt they were making a significant contribution (2004).

In the end, the outbreak of the First World War and in particular the advent of conscription in March 1916 disrupted the cosy relationship British Quakers had enjoyed with the Nation-State. Whilst the Yearly Meeting took a singular position against the war throughout its duration, individual Quakers took one of five positions. Positions varied between individuals and for individuals over time, some changing their position mid-war. Local Meetings held a variety of responses in contrast to the official Yearly Meeting pronouncements. One-third of eligible Quaker men enlisted (Kennedy 2001: 333). Others enlisted in non-combatant units such as the Medical Corps, whilst others joined the newly organised Friends Ambulance Unit (FAU). When the Military Service Act was passed in March 1916, incorporating the right of conscientious objection due to the work of Quaker MPs Arnold Rowntree and T. Edmund Harvey, Quaker conscientious objectors appeared before tribunals and accepted alternative service or, as 'absolutists' refused to take the role of someone who might then be freed to fight, and faced imprisonment. They became outlaws or criminals, instead of citizens, in their refusal to negotiate. Significantly, even whilst the State recognised Quaker conscientious objection, it was not understood or appreciated by the wider population. Quakers lost their jobs and faced vilification for their pacifist stance. T. Edmund Harvey was de-selected from his parliamentary seat in 1918.

This division of Quaker response to war was not new. In the American Revolutionary War, some Quakers had fought for independence. They had been disowned despite their plea for liberty of conscience and became known as the 'Free Quakers', building a Meeting House which still stands in the centre of Philadelphia (Kashatus 1990). Robynne Healey has charted the Quaker involvement in the Canadian uprising of 1837, revealing localised timescales for the shift from sectarian to denominational sensibilities (2006: chapter 7). By the third generation, Healey claims, 'their integration into Upper Canadian society would be complete' (2006: 135): marrying out was permitted in Upper Canada by 1850, a full decade head of Britain. Healey writes:

> The involvement of Friends in the [armed] Rebellion of 1837 was a desperate effort at political change and attests to their transforming identity. No longer was identity as a Quaker exclusive from identity as an Upper Canadian. The rebellion marks the end of the community's second generation. Increased integration into mainstream society brought greater interactions, marriages, and even religious affiliations with those who had similar doctrinal beliefs. (Healey 2006: 189)

This action also marked the end of Canadian Quaker dedication to the testimony against war under any circumstance, creating in its place a version of Quaker just war theory. Healey also makes the connection between this fuller citizenship and the growth in the trust of education (the first school house for the Yonge Street Quaker community was established in 1817), and its perception of value in gaining economic independence.

In the American Civil war, it was said that the Quakers of Indiana were the best recruiters of all the denominations (Hamm 1988: 68). Quakers needed to weigh their opposition to slavery against their historic witness against war and different Quakers came to different positions. Others faced conscription which as a moral issue was easier to oppose.

Organisationally, Quakers maintained their stance against war and sometimes this was taken further by individual Quakers. At the start of the Crimean War in 1854, Joseph Sturge and Robert Charleton and Henry Pease travelled to Russia, with the backing of British Friends, to meet with the Tsar to try and avert prolonged conflict (Brock 1990: 266–268). Prior to the First World War, individual Quakers met with Kaiser Wilhelm II to try and sustain peace (Phillips 2004).

War

Thus, whilst opposition to war has remained a hallmark of the Quaker faith (Muers 2015), its implementation has varied between individual and organisational responses. It has also varied over time. The Free Quakers were disowned but those who enlisted in the First World War frequently were not. Committees were set up to keep in touch with all the Quaker soldiers and the Birmingham one refused to advocate or accept resignation, instead citing integrity of conscience as a greater good than absolute pacifism.

Thomas Kennedy argued that those who took the firmest line against the conflict in the First World War became the interwar leaders of the Society (1989), but this claim needs to be contextualised within a changing attitude to Quaker witness or 'testimony' as outlined by Elaine Bishop and Jiseok Jung (2018).

They cite five major changes within Liberal Quakerism in the way in which testimony operated. The first is that the description of this aspect of witness changed. At the turn of the twentieth century the Quaker opposition to war became replaced with the Quaker advocacy of peace. Whilst the 1883 book of discipline had a section on 'war' (London Yearly Meeting 1883: 153–158), the parallel section in the subsequent 1911 book was headed 'Peace among the Nations' (London Yearly Meeting 1911: 139–146).

Second, the theological basis of this witness shifted in the twentieth century from being rooted in Christianity to it being rationalised in more generalised moral terms, or alternative theological constructions. The term 'spiritual' replaced the term 'Christian' in descriptions of the Quaker stance (Bishop and Jung 2018: 114)

Third, the requirement to subscribe to an anti-war or pacifist position became optional, as we have seen above. A prescriptive teaching and policing of such an ethic became permissive. The pull of citizenship could create a Quaker version of just-war theory (Bishop and Jung 2018: 115)

A fourth shift identified by Bishop and Jung is one in which the area of activity (against war) has moved from the individual behaviour policed within the group to a focus on external activity outside Quaker life, involving, for example, the petitioning of governments and other agencies (Bishop and Jung 2018: 116–117)

Consequent to these four shifts, fifth, the content of Quaker principles became more diffuse. We have already seen how the shift from plainness to simplicity creates a diffused interpretation of what the ideal may mean in everyday life. The idea of peace, as a replacement for anti-war, became complex, individualised, externalised, and diffuse within twentieth-century Liberal Quakerism. Wolf Mendl highlighted the alternative strategies of prophecy and reconciliation (1974), as mentioned above, whilst Bishop and Jung have argued that two forms of peace witness exist within Liberal Quakerism today, 'war-abolishing' and 'conflict-transforming' (2018: 120–121). The first is focused on the components of war, the second on causation and can also be termed 'peace-building'.

Rachel Muers has argued that the peace 'testimony' as with other forms of witness is constructed as much in terms of what it is not, as what it is, what Muers terms 'negative testimony' (2016: 54–70). To move from a position focused on being *against* war to being *for* peace merely masks the negative construction of Quaker witness. In other words, Quakers are against anything which is not towards peace. It is worth noting here that the 1661 statement from the Quakers to Charles II starts with the phrase 'We utterly deny all outward wars'. Muers' conceptualisation of testimony accords with Bishop and Jung's division of peace witness into war-abolishing (the negative testimony) and conflict-transforming (positive testimony).

In the plural and permissive environment of Liberal Quakerism, even one which maintains a commitment to peace, the interpretation of the testimony can lead to a range of ideas and of actions. Does peace principally involve the minimisation of sufferings or the refusal to kill? Does it entail vegetarianism or veganism? This diversity both hinders sectarian prescription whilst also accommodating both soft and hard versions of witness. Some Quakers can oppose cutting an airbase fence in terms of destruction of property whilst others pay the fines for those sentenced. What we find is a continually contested and negotiated interpretation of the parameters of what can be considered 'peace,' both between individual Quakers and between popular expressions and organisational discipline.

On 2 November 1965 outside the office of Defence Secretary Robert McNamara, Norman Morrison, following the example of Quaker Alice Herz and a number of Buddhist monks (Welsh 2008: 55), self-immolated in protest at the senseless suffering of innocent people in the Vietnam war. His widow, Anne Welsh, talks of how supportive Quakers in her Meeting were but how also some condemned the violence of the act. Others were troubled by the fact that he took his daughter, not quite 1 year old, with him. A third problem for some was that he had acted alone without the approval of his Meeting (Welsh 2008: 48).

For some, Morrison represented a pioneer in the mould of John Woolman and Elizabeth Fry, acting outside the corporate discipline and misunderstood by many of his Quaker peers but later heralded as a prophet, a process in part encouraged by the wider view of his actions, in his case the published reflections of Robert McNamara, the positive response from other peacemakers, and the attitude of many Vietnamese (Welsh 2008).

The Quaker response in the monthly magazine of Morrison's branch of Quakerism is interesting. The 15 December issue carried four letters, one of which was critical of the action (*Friends Journal* 15.12.65, p. 621). The following issue, 15 January 1966, ran a positive editorial, two articles and two poems, an article by Norman Morrison, an obituary, and two letters, one of which was critical as Morrison's leading had not been 'tested' by the Meeting (*Friends Journal* 15.1.66, pp. 580–581, 582, 594 and 596) Morrison's demonstration of sectarian 'prophetic' world-rejecting behaviour was generally affirmed. More recently Francesca Montemaggi has found amongst British Quakers that although social justice is a core value, most activism takes place outside Quaker circles (2018: part two). Perhaps this example of activism from within the Quaker world accommodated vicarious activism.

Quaker pioneers have often been treated diffidently by a conservative Quaker organisational disposition but later accorded fame and respect. Anti-slavery activist Benjamin Lay has recently had his termination of membership rescinded 250 years after his disownment. Elizabeth Fry was eldered for her neglect as a mother, due to spending too much time on prison work, when her two daughters married non-Quakers but is today celebrated for her insights and activism.

However, collective activism also erupts even within ostensibly denominational forms. In 1984, British Quakers as an employer refused to pay that portion of income tax collected from its employees that was to be used for military purposes and the two Quakers, representing the Yearly Meeting, went to court to face the charges of withholding revenue. For the Quakers, God's law had taken precedence over the State law. Citizenry was no longer an adequate response and Quakers chose to become outlaws.

The same was true of actions taken within the popular realm of Quakerism: Ellen Moxley and two others threw computers from a nuclear submarine into Holy Loch in 1999, and Sam Walton took part in a physical attack on a war plane in 2016 (both actions upheld by the courts on moral grounds). These examples are instances of a claim that divine instruction is greater than State law. However, in the diverse theological setting of the twenty-first century, this claim is problematic. For those whose Quakerism is atheological, the claim of being led by God's will is meaningless. For these secular Quakers, no longer led by the extra-rational, the law becomes more central: Quaker activists are seen to be choosing to break it. Humanism re-positions the prophet as offender instead of faithful adherent.

Thus even on a central concept of Quaker religiosity, we can locate a diminution of fervour and a complexification of interpretation over time. Organisational and popular response can differ from each other and retain dynamic and different levels of sectarian commitment at any one moment. Conscription in 1916 galvanised an organisational response but the individual response was varied and when it came to the disownment, conscience was given a higher value than pacifism. In 1965, Norman Morrison went further in his witness to the Nation-State than that advocated by his Yearly Meeting, but at the same time reflected the individualism that had become a hallmark of Quaker activism. Thus we can see that sectarian responses still emerge at any point within individual or organisational religiosity even whilst the lure of assimilation continually creates the seedbed for denominational sensibilities. Contrary to Niebuhr (see Chapter 1), zeal need not die out with the second generation and increased wealth or embeddedness in a host culture does not predict total denominationalisation.

At the same time, the extent of denominationalisation partly exists in the hands of the Nation-State. Outlawed groups cannot easily accept 'the world'. The history of responses to Jewish communities in Britain reveals the conditional nature of religious rights. We can see this in wider culture too: British Quakers were given a special clause under which to apply to join the new national ecumenical bodies in 1989 but the Unitarians were not similarly invited to that table. Denominationalisation may not be straightforward depending on wider cultural prejudices and preferences, hence the need to cultivate the spirit of harmlessness and equivalence in those more public-facing settings (whilst, referring back to the conundrum relayed in Chapter 2, still wishing to appear distinctive and salient to would-be converts).

Thus, we need to look at sect/denomination/church typologies in terms of public reaction as well as organisational change. Here the popular and organisational elements of religiosity become significant. When Morrison self-immolated, did the group 'own' and sanction his action or distance itself from an individualist act? Did Quakers as a body support absolutist non-compliance with conscription and alternative service or take a more seemingly harmless position to maximise public acceptance? These are the kinds of choices each religious group needs to regularly face, especially where a subjective interpretation is encouraged.

We can see that organisational and popular elements of religion are in constant negotiation with each other and that in turn each is in constant dialogue with the State and wider culture, which too are in a dynamic relationship. Figure 4.1 shows the old model of religion inter-relating with 'the world', whilst Figure 4.2 illustrates this more complex model outlined here.

FIGURE 4.1 Quakers and the world

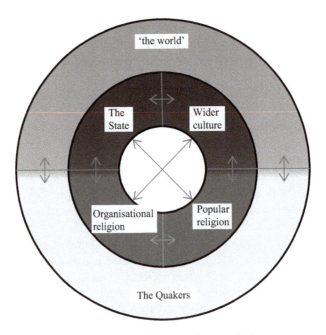

FIGURE 4.2 The elements of Quaker religion and non-religion

Patterns of institutional assimilation

In summary, we can locate a shift from world rejection towards world affirmation as early as 1656. Co-leader of the Quakers, James Nayler rode into Bristol with other Quakers waving branches before him and shouting 'Hosanna Hosanna'. He was charged with blasphemy for believing he was Christ and as a second offence, faced the death penalty. His case was tried by Parliament and George Fox wrote to Oliver Cromwell saying that they needed to do as they saw fit. This may be interpreted as Fox at his least charitable towards a leadership rival or it can be seen to denote the fragility of the moment for the Quaker movement. At this key moment, following Nayler's prophetic act, Quakers took a reconciliatory line. Nevertheless, three years later, Dorothy White told Parliament in prophetic terms they must repent for the day of judgment was at hand. This contrast with the events of late 1656 support Björkqvist's view that groups move along an axis between twin dispositions of world rejection and affirmation. I have written that as the State tolerated Quakers, so the Quakers tolerated the State (Dandelion 2007: 131) but in Mendl's terms, Quakers have continued to operate in both prophetic or reconciliatory ways. Quakers still both reject and accept 'the world' along both organisational and popular axes and need to negotiate with both State and wider cultural positions.

This pattern of increasing assimilation is not unusual and obviously other scholars have identified a similar pattern of the tendency to denominationalisation alongside multiple streams of religiosity. One of the most notable examples is Roland Robertson's study of the Salvation Army (1967). A persecuted group in the 1880s, the Salvation Army received royal and State acknowledgement in the early twentieth century. Robertson claimed that in turn the Army has become 'more tolerant of worldly affairs' whilst retaining its own identity through the 'institutionalised pragmatic interpretation of doctrine and teaching, the 'military' form of government and the social welfare services' (1967: 50). In Wilson's terms, the Army is an established sect, rejecting secular forms. Robertson claimed that a simple straightforward theology gave less opportunity for schism (1967: 67) Robertson identified three main positions within the army: *Old-guard* or the traditionalists; *Acceptors* who are pragmatic and neutral; and *Modernists* who want to revitalise and reshape its identity, re-evaluate doctrine and practice (e.g. uniform wearing) (Robertson 1967: 104). Thus we see a strong dynamic relationship between parts of the Army and a more stable one between the group and wider society.

The Exclusive Brethren and the Mormons represent two counter-examples to the pattern of inevitable denominationalisation. Writing about the Brethren before a major schism in the 1970s, Bryan Wilson described the group as a 'strictly separated sect' who emphasised inner sanctity and exclusive possession of a distinctive theology, soteriology and eschatology (1967b: 309). The group maintained its own version of the hedge and engaged in a collective practice of 'withdrawing from' an evil-doer (Wilson 1967b: 310–311). Equally, doctrine is flexible and malleable: 'members are held to the sect not by the fixed knowledge of an established set of truths, but also, and perhaps more, by the evolution of doctrine, and the changes in sect life and practice which represent a type of 'progress' for the fellowship'. (Wilson 1967b: 317)

According to Wilson, the Brethren have maintained sectarianism and intensified it (1967: 319): 'There is very little in which an adherent can be engaged that is not under the complete regulation of sectarian principles' (1967b: 326). Avoiding association with the world is key to the religiosity of the group. Group members do not share property with non-members (so no semi-detached houses or flats or staying in hotels), they do not share drains (1967b: 327). Children tend to go to Brethren schools and members are not permitted friendships outside the group. They tend to avoid public transport. There are processes of exclusion for those who are perceived to have fallen short. Money is only borrowed within the group, and cinema, theatre, television and radio are eschewed, as are mobile phones and computers. Women wear headscarves but there is otherwise no strict dress code. The group has opposed military service on the basis they wished to live out the Sermon on the Mount.

As Wilson states, 'The case of the Exclusive Brethren is one which completely falsifies the proposition that sects necessarily evolve into denominations in the course of two generations' (1967b: 334). Rather, the Brethren exhibit 'intense introversion' claiming that their fellowship provides 'the only effective place of salvation' (1967b: 335).

Wilson was writing 50 years ago but the Exclusive Brethren may still be seen as a counter-example to the received sociological wisdom that sects denominationalise. They have maintained their 'doctrine of separation' in a variety of clear ways and this is emphasised in the self-presentation of the group. However, there are also signs that this group is becoming more permissive (Mytton 2008).

Armand Mauss studied the tension between Mormonism and assimilation (1994). Received sociological wisdom would suggest that Mormonism survived through assimilation and the disavowal of its most unpopular practices, emerging into a place of respectability and acceptance by wider society. Mauss suggests that assimilation was not total and in recent decades has been less complete as 'peculiarity' has been revived and reaffirmed within the Mormon movement.

Mauss suggests that faced with innovative religious movements, the need for harmony lends the host society an impetus to assimilate or repress (1994: 4). Building on the work of Rodney Stark and his theoretical work on how religious groups 'succeed', Mauss claims that survival of the faith group depends on its balance between assimilation (respectability) and distinctiveness and separation (1994: 5) (essentially the conundrum outlined in Chapter 2 of this volume, although Mauss depicts the wider culture as static with the faith group managing this balancing act between respectability and disrepute and choosing which traits to emphasise to achieve the desired direction.)

Thus Mauss accepts that sects typically evolve into churches as a means of survival but suggests that the Mormons represent an anomaly with a retrenchment of peculiarity and an increase in tension with societal values. This contests classical sect/church theory but does suggest the continual rebalancing required: 'the theory advanced here is that religious movements must strategically reverse course from time to time as a condition of meaningful survival and success' (Mauss 1994: 8).

Mauss indicates an 'official response' to assimilation (1994: 77): 'Mormons have felt the need since the sixties to reach ever more deeply into their bag of cultural peculiarities to find either symbolic or actual traits that will help them mark their subcultural boundaries and thus their very identity as a special people.' They have used the following mechanisms to enhance a distinctive Mormon identity:

1. Continuing revelation over and against Protestant Bible-centricism, also new and adapted doctrine, and emphasis on the Book of Mormon instead of on the Bible.
2. Renewed emphasis on genealogy and temple work, and temple building.
3. A missionary programme.
4. Family renewal facilitated by an increase in discussion of, e.g. marriage, patriarchal order, parenthood, sexual sin, etc. (1994: 93).
5. An emphasis on religious education, including more financial support for Mormon institutions such as Brigham Young University, and a move away from worldly scholarship.

Mauss claims that nowhere are church–State relations more explicit than in the political arena. Perceived deviance and political leverage, he suggests, are in inverse relationship (1994: 108). Former versions of Mormon polygamy served as a catalyst for deeper concern over religious separatism. Explicit political involvement is more limited to particular individuals rather than a church role, with the exception of local politics in Utah and neighbouring States, only to be expected given the percentage of the population who are Mormon (1994: 108).

Mormon theology supports a conservative ideology in terms of family values and the discouragement of gambling, alcohol and other addictive substances. In general they wish to maintain the 'wall of separation' between church and State enshrined by Presidents James Madison and Thomas Jefferson and which had been most visible in the disestablishment of those States which had as colonies had maintained an established church. (Connecticut, for example, was disestablished in 1818, one of the last US States to do so.)

Mormons wish to keep war to a minimum but in 1898 with the advent of the Spanish-American War, and in both World Wars, Mormon leadership encouraged the faithful to enlist to, Mauss suggests, clarify for the American public that Mormons were patriotic (1994: 112). Mauss suggests that throughout the early twentieth century, Mormon sensibilities followed the national consensus, revealing high levels of assimilation (1994: 115). In the latter half of the century, Mormon conflict with the wider cultural consensus became more pronounced, particularly over issue of equality. Only in 1978 did Mormons rescind their earlier teaching that prohibited its Black members from joining the priesthood. Mormons also opposed the Equal Rights Act and pro-choice abortion legislation (1994: 116–119), positions which revealed a stronger sense of retrenchment after a long period of assimilation.

Mauss cites retrenchment as an internal reaction to assimilation as well as to an eightfold growth in membership, whilst also suggesting that shifts in wider culture (the moral revolution of the 1960s, for example) acted as an external catalyst, as it did for many conservative religious expressions (1994: 120) in enhancing distinctive religious identity:

> a religion's institutional identity is internalized by the individual member in the form of a clear and satisfying personal identity, as in the case of Hassidic Jews. Without the moral boundaries, the demands for personal investment, and the distinctive (even stigmatizing) traits of a sect or cult, its members do not enjoy a clear and separate identity at the individual level. (Mauss 1994: 9)

Thus, we can suggest that Mormons have prioritised separation (recruitment) rather than assimilation (harmlessness and equivalence).

Future research may want to look at the role apocalyptic thought plays in these patterns of assimilation and retrenchment. Elizabeth Cooksey and I have suggested (2010) that the Quakers had assimilated more than the Amish because the initial theological premise for separation had been intertwined with a sense of living in the end times whereas for the Amish the end times had always been a future event. For the Amish that hope remained and their degree of separation was more or less sustained. The Quakers on the other hand needed to reconfigure their identity and without a theology of realising eschatology had less upon which to justify extreme separation. 'Holy Nation' rhetoric (Crabtree 2015) can be seen to be a secondary eschatological trope once the initial experiential basis of eschatological thought had diminished. When that too ended, separation becomes less obvious a strategy. It is interesting here that Bryan Wilson noted of the Exclusive Brethren that they had no form of eldership as they believed there is no office-holding in 'the last days' (1967b: 324).

Chapter summary

From this chapter, we can see how Quakers have been used as an example of denominationalisation, although scholars have timed the transition in different ways. Nevertheless we can see that Quakers have over time received more rights from the State and have at the same time become less hostile to 'the world'. They have moved into an acceptable and accepting part of the religious landscape, thus affirming the received sociological wisdom about denominationalisation. However, assimilation is never complete and on key issues, particularly war, Quakers, at both an organisational and popular level, have maintained a counter-cultural pre-disposition which has been expressed in both denominational and sectarian ways. Other groups, such as the Brethren and the Mormons, also exhibit forms of religiosity that contest denominationalisation theory.

The next chapter builds on Thomas Tweed's use of fluid dynamics to theorise religion in terms of 'confluences of organic-cultural flows' (2006) to model this more complex view of religion/non-religion relations, and to introduce the presence of turbulence and 'incoherent motion'.

Note

1 This involved the arrest and trial of prominent Quaker leader James Nayler following his enactment of Christ's second coming by riding a horse into Bristol, other Quakers waving branches before him. This was a fragile moment for the movement.

5

MODELLING TURBULENCE

From the previous chapter, we can see that the relationship between Quakers and non-Quakers (or religion and non-religion) has at least four components: organisational Quaker life, popular Quakerism, the Nation-State and wider culture. These can also be broken down into regional or sectional variants. Each is in constant negotiation with each other creating a dynamic set of inter-relationships (see Figure 4.2). Sectarianism can erupt at any point given particular conditions.

In wishing to create a more dynamic metaphor for the intersection between the religious group and wider culture than the binary notion of 'the hedge', one that encompasses external disposition as well as internal, various options have been suggested. Perhaps we could think of these two cultural sites as cells with permeable membranes through which different substances can pass at different rates simultaneously. This captures the permeability and malleability of cultural states well but tends to suggest a static body to which change happens rather than an ever-changing dynamic within cultures as well in terms of outside influences.

Fluid dynamics appears a better metaphor. As Hughes and Brighton state in an introductory text to fluid dynamics 'a fluid is a substance which cannot resist a shear force or stress without moving' (1999: 1) as opposed to a solid. A liquid possesses volume but no fixed shape, rather it can take different shapes whilst retaining its volume. Unlike a gas, a liquid does not dissipate in all directions but it has an internal coherence which maintains a particular volume. Thus we can imagine a social group with its own internal prescriptions and proscriptions as behaving in ways similar to a fluid. It might be compressed out of existence by State persecution but equally it resists such compression, potentially reshaping itself to fits the new container it is given.

In thinking about fluid dynamics, we are also looking at continuum rather than at individual particles, ideal for the sociological imagination which looks at group dynamics rather than individual actors. In fluid dynamics as in sociology, we can assume that particles or actors act in similar ways, that the 'distance' between them is very small in relation to the generalised behaviour we are observing and analysing.

Thomas Tweed has usefully used the idea of flow in terms of his theory of religion (2006), and building on Thomas Tweed's theorising of religion in terms of flow and confluence, this chapter emphasises the importance of modelling turbulence and outlines a new terminology for the dynamic inter-relationship between the Quakers, and religions in general, and wider society. The first part of this chapter, however, rehearses the nature of fluid dynamics as a dynamic system.

Dynamic systems of flow

Rickles et al. talk of a system in the following way:

> A system is simply the name given to an object studied in some field and might be abstract or concrete; elementary or composite; linear or non-linear; simple or complicated; complex or chaotic. Complex systems are highly composite ones, built up from very large numbers of mutually interacting subunits (that are often composites themselves) whose repeated interactions result in rich, collective behaviour that feeds back into the behaviour of the individual ... A dynamical system is a system whose state (and variables) evolve over time, doing so according to some rule. (2007: 933)

Thus we can think of flow as a dynamic system that changes with respect to time and that is not in a constant state. Hughes and Brighton state: 'An "ideal" flow, then, has no internal friction and hence no internal dissipation or losses. Actually, no fluid is ever really ideal' (Hughes and Brighton 1999: 4). Changing pressures on fluids affect its acceleration (Hughes and Brighton 1999: 3). Other variables include the viscosity of the fluid, itself affected by temperature: higher temperatures reduce viscosity.

Those involved in fluid dynamics talk of two main kinds of flow: laminar and turbulent. Laminar flow is where the fluid flows in layers, as opposed to turbulent which involves fluctuations.

> A stream of dye or ink inserted into a laminar flow will steak out a thin line and always be composed of the same fluid particles. However, in turbulent flow the dye line would quickly become tangled up and mixed in with the fluid as it flows along, and we would see myriads of threads and clouds ever widening and dispersing as the fluid flows along. (Hughes and Brighton 1999: 4)

It is very difficult for flow to remain laminar even under highly specified artificial conditions (Acheson 1997: 133–151). Turbulence normally exists at the edges of even ideal flow (Hughes and Brighton 1999: 9) and in general we can say that turbulence follows transition. As flows meet a boundary layer or edge, initial flow is laminar but a transition region and turbulent flow follow just behind:

> The transition region actually consists of bursts of turbulence which spread until they intermingle to result in a fairly turbulent region ... These turbulence bursts do not have fixed locations but continually move.
> (Hughes and Brighton 1999: 103)

Turbulence can also involve 'reversed flow' especially at separation points of the flow, e.g. as flow hits an object (Hughes and Brighton 1999: 113). Turbulence then is essentially 'irregular flow' or random variation in the conditions for laminar flow (Hughes and Brighton 1999: 245): 'Turbulence is 'a mess of disorder at all scales, small eddies within large ones. It is unstable. It is highly dissipative, meaning that turbulence drains energy and creates drag. It is motion turned random' (Gleick 1988: 122).

In short, changes in velocity or pressure disrupt laminar flow and create turbulence. As internal disturbances extend in magnitude, flow becomes 'unstable', and can then return to laminar or grow in instability and become turbulent. In fluid dynamics, 'the study of the response of fluids to disturbances or perturbations is known as *stability theory*' (Hughes and Brighton 1999: 246). We might suggest that sociology is an investigation of cultural stability theory.

The challenge of stability theory within fluid dynamics is to gauge the conditions in which instability begins. Fortunately sociologists do not need to measure with such accuracy or work with predictive equations.

Thus we can begin to imagine the cultural dynamics of a social or religious group in terms of a distinct fluid, interacting with wider culture as a separate fluid, within which various other sub-cultures exist as their own fluids. In the complexified model of relations between religions and the world outlined in Chapter 4, we can think of two significant fluid interactions; that between the group, itself divided between organisational religion and popular religion, and wider culture divided between governmental regulation and public opinion.

In this study of religion and non-religion, we can imagine the two aspects as two flows that may or may not be operating in laminar or turbulent forms.

> ... there are two states, laminar and turbulent, in which flows can occur: the transition between these two states is a definite point and the point is dependent on the situation through which the flow travels. If a social situation is laminar, we would expect that there would be an orderliness about it and that things would stay where they were. As it comes under pressure the orderliness would increase. However, when the pressure is too strong then turbulence will occur as the order breaks down. Finally, we would expect

that the surrounding social situation will alter the point at which the change
from laminar to turbulence occurs. (Russell 2015: 169)

Thus, we can see how the interaction between the flow of religion and the
flow of non-religion, which themselves may be laminar or turbulent, is crucial
in determining the style of confluence that is created by the two flows. Jean
Russell explains:

> The difference between laminar and turbulent normally starts in the
> boundary layer ... the boundary layer is where the behaviour of the liquid
> is significantly different from the central flow as the molecules are in a
> state of transition between the flows. That is, molecules in the boundary
> layer are in a state of transition between the flow in the core and the
> currents that surround it. It should be noted that some currents from
> outside that enter the flow will be in a similar orientation to the internal
> direction of the flow. Equally, some are going in a direction significantly
> different to it. Those that move in a similar direction are easily assimilated
> into the flow. When those whose trajectory is across the direction to the flow
> enter the boundary layer, they cause more disruption and thus there is often
> turbulence in the boundary layer ... The boundary layers also come in two
> forms. There are those boundary levels that are smooth, where the turbu-
> lence caused by the surrounding currents is not transmitted to the core flow
> of the fluid. Also, there are rough boundary layers where the turbulence at
> the edge is not absorbed within the boundary layer, and the changes are
> transmitted to the core flow. Therefore such areas tend to be more turbulent
> than the central flow as the molecules are subject to forces that drive both
> the flow and also the surrounding currents. Therefore, in fluid dynamics,
> boundaries are significant areas of transition. (Russell 2015: 169–170)

In social terms, it becomes important to recognise how ordered and cohesive are the sites of religion non-religion, or how the nature of these states
will affect the consequent interaction within the complex set if dynamic
relationships between the components of religion and non-religion.

Fluid dynamics concerns itself with spatial and temporal instability
(Hughes and Brighton 1999: 333) as well as two types of instability: 'convective' and 'absolute'. 'Convective instability occurs when a disturbance is
inserted into the fluid and it grows as it propagates downstream ... Absolute
instability occurs when the entire fluid domain becomes unstable, and as time
progresses the entire fluid field changes' (Hughes and Brighton 1999: 333).
Given our interest in changing social dynamics, within a generally stable
situation, we are interested here in when the relationship between religion
(organisational and popular) and non-religion (State and culture) moves from
being laminar to turbulent, when that dynamic creates convective instability
by a change in position of one of the components of church and non-church

flow. This will be particularly crucial at the edges of the interaction of the flows or at the boundaries of inter-relationship.

Jean Russell uses fluid dynamics in her work on Congregationalist church life.

> If we are standing at the edge of flows, we can distinguish two types of flow. A smooth or laminar flow is one moving in a direction in an orderly manner. A turbulent flow has whirlpools and eddies; thus the path of a single particle may not be in the bearing of the overall flow. At the molecular level, a smooth flow is where the relationships between the particles in the flow are stronger than the connections to the surroundings. Thus, the momentum of the flow dominates the direction of flow of the particles. Turbulence is a result of particles in the flow being influenced by particles in other flows which have different velocities. So, within a congregation, while we would expect things to be smooth, at some level there will instead be places of turbulence. (Russell 2015: 126)

Of interest here is that once turbulence is created it requires a force larger than the one which initiated it to overcome it. Acheson, in his mathematical modelling of turbulence, claims that a small or incremental disturbance in particular conditions can create a sudden or 'catastrophic' change. Imagine holding a piece of bicycle brake cable with pliers near its top and letting it hang vertically under gravity. Move the pliers down the cable and the wire still remains vertical but at some point as the piers are moved further down, the top of the cable bends over and hangs down. Reversing the process does not reverse the effect. Moving the pliers back up a little does not cause the wire to bend back up. Only when the length of cable above the pliers is less than the length below does it return to the upright. This pattern of non-reversibility when a parameter is increased and then decreased again is called 'hysteresis' and the mapping of the phenomenon creates a 'hysteresis loop' (Acheson 1997: 141–142).

Hysteresis is a term derived from the Greek word to 'lag behind', and is used in a variety of fields to show that effects lag behind causes and that reversal of effects lags behind a reversal of the inputs. It is used in economics and one example is how when recession creates unemployment, long-term unemployment remains at increased levels beyond the parameters of the recession as businesses try to maintain their reduced costs even as demand increases again. Hysteresis works with the history-dependent nature of the matter it is referring to.

We can see this effect in social situations as well. In a simple example, we can think of a school staff that together create a particular ethos. The ethos can remain as one or two staff members leave but could be ruptured when a critical number have left. Replacing or even replacing one or two staff will not recreate the ethos.

Once laminar flow has become turbulent, it takes a relatively large effect for it to collapse back from turbulent to laminar again. Thus the relationship between laminar flow and turbulence exhibits hysteresis (Acheson 1997: 149–150).

Where a hysteresis loop is completed or where the original situation is never replicated, i.e. there is no return to the original state, the phenomenon is called 'hysteresivity'. In physics, this may be because the action resulted in heat or energy loss that cannot be recovered. In social situations, we may argue that social relations are never exactly replicated but flow on in new forms. We can define social life in terms of hysteresevity. History is hystoretic.

Cultural flows

The idea of cultural 'flows' is one that is frequently used in the social sciences. Doreen Massey argues for understanding space as interconnected with time; things are not static but in motion (2005). Doreen Massey argues that the concept of 'space' with its eternal openness creates a location for engagement. In space, anything can happen. It is not yet mapped, defined and bounded. Rather, space is about the interactions of coexisting lives: it is 'the sphere therefore of coexisting heterogeneity' (2005: 9).

Arjun Appadurai suggests that there are certain fundamental disjunctures between economy, culture and politics that might be explored using five types of global 'cultural flow': 'ethnoscapes', 'mediascapes', 'technoscapes', 'financescapes' and 'ideoscapes' (2008: 33). An ethnoscape is about the landscape of persons who constitute the shifting world: tourists, immigrants, refugees, exiles, guest workers and other moving groups. Still some stable communities but, Appadurai claims, 'the warp of these stabilities is everywhere shot through with the woof of human motion, as more persons and groups deal with the realities of having to move or the fantasies of wanting to move' (2008: 33–34). Technoscapes are about technology, financescapes about money, mediascapesthe distribution of capabilities to produce and disseminate information, ideoscapes are about ideologies and counter-ideologies (Appadurai 2008: 35–36). Appadurai uses the suffix 'scape' to emphasise the fluid and irregular shape of these landscapes that appear differently from different angles, and that they are 'deeply perspectival constructs' inflected by broad and multi-faceted contexts and a variety of actors who navigate them (Appadurai 2008: 33). Appadurai argues that these flows are in fuller force than ever before (Appadurai 2008: 37), and links them to the globalised deterritorialisation of populations, which creates markets for mediascapes to transmit 'homeland' to the new temporary or diasporic (displaced) locations.

Zygmunt Bauman coined the term 'liquid modernity' to describe the way in which the differentiation of institutions within modernity has given way to less enduring structured forms in which the individual is required to make choices without the patterns, codes and rules they once relied on.

It is the patterns of dependency and interaction whose turn to be liquefied has now come. They are now malleable to an extent unexperienced
by, and unimagined for, past generations; but like all fluids, they do not
keep their shape for long. Shaping them is easier than keeping them in
shape. (2000: 7–8)

For Bauman, the way in which late modernity is increasingly arranged around
individualised and private choice-making gives it this liquefied quality in which
societal shape-shifting becomes normative. Workplace, neighbourhood, family
and religious affiliation no longer represent lifetime certainties but have given
way to forms that are provisional with identities and conceptions of community
constantly re-negotiated. Bauman presents this picture of constantly changing
social forms in negative terms, in terms of loss, rather than celebrating new
forms of cultural flexibility.

Russell likens high or late or liquid modernity to a change in the viscosity
of cultural flow:

All fluids have a viscosity, that is, resistance to changing flow. Fluids will
keep flowing at a constant speed in the same direction unless they
encounter some obstacle or force that acts against their flow. Equally,
stationary fluids will not suddenly start flowing in the absence of force.
Indeed without a force acting on them fluids will tend to experience
laminar flow … if we work correctly with fluid dynamics, what has
changed in modernity is the viscosity; we have moved from a time when
modernity had a high viscosity to one which is lower. Thus, Bauman is
looking at is the difference between high viscosity and low viscosity …
and society is changing to absorb this new situation. (Russell 2015: 211)

Russell comments on the use of flow by social scientists:

In using 'flow', these authors want to make two statements: that things
are not static and that things get dispersed … These theorists seek to map
currents much like an oceanographer … or meteorologist. Mapping currents is not mapping stasis but mapping dynamics. (2015: 73–74)

Thus, in changing relationships between religious groups and wider culture,
incremental changes can create large net effects to create new states which do
not collapse back to their original situation. The role of social scientists is to
map these flows and to theorise about them.

James Gleick in his account of the development of chaos theory relates
how scientists found regularity and pattern in the random nature of turbulence. The study of the boundary region between laminar and turbulent flow
by Mitchell Feigenbaum led to the understanding of a constant at play that
moved the laminar into turbulence. Amidst the random nature of turbulence

lay a regularity of the timing and rate (scaling) of turbulence (Gleick 1988: 172–175). In other words, there is structure in non-linear systems (Gleick 1988: 183). Similarly, social life is not chaotic, but social systems still seem to follow rules, and perhaps the constant that moves social life into turbulence and creates new regular patterns is that of collective dissonance between the components of social life we have identified here as parallel flows.

Applying flow and turbulence to religious groups

From the work in the previous chapters, I find three potential deficiencies with the sociological theory and the work on sects and wider society.

All of the typologies of types of religious group contain within them a fundamental assumption of a movement from radical sectarianism towards conformist denominationalism. Sects become denominations, not the other way around. Even in Martin's terms, groups may start life as a denomination (1962) but they do not then become sects. Indeed the question arises whether the denomination is a modernist form, rooted in rationalism and a sense of (mutually accepting) differentiation. World-rejecting groups become world-accepting or world-affirming. The scholarly debates have been only over the naming of the organisational types of religious life and the timing of these processes of transition.

Equally, all the work to date on e.g. Quaker attitudes to 'non-Quakers' has drawn on a trajectory of increasing conformity to the State, that as the State has increasingly tolerated Quakers, so Quakers have increasingly tolerated the State. Indeed, the view from 'the other side' is rarely featured, except where, e.g. in the case of Thomas Clarkson's *Portraiture of Quakerism* (1806), it feeds a positive interpretation of Quaker faith.

In most of these models of inter-relationship between Quakers and nation, the State is depicted as a static entity to which the faith group responds. Calvert's work on the broad political maelstrom of colonial Pennsylvania is a notable exception. Only with accounts of the Quaker opposition to the Military Service Act of 1916, entailing conscription, is a dynamic relationship clearly visible as Quaker MPs amend the wording of the legislation. In other words, historians of Quakerism have only become historians of the politics of nationhood when Quakers have become part of the government apparatus.

I propose in contrast a dynamic and flexible model building on the work of Thomas Tweed and the descriptions of fluid dynamics above. The model frames the navigation between citizenship and public appeal as a combination of dynamic processes within the Quaker group as they relate to those *equally* dynamic processes within the State and the public square, resulting in differing levels of engagement on different aspects of church–State and church–world relationship at different times. Thus, I am proposing a model that can accommodate how Quakers may argue with Quakers over what 'purity' may consist of, and on the importance and content of strategies for State acceptance and public appeal.

Tweed's work is crucial here. In his pioneering volume *Crossing and Dwelling: a theory of religion* (2006), Tweed defined religions as 'confluences of organic-cultural flows that intensify joy and confront suffering by drawing on human and suprahuman forces to make home and cross boundaries' (2006: 54), where confluence refers to the joining together of separate systems of flow. In much the manner that I have illustrated above, Tweed claims his definition 'draws on aquatic metaphors in order to emphasize movement, avoid essentialism, and acknowledge contact' (2011: 21). For Tweed, 'Each religion, then, is a flowing together of currents—some institutionally enforced as "orthodox"—traversing channels, where other religions, other transverse confluences, also cross, thereby creating new spiritual streams' (2011: 21).

Tweed claims:

> Religions cannot be reduced to economic forces, social relations, or political interests, but they always emerge from the swirl of transfluvial currents, as both religious and non-religious streams propel religious flows. These flows are also 'organic-cultural,' in my view, so I invoke the hyphen to suggest that both natural forces and cultural processes are at work in religion: we can talk about constraining organic channels and shifting cultural currents. So religions are processes in which social institutions (the state, the temple, and the family) bridge biological constraints and cultural mediations to produce reference frames that yield a variety of representations (rituals, artifacts, and narratives) that draw on suprahuman agents (gods, buddhas, or bodhisattvas) and imagine an ultimate horizon of human life (Amida Buddha's Pure Land or the Kingdom of God). (2011: 21)

Tweed very helpfully introduced the idea of cultural and natural flow and confluence as metaphors to describe the dynamic nature of religion (2006, 59). For Tweed, 'religious women and men are continually in the process of mapping a symbolic landscape and constructing a symbolic dwelling' (2006, 73–74). It is this constantly negotiated process, critically in combination with the confluence and flows of the State and the public arena, that means, after Michel de Certeau (1984), that place is continually practised in new ways, that the space around expressions of full (and harmless) citizenship is continually changing for religious individuals and organisations (as are thus the consequences for secularisation). Although overall shifts over time or particular stances at particular moments can be identified, I suggest there is no causal or pre-determined route. I agree with Tweed that maps are continually redrawn. Sectarianism for example, as we have seen in Chapter 4, re-emerges on a particular issue at any moment and changes the way the group needs to be treated sociologically.

As mentioned above, Wolf Mendl suggested that the Quaker peace witness comprises two contrasting tropes, one of prophetic witness, one of reconciliation. The prophetic is fixed on the vision of holy horizon, the prophetic task to call others towards that destination (Mendl 1974). The reconcilia-tory is concerned with the means to that end. These are often in tension. We might see the theatrical anti-slavery direct action of Benjamin Lay as prophetic, John Woolman's desire for obedience to the divine as equally so (Kershner 2018), but Anthony Benezet's approach more pragmatic and reconciliatory (Carey 2016 and Chapter 3 above). We could categorise Richard Nixon in his ground-breaking visits to China as reconciliatory and the self-immolation of Norman Morrison on the steps of the Penta-gon in protest at US war policy prophetic. As Morrison's example shows us, even as an individual act unsanctioned by his Quaker Meeting, the desire amongst religious groups to cultivate conformity to win rights and the regulation of that conformity by the State in order to co-opt dissent and maintain harmonious society, is never completely predictable. Thus, looking at the anti-war witness of Quakers, perhaps the last collective trope of anti-worldliness within global Quakerism, offers a broader per-spective as to how we might approach Quaker relationships with the State. It highlights the reality of opposing and contrasting moments of laminar (undisrupted) flow between church and State with at other times opposi-tional movements.

However, Tweed's ideas of flow and confluence appear uni-directional and denote co-operation. Whilst he talks above about the 'swirl of transfluvial currents' and introduces the idea of 'transfluence' between religious and non-religious streams (2006: 60), his use of transfluvial, of one flow crossing another, to represent intercausality underplays the potential for disturbance and disruption. For Tweed, the crossing of currents produces only 'new reli-gious streams'. Tweed is in the end more interested in the dynamics of reli-gion rather than the relationship between religion and political 'other'. To encompass the religion/secular inter-relationship, we need to add ideas of conflict, of dissonance, and of turbulence.

We can think of conflicts between the religious and non-religious in terms of backwash or a concept of 'the bore', the tidal backsweep that pushes back up tidal rivers such as the Severn in England from time to time (130 days a year in the case of the Severn). It may be a good metaphor for the way sects have chosen to 'swim upstream' in their relationships with 'the world'. The plumbing terms of 'backflow' or 'reflux' may work better than confluence alone to recognise the uneasy and unexpected meeting of flows from both religion and the State, the unpredictability of the mix of sudden party-political or pro-phetic inspirations, and the unwanted sense of contamination that either side may imagine the other heralds. The meeting of the two ideologies may not be smooth but one of turbulence. The interaction may be similar to a vortex where one party holds a static position and the other swirls around it (perhaps Morrison's lone action against the Johnson govern-ment), with the political forces of what physicists term 'diffusivity' acting on the vortex to calm it down (Hunt et al. 1988).

Typically though, we may most appropriately see the interaction between the religious and non-religious in terms of multiple eddies or patterns of multiple turbulent flow, described as follows by A. K. M. Fazle Hussain.

> A turbulent flow can be viewed as a tangle of vortex filaments. Even in transitional flows, initially rolled-up two-dimensional vortical structures develop three dimensionality through secondary instability and then undergo interactions. A study of vortex interactions is obviously crucial to understanding transition processes as well as basic turbulence phenomena (1986: 338)

A. K. M. Fazle Hussain's work on coherent vorticity (the interactions around a vortex) and incoherent turbulence (1986), whilst complexifying the nature of turbulence within his own discipline, suggest to me patterns of coherent flow, more generally, and incoherent flow. This is using the terms coherent and incoherent in a different way from Hussain's focus on types of turbulence but is using them to refer to patterns of generally laminar and general turbulent flow.

'Incoherence' denotes a lack of connection, cohesion and harmony. In this context, it is about dissonance between State and faith group, but one rooted in ever-changing social stances. Whilst we may still be able to identify an overall trajectory of increased conformity or confluence, this is a trope of coherence within which incoherent turbulent motion may erupt at any stage from either church or State, a potential for non-conformity within (increasing) conformity. 'Ideal flow' as we know, is very rare.

If we accept this model of multiple patterns of laminar and turbulent flow, which we can now understand in terms of multiple arenas (organisational religion, popular religion, State, popular culture at least, more if we include geographical or historical diversity), we can chart the relationships between the Quakers and the State, or the Quakers and the general population, in terms of varying degrees of coherent and incoherent flow. Equally, we can chart different axes of coherent and incoherent flow. Thus by the time of the First World War, to revisit the earlier example, Quakers in Britain cohered on just about every dimension of State law until the introduction of conscription at which point an axis of incoherent flow was introduced. Flow turned to backflow in this aspect of church/State relations.

Backflow necessarily creates its own reaction as it pushes against the dominant flow. It creates its own return flow and we can see this in terms of the imprisonment visited upon the absolutist conscientious objectors who refused to recognise the authority of the tribunals. Multiple turbulent flow is created and the relationship between church and State becomes incoherent, lacking connection, cohesion and harmony. Coherent flow was only re-established after the end of the war, probably by about the mid-1920s.

Thus I am suggesting this model of flow and backflow, coherence and incoherence to present relationships within religious groups and between religious
groups and wider society (both State and popular culture) in a more variously
dynamic way. This model needs to be understood along the two axes of the
negotiation of (a) purity and public appeal, and (b) the desire for citizenship
and State appeal, and be applied to both sides of each of these relationships.
This model offers greater analytical power than earlier models of sectarian
interplay with worldliness which assumed a one-way route to acceptance of the
world and worldly acceptability and which presented the 'world' (either State or
public) in static terms.

As Tweed himself wrote in a paper following his original theory, 'Religions, as
I understand them, negotiate power as well as make meaning … there are no
unimpeded flows. The flows—of people, things, and practices—are propelled,
compelled, and blocked, directed this way and that, by institutions' (2011: 25).
Tweed likened the control of religious institutions to the maintenance of a dam,
controlled by an authorised adherent whose personal preferences are constrained
by their responsibilities to the organisation and the role allocated to them (2011:
26). However, whilst this accommodates the potential for turbulence within the
religious life, it still omits the possibility or probability for turbulence when the
religious collides with the non-religious, either wishing to apply a brake to social
reform (increase the viscosity of modernity) or move ahead of societal conservatism (one flow moving at a higher velocity than another). These interactions in the boundary layers of the religious and non-religious are almost
inevitably likely to tend to turbulence or incoherent flow rather than ideal laminar flow, especially as we sub-divide these two categories into component flows
of state and wider culture, and institutional and popular religion. At the same
time, the presence of turbulence does not interrupt the trend to assimilation.
Indeed it is almost a hallmark of it: for groups less integrated into wider society,
such as the Amish, the direct effect of turbulence may be less as the interaction
between religion and non-religion is less direct. Sects are not necessarily against
the government as much as disinterested: they simply ignore and eschew the
world. Assimilation brings intimacy and probably rights but also the likelihood
of greater turbulence, either visited upon the group by State direction or popular
challenge, or created by the group itself in its more sectarian presentations.

Linda Woodhead has introduced the idea of strategic religion and tactical
religion (2013) as a way to better explain the internal dynamics of faith
groups. Following Michel de Certeau, Woodhead suggests that strategy is the
prerogative of the powerful, whereas the weak are forced to react rather than
command. For de Certeau, a tactic is 'determined by the *absence of power*
just as a strategy is organised by the postulation of power' (1984: 38, original
emphasis) The weak are necessarily tactical in their responses. Woodhead
claims that 'strategy and tactics form and shape one another dialectically' and
'form the conditions of the other's possibility' (2013: 16). The tactical will
always be finding ways to resist the strategist and shifts in the balance of

(unequal) power may blur the mode of operation. In religious terms, the strategic delimits faith and guards its sacred spaces and other forms of representation. Woodhead gives the example of the priesthood's control of the liturgy, the liturgical year, and liturgical space. The tactical, she suggests, subverts the power of these rites, times and places by re-imagining the sacramental, by making it portable or temporary or internal. Historically, we might imagine reforming tendencies as tactical in their attempts to subvert dominant religious strategic religious authority. Alternatively we can see 'the dance between the strategic and the tactical' (2013: 18) in the dialectic between popular and institutional religious expression. In the terms discussed above, it is at the interface between institutional and popular religious flows with 'the dance' as a form of ongoing incoherent fluidity. Woodhead also suggests that in terms of religious healing, the State strategised about faith forcing the churches into tactical role (2013: 19). Thus we can also see the inequalities of power between religion and the State in terms of the strategic and the tactical or, we can find her a confirmation of the need to consider differing types of flow with different agencies operating within religion and between religion and the components of non-religion.

Jean Russell explores Kim Knott's exploration of the crossing of the sacred/ profane within a congregational environment. Knott talks of 'right-handed' faith that approaches the divine by separating out purification rites and so on from the everyday (Knott 2005: 133–148). Russell suggests that this is in some ways what is expected: a divide where the maintenance of the boundary is clear to all. Knott also discusses what she terms the 'left-handed'; the way to the divine through the deliberately profane (Knott 2005: 146–169). Russell argues that instead of this representing an either/or situation, that these are held in tension in many congregations: 'They could both maintain the "left hand" argument that the communion table was just a table, but also make sure it was made of oak' (2015: 152). Here again, we see contrasting flows of interpretation and agency operating alongside each other. In Tweed's terms, religious life is both about crossing and (re)creating, and dwelling and stabilising representation.

The organisational, within a secular democracy, is both about maintaining good reputation of religious citizenship as well as advocating and enforcing purity and authenticity amongst adherents. Adherents interpret the organisational and create their own 'lived religion'. Neither is static, even whilst the organisational may move more slowly or attempt to create a single theological dwelling place. Henri Lefebvre talked of conceived and lived space, the difference between an imagined representation of space and a space of representation (Stanek 2011: 129). We can borrow these terms to think about conceived and lived religiosity (Dandelion 2017). The organisation conceives and attempts the strategic role, lived religion is about the tactical interpretation.

Within fluid dynamics, it is interesting that the particles in the middle of flow down a pipe are travelling more quickly than those at the (trailing) edge where there is greater friction. Where flows interact, they move more slowly as flow is disrupted or interrupted. Frances Handrick in her work on Amish life discusses the signifiers of Amish religiosity in terms of solid and liquid (2016) but also in terms of centre and 'edge' (2017), where the edge represents tactical religiosity. For all Amish, non-Amish are 'the English': that is solid, but their interpretations of the use of phones or labour-saving devices maybe more liquid. These new modes of expression are not perceived by their advocates as apostasy or atheism but as fresh expression of faith. Quakers in the 1860s felt it was appropriate and authentic to move away from the mandatory requirement of plain dress.

Of course, not all participants interpret their faith in similar ways, so there may be multiple 'edges' or gradation of 'edge'. Here it is of note that smaller particles move more easily than big ones, e.g. pebbles over rocks, so flows of mixed-size particles move at different rates. Religious life is made up of multiple flows constantly engaging with each other, and non-religion, in changing patterns of coherent and incoherent flow.

Chapter summary

In summary, the use of 'flow' is a very helpful way of viewing the currents of religious life and the use of multiple flows works well to help describe and theorise the dynamic relationships between elements of religious life and culture and elements of non-religious culture. Flow is rarely 'ideal' and laminar flow can easily become turbulent, an analogy we can use to depict the relationship between religion and State or religiosity and popular culture. Building on Thomas Tweed's work on religion in terms of 'confluences of organic-cultural flows', I have suggested here that we need to take more account of turbulence or of when flows fail to cohere, of incoherent flow as well as coherent flow. We can apply this in turn to other theorisations of religion such as Woodhead's suggestion of tactical and strategic religion and start to locate the causes of turbulence within the dynamics within religion and between faith and 'world'. We will use this modified view of religious coherent and incoherent motion in the following section which starts to theorise about non-doctrinal Quakerism and its potential for internal secularisation.

PART III

New theory: a future of religiosity

6

QUAKER CULTURE AND NON-DOCTRINAL ASSIMILATION

This final section of the book suggests new sightings, new theories about the nature of British Quakerism and how it manages the conundrum outlined in Chapter 2 and about the elements, mechanics and flows of internal secularisation more broadly, taken as an end point of extreme assimilation. Taken together, these chapters suggest one future of religiosity.

This chapter[1] offers an overview of the current 'Liberal' incarnation of British Quakerism. Quaker believing is today expressed in diverse and thus post-(solely) Christian language, and doctrine is marginal to the construction of Quaker identity. Caroline Plüss has termed Liberal Quakerism 'non-doctrinal' (2007) and Peter Collins and I have termed it a 'liquid religion' (2014). British Quakers today do not make universal belief claims, and exhibit highly diffuse (and permissive) patterns of belief. Quaker culture is less permissive in terms of its processes and form, what I have termed a 'behavioural creed' (orthopraxy) and the way in which these beliefs are held, an 'orthocredence', also acts as a boundary marker of Quaker identity. Orthopraxy and orthocredence offer the kinds of distinctives which appear to have stemmed the advance of secularisation and have, curiously given Steve Bruce's theory about the decline of liberal religion, secured an ongoing appeal amongst non-churchgoers. However, using data drawn from the British Quaker Survey of 1990, 2003 and 2013 and interview data from 2014, this chapter also argues that high levels of recruitment do not necessarily counteract theories of religious decline but can be represented in terms of other attractions such as heterotopic space in which individualism is celebrated (after Gay Pilgrim's work – see Chapter 4), counter-cultural values, and the absence of collective doctrinal boundaries. High levels of conversion along non-religious axes indicate the potential for internal secularisation as well as offering participants the possibility of uncomplicated departures.

The Liberal project and the primacy of experience

Liberal Quakerism is essentially modernist in its origins, whilst expressed through the traditional Quaker forms of silent worship and world-ambivalent attitudes. As Elizabeth Isichei (1970), Martin Davie (1997), and Thomas Kennedy (2001) have shown, the seeds of liberal Quakerism can be found in the controversy surrounding Manchester Quaker David Duncan which emerged in the late 1860s. Duncan suffered the indignation of fellow Quakers for his rational approach to the scriptures and his enthusiasm for biblical criticism and Higher Scholarship (Dandelion 2007: 117) and the establishment of a periodical, *The Inquirer*, and discussion groups to promote these ideas. Duncan was merely 20 years ahead of his time. In 1888, London Yearly Meeting rejected the proposal to unite with the 'Declaration of Faith' agreed by representatives from evangelical 'Gurneyite' Yearly Meetings in Richmond, Indiana in 1887. Partly, it felt too credal to many, partly British Friends were already moving away from the evangelical certainty of its expression. In 1895, at the 'Manchester Conference' established to reflect on what British Friends had to say to wider society (itself symptomatic of a post-hedge sensibility) modernist thinking was expressed on equal terms with evangelical religiosity. A meeting between the British Quaker J. W. Rowntree and American Rufus Jones in Switzerland in 1897 proved a critical moment in the formulation and spread of the vision from Britain across the Atlantic and in the combined energies to realise that vision through educational initiatives such as summer schools resulting in a permanent settlement for this kind of teaching and learning, a new history of the movement, and an annual lecture series known as the 'Swarthmore Lecture'. The idea was that if Quakers knew their tradition better, the renewal of key distinctives would follow.

Martin Davie (1997: 67–72) sets out a list of features which characterised the Liberal Quakerism which emerged in Britain and parts of America at the end of the nineteenth century. Theologically, there were four main motifs to the modernist vision:

a   that experience was primary
b   that faith needed to be relevant to the age
c   that Quakers were to be open to 'new Light'
d   that new revelation had an automatic authority over old revelation and that God's Truth was revealed to humanity gradually over time: the idea that Isichei has termed 'progressivism'. (1970: 34)

Liberal Quakers wanted to accommodate the new scholarship and circumvent the problems it raised about scriptural authority. The solution was found in the writings of the first Quakers and their emphasis on the primacy of spiritual revelation. The primacy of experience accorded with the foundational experience of George Fox of 1647. Then, in a period of deep depression and having 'nothing outwardly to help me nor could tell me what to do, then, oh then,' George Fox 'heard a voice which said, "There is one, even Christ Jesus, that can speak to your condition". And when I heard it, my heart did leap for joy' (Nickalls 1952: 11). Fox's experience signalled the possibility and reality of a direct inward connection between humanity and God. It required no human or textual mediation. However, unlike Liberal Quakers, Fox also claimed that everything revealed to him was later confirmed by the scripture (Nickalls 1952: 33). What was new about Liberal Quakerism was the authority given experience alone.

The other three aspects of the Liberal project (that faith be relevant to the age; that Quakers be open to new light; and progressivism) also contested received historical Quakerism. Quakers, whilst opposing the evangelical sensibility of their parents, did not want to return to the hedged-in Quakerism of their eighteenth-century forbears. They did want a return to plain speech and plain dress but wanted rather to enjoy the citizenship they were finally free to inhabit. They wanted to be 'of the age' and of the Society. Equally, they did not want their intellectual and spiritual endeavours to be constrained. In 1662 when John Perrot returned from the unsuccessful mission to the Vatican and questioned Quaker 'hat honour' (that hats would only be removed before God, typically in prayer, not before another human as was customary etiquette) and suggested shoes could be removed instead when someone was in prayer, Fox was clear that Quakers had already been given their dispensation and that such innovation was inappropriate (Gwyn 2000: 344). Whilst Quaker theology has changed numerous times in the seventeenth, eighteenth and nineteenth centuries, such shifts had been protracted and sometimes bitter processes rather than the result of an innate flexibility about doctrine. Such shifts were about one theological emphasis replacing another. Whilst taken by Liberal Quakers today as normative, the phrase 'be open to new Light' was adopted by London Yearly Meeting in 1931 (Punshon 1989: 15). Progressivism established a chronological authority to revelation – given the unfolding nature of divine plans and preferences, recent discernment would have a necessarily greater authority than earlier discernment. Faithful Quakers would necessarily know more in 1920 than they ever could have known in 1820.

Taken together, theologically, these elements do not tie Liberal Quakerism to anything in terms of doctrine; to no particular text, no particular rendering of the tradition. Whilst based on interpretations of the past, they allow, encourage and accommodate a Quakerism potentially forever on the move. These characteristics both represent a deviation from erstwhile Quaker theology and are also difficult to regulate, lacking as they do any accountability beyond the collective interpretation of pure experience. In some ways, this reaction to the Evangelical Quakerism of the Liberal Quakers' parents looked like a reclamation of early Quakerism but the emphasis on this set of characteristics was to create the biggest deviation from early Quakerism to date.

Diversity and post-Christianity, the marginalisation of belief and the liberal belief culture

Given that spiritual experience can be articulated in different terms and ways, it was perhaps inevitable that this central role given experience, without any policing of doctrinal parameters, would lead to a pluralistic popular Quaker theology and an organisational one that celebrates diversity and proscribes the prescription of doctrine. Martin Davie has articulated the shift to pluralism as being a movement from 'conservative' to 'radical', most visibly seen in the move from a Liberal Quakerism which assumed the Christianity of its members to one in which it did not matter (1997). As early as the 1930s, the question was raised as to whether someone had to be a Christian to be a Quaker. In 1966 at London Yearly Meeting, British Quakers rejected draft membership regulations as too doctrinally Christian and one Quaker 'appealed for a place in the Society for those who, like himself, were reluctant to define their attitude in terms only of Christian belief' (*The Friend* 124 (1966), 672). Davie (1997) cites Janet Scott's 1980 Swarthmore Lecture *What Canst Thou Say? Towards a Quaker Theology* as symbolic of this shift. When faced with the question as to whether Quakers need be Christian or not, Scott answered that it did not matter: 'what matters to Quakers is not the label by which we are called or call ourselves, but the life' (1980: 70).

After the Second World War, particularly as the endogamous and dynastic Quakerism was replaced by an increasing number of Quakers joining as adults, belief diversified. Nearly 90% of participants now join as adults (Hampton 2014: 21), In 1990, 47% came directly from other churches, the rest with no immediately prior religious affiliation (Heron 1992: 13), but by 2013, this figure had reduced to about 33% (Hampton 2014: 66). In a group with a diverse and consequently diffuse belief system, these converts interpret Quakerism in the context of their own faith experience. As the diversity of belief increased, so too did the points of contact for a wider diversity of new participant. By the 1990s, Muslim, Hindu, Buddhist (Huber 2001), and non-theist Quakers (Rush 2002) were all explicitly present in the group.

I have suggested that the British Quaker group is most accurately described as 'post-Christian', given the large numbers of alternative theologies present within the membership (Dandelion 1996). Belief, in the permissive Quaker 'liberal belief culture' (Dandelion 1996: 123), is thus diverse. Unlike other religious groups, belief does not play a central defining role (see below). Indeed, accommodated by an historical critique of credal systems of belief, belief is marginalised as a concept and in terms of content. This phenomenon of where groups refrain from 'authoritatively defining the content of their beliefs' and where 'they recognize a plurality of religious meanings that practitioners may transform' has been described by Caroline Plüss as 'non-doctrinal' (2007: 253).

Conformity and the behavioural creed

Eleven reasons for not adopting a credal system of belief come easily and readily to Liberal Quaker groups (Dandelion 1996: 94–95). These can be grouped into five categories as follows:

1   The Limitations of Language.
   a   Religious experience is beyond linguistic codification and definition.
   b   Credal statements demean, in their limited linguistic form, the depth of religious experience.
2   The Limitation of God's Word.
   c   Credal statements operate to close off new religious expression and revelation.
   d   Credal statements encourage a complacency of attitude to religious life by giving an impression of finality and surety.
   e   Credal statements take on an authority of their own, belying the authority of God.
3   The Limitation of Quakerism.
   f   It would be impossible, inappropriate and dishonest, because of the diversity of individual belief, to adopt a credal statement.
   g   Credal statements, even if possible, would misrepresent the nature of Quaker religion.
4   The Exclusive Nature of Credal Statements.
   h   Credal statements operate i) to exclude those outside the group, and ii) alienate those within the group, who cannot subscribe to them.
   j   A credal statement would separate the group from those of other faiths by identifying the group with one particular faith.
5   The Practical Points.
   k   There is no structural need to adopt a credal statement, e.g. a basis for Membership.
   l There is no mechanism for adopting a creedal statement.

What is interesting in the way Liberal Quakers collectively and clearly agree and affirm these 11 values, even when faced with suggested counter-arguments as to the value of credal statements (e.g. Ambler 1989). The paradoxical collective affirmation of belief in not having creeds suggests the idea of a 'behavioural creed' (Dandelion 1996: Chapter 3) In other words, a credal attitude to form or practice (in this case the lack of the need for formal credal statements) exists, visible through its opposition to more traditional kinds of creed. If we take the 11 reasons against credal systems of belief and apply them to attitudes to Quaker worship, the keystone of Liberal Quakerism given that it is the means to spiritual experience and thus primary spiritual authority, we find that the opposition falls away. Liberal Quakers do not feel concerned that maintaining a similar system of worship for 350 years demeans the experience of worship, undermines progressive revelation or leads to complacency and a false sense of surety. These Quakers do not feel silent worship misrepresents Quakerism and its diversity or inappropriately links Quakerism with particular faith. If it excludes those outside the group or alienates those within, this does not seem to concern these Quakers. Thus, 'Orthopraxy' is used as a basis for Liberal Quaker commitment and membership and passages on practice that form part of the Yearly Meeting book of discipline are prescriptive rather than permissive. In other words, the concerns over the consequences of credal statements of belief are ignored when Liberal Quakers reflect on their adherence to a particular form. This too fits with Plüss' work on non-doctrinal religion in which the socialisation within non-doctrinal groups centre on an interiorised and shared definition of group behaviour rather than shared beliefs (2007)).

The Quaker double-culture

This contrasting pattern, of a permissive approach to belief content and a conformist and conservative 'behavioural creed' comprising a 'double-culture', is sociologically fascinating. First, it is the behavioural creed, the way in which Quakers are religious, which acts as the social glue. Second, it is possible to suggest that the two aspects of the double-culture operate in inverse relationship, so that when one is weak or permissive, the other is strong. Thus, we might identify a proto-behavioural creed in the Quietist period. The 'peculiarities' of plain dress and plain speech were the outward mark of the inward Quaker spirituality and they operated as a boundary marker of who was in and who was out of the group. The Evangelicals with strong belief content felt able to abolish the peculiarities and relax the behavioural creed surrounding worship, even in some cases replacing traditions such as unprogrammed worship. The Liberal Quakers with a permissive attitude to belief regrouped, according to Kennedy, on the peace testimony (2001) and latterly, according to my work and that of Caroline Plüss (1995) on process rather than belief content.

The ways in which the two dimensions of the double-culture relate is illustrated in Table 6.1.

Georg Simmel argued that in differentiated groups, there is a lack of individual differentiation. In undifferentiated groups in contrast, the lack of a shared and distinctive cultural identity allows the individuals to be differentiated (Levine 1971: 257). He used the Quakers as an example to illustrate this formula:

> The specific manifestation of this is as follows: in the affairs of the congregation, in the assemblies of worship, each person may act as preacher and say whatever he likes whenever he likes. On the other hand, the congregation

watches over personal affairs such as marriage, and these cannot occur without the permission of a committee that is appointed to investigate each case. Thus the Quakers are individual only in collective matters, and in individual matters, they are socially regulated. (Levine 1971: 258)

TABLE 6.1 The Quaker double-culture

Liberal belief culture	Behavioural creed
i.e. Belief	Form
Non-credal	Credal
Religious basis	Pragmatic basis
Individually decided	Collectively agreed
Individually held	Collectively operated
Open to individual reinterpretation	Collectively changed
Accommodates diversity	Requires conformity
Diversity between participants	Commonality of practice
Inclusivist	Exclusivist
Syncretic	Conservative
Permissive	Conformist
Change of paradigm in last 30 years	Basically unchanged for 350 years
No official control	Official control (e.g. Clerks and Elders)
Unofficial leadership ('weighty Quakers')	Rule-defined (book of discipline)
Not discussed in Quaker-time	Discussed frequently
Not required for membership	Required for membership
Not central to perceived meaning of Quakerism	Central identification with Quaker identity
Subordinate	Dominant
Does not function as a framework	Meta-narrative

In other words, the distinctive cultural identity proscribes individualism in matters of lifestyle, whereas within the group a certain lack of differentiation (such as the freedom to offer vocal ministry in Meeting) can be identified. However, whilst the content of vocal ministry is rarely policed, the mode of vocal ministry is highly regulated (Collins and Dandelion 2006). What serves better to support Simmel's argument is the contrast between personal and private belief stories and the public expression of faith in Meeting or in lifestyle. In terms of sect typology, Quakerism appears highly differentiated from wider culture in terms of its forms and modes and yet undifferentiated in terms of its permissive belief culture.

Indeed, in terms of sect/denomination typology, it can be argued that Liberal Quakers operate as both a sect and a denomination. The inclusive permissiveness afforded to belief content places low demands on participants:

there is nothing to learn or get right, and no requirement for a confession of faith or conversion narrative. Quakers in this regard are 'world-accepting' and such a permissive attitude to doctrinal diversity is inherently denominational. At the same time, participants are required to learn the rules of worship and 'Meetings for business'. (Whatever their personal position, they are also expected to at least support the continuation of the historic Quaker witness against war.) These collective acts of worship and witness are by default more public and more central to Liberal Quaker identity. When present-day British Quakers respond to questions about Quaker belief with a list of negatives about not singing hymns or having outward sacraments or a separated priesthood (Dandelion 1996: 302), it may appear as if they are avoiding the question. I suggest instead that they are answering the question they think is being asked, 'What is at the core of your religion?'; in other words, what defines Quakers as a distinctive set of believers? Silent worship, in its open and inward form is what defines this form of Quakerism. It is the means to the experience, central to the Liberal Quaker project. These elements are set over an against what 'the world' classes as significant.

These twin cultures of permissive belief culture and conformist behavioural mores, which also place Quakers in two contrasting places in Beckford's typology (see Chapter 2 of this volume), and play out in terms of leadership and authority. Explicit Quaker leadership roles are limited to those concerned with the maintenance of form, and to step beyond those limits is itself breaking the form and can lead to censure. However, informal leadership by 'weighty Quakers' (those whose words carry weight) is unconstrained on matters of belief. Resignations also follow the dichotomous pattern of permissive attitudes to belief and conformist and conservative attitudes to form. Attempted resignations which emphasise a crisis of faith or doubt are less likely to be immediately successful. Crises of faith do not contradict the liberal belief culture in which doubt is valid (*Advices and Queries* 1995: No. 5). However, when one participant criticised Quaker process as 'undemocratic', a tension was exposed between the individual and the (pneumocratic) behavioural creed. The individual was encouraged to worship in another church.

Interestingly, in a group which places so much emphasis on continuing revelation, individuals resign not only because they feel disenchanted generally but because they feel left behind by a group on the move. Equally they can feel 'left ahead', that the group is moving too slowly in spite of being 'open to new Light'. Each of these three types of resignation operates in each aspect of the double-culture, belief and practice (Dandelion 2002).

The culture of silence and the potential for heteropraxis

The double-culture also underpins the way in which silence has masked and accommodated the pluralisation of belief within British Quakerism and other Liberal Quaker groups in the last 50 years. A 'Culture of Silence' (Dandelion 1996:

chapter 6) is created through the high value given silence, the low value given language, and the consequent rules about breaking the silence. Superficially, silence marks the boundaries of the collective worship. It is also, in Quaker orthodoxy, the medium through which God's will is heard, voiced and discerned.

Quakers claim that it is through the silence that:

1. God is experienced by the individual and thus, authority for belief in God is given.
2. The silent approach to discerning God's will is validated through the fact that participants claim they experience God in the silence.
3. God's will is discerned by the individual through 'leadings'.
4. Ideas of what might constitute God's will are shared and tested through 'ministry'.
5. Action consequent to God's will is devised and accepted through 'business Meeting' decisions.
6. The names of those serving roles are discerned and appointed in business Meetings.

Within the Liberal 'liturgy of silence' (Dandelion 2005), speech is devalued by consequence of the theological role given to collective silence. Its status is also diminished by the popular Quaker view on the impossibility, and the inappropriateness, of speech, as described in the attitudes to credal statements above, to communicate belief. Words are not of practical use in expressing spirituality. Second, it is not appropriate to try and verbalise religious belief. This view is based on the premise that the nature of language and the nature of God are qualitatively distinct. Language limits the understanding of God.

> For many of us, I feel sure, putting 'God' into words at all is to trivialise the very thing we are seeking to convey ... the silence of meeting means so much to me. Where else can I go to share with others what is beyond words? (Letter to *The Friend* 150 (1992), 471)

In this sense, this Quaker group sets itself apart from both a text-bound tradition and an oral one.

The value placed on silence devalues speech and also increases attention on the role of vocal ministry (Kelly 1944: 12). Present-day Quakers are confronted by two challenges. The first is to identify what is and what is not true ministry. The second is to deliver God's word in the right way. Zielinski neatly summarises the problem of discerning the legitimacy of vocal ministry: 'if there is any doubt in the mind of the speaker as to the value of his message, then he [*sic*] should remain silent' (1975: 31).

In addition to discerning whether or not the message is from God, Quakers need to submit to the cultural and theological rules around when and how the silence can be broken by speech if they are not to risk public interruption or a private word from an Elder. Seven aspects of normative ministry are readily identifiable. They are: (i) length; (ii) style; (iii) frequency; (iv) timing; (v) content; (vi) thematic association; (vii) linguistic construction. In 1988 Alan Davies, then in linguistics at Edinburgh University, was given permission to tape-record 13 Quaker Meetings in order to analysis the vocal contributions made during the hour of silence. He was able to look at the pattern and duration of these contributions as well as the way that themes threaded through a series of contributions in any one Meeting and across Meetings. Davies found that the total length of ministry ranged between 7.5 and 20.25 minutes for a whole Meeting. Individual ministries ranged between 0.25 and 10.25 minutes. Seventy per cent of the spoken contributions were less than three minutes in duration (1988, 123). Ministries which are of a length greater than 10 to 15 minutes are subject to public interruption by an Elder. There was a 'heavily marked style' to contributions (Davies 1988: 133). People only spoke once in any Meeting and never usually right at the beginning or end. Certain topics are what Davies referred to as 'non-mentionables' (Davies 1988: 131).

There are four consequences to the rules around speech and silence in worship. The first is that the correct use of silence and speech is a skill to be learned. Second then, conversely, silence can be misused. Participants try to minimise differences between their 'performances'. Third, fear of not having learnt the normative style of, or misusing, speech acts as self-censor within worship. Fourth, fear of conflict and ostracism within a pluralistic group where theology is often kept private impedes 'talking-God' outside the worship event. If theology is not mentioned within ministry, it is even less likely to be mentioned in contributions which lack the divine potential of ministry. It is not only fear of getting the form of ministry wrong which constrains, said the participants, but fear of expressing ideas which will not be approved of. Quakers learn in silence too. Over half of those who have been involved with Quakers for less than three years have not ministered (Dandelion 1996: 254). Thus, changes in belief content remain hidden.

Quaker religious experience occurs within the silence, and types of individual belief are self-constructed to help make sense of that experience. Belief may be vocalised in ministry but frequently is not, either through a lack of opportunity or lack of courage (with the silence used as a form of self-censor or defence against ostracism) (or, theologically, because God has not demanded it). The lack of regular and explicit vocalisation of belief means that there is no public reaction in these terms. Silence represents the medium, the message and the response. In this way, changes to popular belief, as newcomers enter the group or as participants change the language of the theology, occur covertly. This process can recur infinitely with changes in individual and group belief remaining hidden whilst the common form of worship presents a picture of unity.

Orthopraxy accommodates heterodoxy and creates coherence in a group without an orthodoxy. Orthopraxy conceals diversity but may get unpicked by it: whilst the form of worship operates as a means of cohesion for the group, its varying interpretations may at some stage begin to unpick the form. The Meeting for Worship for business, for example, also based in silence, has been traditionally seen as a means to the discernment of the will of God. For those modern Liberal Quakers without a God or without a God with a will, this formula becomes anachronistic. Instead, for some of these Quakers, the business method becomes a secular process, a temperamental or political preference. Whilst still appearing a unified process, orthopraxy may covertly become heteropraxy, especially given regional variation.

The prescription of seeking: the absolute perhaps

To try and understand its shifting dynamics, there have been various attempts to model Liberal Quakerism. In 1992 Fran Taber suggested a dynamic Quakerism in tension between Liberal and Conservative impulses (1992). She argued that this was a healthy Quakerism with spin-offs or aberrations the result of losing the counterbalance. In the British context, however, the model fell short as much of what was normative in Britain had been described by her as an aberration.

Emlyn Warren focused on the nature of believing within Liberal Quakerism. His models depict a shift from a Quakerism with a central core of belief in the 1660s, to one with a more diffuse pattern of believing in the 1990s. His projection was of different clusters of belief affinities operating in the periphery of Quakerism, independent of each other (Dandelion 1996: 299).

This is similar to Gay Pilgrim's model of the future of Quakerism (2003, 2008). Pilgrim argues that for world-affirming Liberal Quakers in a Quaker-affirming culture, the heterotopic impulse has become turned inward. In other words, the desire to create difference and dissonance becomes internalised when the world no longer readily affords Quakers the possibility of defining themselves in opposition to it. This results in the celebration and even prescription of mutual difference between participants. The ability to be different has become a normative expectation. She argues that three kinds of Quakers have emerged as distinct groupings, akin to Warren's clusters, and mirroring to some extent Robertson's work on the Salvation Army (see Chapter 5). The first group are 'exclusivists', who maintain a doctrinal unity, some of whom have left the 'larger body' such as the Yearly Meeting of Friends in Christ. The second group is that of the 'inclusivists' who manage the liberal belief culture by continually adding new layers to their theology but who also uphold the conservative and conformist behavioural creed. The third group is that of the 'syncretists' who follow a self-serving path through Quakerism, picking and choosing their personal theological identity.

The main problem with all these models is that they are focused on *belief content*. It is the behavioural creed which remains definitional for Liberal Quakers, with belief, 'belief stories' of semi-realist[2] interpretation, marginal and individual. Only the idea of 'that of God in everyone' is shared, acting as (i) an underpinning of form (e.g. the free ministry), (ii) an underpinning of testimony (e.g. attitudes to equality and war), (iii) a common element of the belief stories, and (iv) a boundary function in that anything which transgressed this idea would be challenged. Its meaning, what the 'that', the 'God' and the 'everyone' means, nevertheless remains individual.

An additional boundary function to Quaker identity can be identified in the prescription of seeking as the normative mode of belief, which ultimately makes Liberal Quakerism less permissive than it first appears (Dandelion 2004). In other words, apart from the behavioural creed related to the mode of worship, Liberal Quakerism is held together not by what it believes but by *how* it believes. Caroline Plüss identified this epistemological collectivism in the 1990s (1994) but I have suggested that it has since become prescriptive (Dandelion 2004). The set of four characteristics identified by Martin Davie that allowed this kind of Quakerism to be forever on the move have become normative. The possibility of difference has become a prescription. The idea of progressivism and of being open to new Light has become translated into the idea that the group cannot know Truth, except personally, partially or provisionally. Thus Liberal Quakerism is not just about the possibility of seeking, it is about the certainty of never finding. All theology is 'towards', a 'perhaps' kind of exercise. In a rational philosophical understanding of the nature of religion, religious truth claims are problematic, perhaps even neither true nor false but meaningless. From outside the religious enterprise these Quakers are sure of this. In other words, they are absolutely certain (rationally from within their modernist outlook) that they can never be certain (theologically as liberal believers). They operate a prescriptive doctrine of what I have termed the 'absolute perhaps'. In other words, these Friends are zealous, even fundamentalist, about their permissive theological stance (Dandelion 2004). Those who find theological truth or who wish to share it with the rest of the group feel increasingly uncomfortable. One of the ironies for such a permissive group is that this position holds that any group or any individual who claims to have found the final truth, for all people or for all time, is wrong. Additionally, all religious groups have to be partly wrong theologically: thus Liberal Quakers operate an *orthocredence*, a conformist approach to how beliefs are held. The 'absolute perhaps' is a defining characteristic of the Liberal Quaker and is the key difference between these Quakers and the whole of the rest of Quakerism, worldwide today and historically. (It is also distinct from a purely rational openness to critical enquiry as might delineate Unitarians for example, given the theological framing of progressivism.) For Plüss, it is this very 'diffuseness' that acts as an 'integrative social principle', 'a cognitive and ideological means to assure group unity through legitimizing institutional conduct in ways that transcend the belief and intentions of any one group participant alone' (2007: 270). This works within non-doctrinal religion as beliefs are marginalised and privatised: belief is not the most relevant feature of the group.

Historically, Liberal Quakerism has shifted away from Christian theism in the last 50 years towards a seeker spirituality (Roof 1993). This contradicts the work of Paul Heelas and Linda Woodhead who in their work on the town of Kendal (see Chapter 2) identified Quakerism as part of 'religion', i.e. emphasising the sacred as transcendent or 'other', rather than 'spiritual' where the sacred is part of the subjective (Heelas and Woodhead 2005: 6). Heelas and Woodhead are right to include organisational Quakerism at the experiential end of religion (Heelas and Woodhead 2005: 21–22) but wrong not to have its popular expression overlapping into their 'holistic milieu'. Those who are more exclusivist, in Pilgrim's terms, leave from either end of the Quaker theological spectrum. Pilgrim's inclusivists and syncretists can lie at any place on the spectrum but those believing in a corporate structure based on divine guidance are likely to be grouped more towards the traditional end with more diffuse spiritualities towards the innovative end.

The model of orthocredence is helpful in letting us see that whilst particular theologies within Liberal Quakerism may not be distinct from those of other Christians or Buddhists, the form of Quakerism as a whole transcends any single faith definition or identity.

Shifting markers of Quakerism

As the last two decades have shown, Liberal Quakerism is highly adaptable. Freed from the constraints of a singular or fixed pattern of believing, it can mould its interpretations of the divine in wide variety of ways. Even form can ultimately be changed, as the growth of all-age or semi-programmed worship in some local Meetings reveals. Indeed, the boundary function of the 'absolute perhaps' allows Quakers to now experiment more fully with form, given that the creation of coherence has, in my view, shifted from orthopraxis to orthocredence, a normative approach to the credibility of belief, if not belief content.

This shifting pattern around creating coherence, internal coherent flow suggests that Collins' ideas of plaining and of a Quaker habitus, and Pilgrim's ideas of heterotopia may need to be revisited as tropes which cut across centuries of Quakerism, or at least as ones which can be predicted to continue to operate as normative and foundational. In this reading, Liberal Quakerism and its enshrinement of seeking means it is far too flexible to be tied to any one particular form of coherence-creation, especially if they have been historically normative.

Indeed, Peter Collins and I have argued that British Quakerism can be viewed, in Zygmunt Bauman's terms (see Chapter 5), as a constructive example of a liquid religion (2014). The argument is that as well as liquidity being self-evident in the privatisation of belief stories, practice too is open to 'significant liquidity' (2014: 297). This is particularly evident in dual faith identities where an adherent's Quakerism sits alongside an alternative affiliation such as paganism (Vincett 2008) or Anglicanism. Over 16% of respondents to the British Quaker Survey in 2013 claimed an active dual affiliation (Hampton 2014: 66). Thus Quakers can be liquid in terms of their own spiritual practice and the combinations they create. At Quaker young adult events, practice often differs from that of older Quakers. Simon Best contrasts a 'culture of contribution' amongst younger Quaker with the culture of silence of older ones (2010). Local Meetings are free to experiment with different forms too and there are many recent examples of the introduction of elements of 'programming' such as readings at the start of Meeting, or 'all-age worship' designed to be inclusive across the generations. The next section suggests that this liquid accommodation of the non-doctrinal may be attracting a new set of recruits.

The curiously compelling nature of non-doctrinal religion: Quakers and secularisation

Membership is falling in Britain Yearly Meeting in line with Bruce's predictions that liberal religion is contributing to its own demise through diffuse belief systems, poor belief transmission, and the lack of seriousness identified by Kelley (1972) that encourages conversion. Liberal Quakerism *does* offer a stepping stone on the ladder of religious seriousness to the 66% who come from no immediately prior religious affiliation (Hampton 2014), but in time some leave because of the very permissiveness which first attracted them (Dandelion 2002). The 'absolute perhaps', the zealously held doctrine of uncertainty, requires conformity amongst participants in the Quaker group and the demands placed on members may be less denominational than the idea of a liberal belief culture might at first suggest (Dandelion 2004). As stated above, today, whilst overall numbers of Quakers in Britain fall, nearly 90% of participants convert into the group as adults suggesting that Quaker distinctives offer unique claims which are taken seriously by outsiders.

Of the converts, the average age of first attending is 43. In the last 20 years, the average age has remained around 64. Thus the membership does not represent an ageing and diminishing generational cohort. Rather, recruitment appears to be consistent. Different belief clusters identified through a latent class analysis in Jennifer Hampton's work consisting of 'traditional', 'liberal' and 'non-theist' categories are cross-generational (2014). Younger Quakers, under the age of 30, are just as likely to be 'traditional' (with a high belief in God, a regular prayer life with the belief that prayer can affect the ways things are on earth, and higher levels of Christian adherence) as 'non-theist' (with low levels of belief in God, low levels of Christian belief, and almost non-existent patterns of prayer).

In 2017 the number coming into formal membership (290) was less than the number of Quakers who had died in the year (310) (*Patterns of Membership* 2018: 5). An additional 235 left formal membership, either by their own initiative (resignation) or their Meeting's (due typically to prolonged non-attendance or less frequently, 'disownment' in recognition that the 'spiritual bond' between member and Meeting had been broken). This is a pattern that is typical of the previous decades and, overall, membership numbers have fallen in most years since 1970 and in every year since 1991. The number of 'Attenders' (those who attend regularly but who are not formal members) has fallen in most years since 1991 (*Patterns of Membership* 2018: 5). Nevertheless, recruitment has remained relatively high and one-third of the group has participated for less than ten years (Hampton 2014).

Thus, even as a very permissive religious group in the twentieth century, Quakerism has defied secularisation theory by continuing to offer distinctive practices and forms, such as silent worship and voteless decision-making, which have buoyed recruitment. 'Harmlessness' has been in counterpoint to the maintenance of unique truth claims around worship, the nature of belief (orthocredence), and witness including the Quaker opposition to war.

As mentioned above, Francesca Montemaggi in a survey and interview of 'new Quakers' (those involved for less than three years) found that new adherents valued the theological openness of the movement, that they felt valued as individuals, and that the silent rite was central to Quaker identity, as was social activism although activism typically took place outside of Quaker settings (2018: part two).

Quakerism in its denominational form may indeed look very attractive to spiritual seekers. Whilst the formal literature of the organisation still maintains a transcendent reference point, classifying it as a religion in Heelas and Woodhead's terms, popular Quakerism is often focused on 'the subjective turn' and very much fits their definition of spirituality. The non-doctrinal form accommodates, as we have seen, huge possibilities in terms of personal doctrinal emphasis. The lack of a confession of faith may be the doctrinal equivalent of the 'anonymous Christian' who enjoys cathedral services where they can remain unidentified (Davie 2015: 138). As in the cathedral setting, the liturgy is predictable and the services experiential rather than dogmatic. The buildings are often beautiful or aesthetically satisfying (Homan 2006b).

As we saw in Chapter 3, changes in the last 150 years have also moved the outward form of Quakerism out of its sectarian practices such as 'plain dress' and 'plain speech': the spiritual journey for the Quaker convert no longer needed to start in the tailor's shop. After 1859 Quakers could marry non-Quakers and the present decline of dynastic Quakerism has created a new phenomenon known within the group as a SQUIF (single Quaker in family). Quakers no longer claim to represent the true church and today would not insist a moral life required membership of any spiritual group. Quakerism is an option within the option of faith.

The British Quaker Survey (Hampton 2014) asked respondents what initially attracted them to Quakerism. They were allowed to tick more than one item. The only purely doctrinal element, 'the idea of the inward light' received a 27% positive response, the form of worship 62%. The full results are reproduced in Table 6.2.

These responses can be considered alongside patterns of response to questions about God, Jesus and prayer over the past 20 years (1990, 2003 and 2013 surveys). The items listed in Table 6.3, 6.4 and 6.5 are the responses where a significant difference was recorded. We can see that the most explicitly religious options fall away in popularity over the three surveys.

Table 6.6 illustrates the significant differences in Quaker self-definition. Only two descriptions changed significantly across the three surveys, those of 'Christian' and 'Universalist'. The former fits the decrease in explicit and traditional faith descriptions amongst the group, the latter a reflection of the way in which

TABLE 6.2 Initial attraction to British Quakerism (respondents were allowed to tick more than one response)

Percentage	Response
41%	Peace and social testimonies/political viewpoint
62%	Form of worship
40%	Quaker way of life
67%	Lack of religious dogma
18%	Position of women within the group
12%	Position of gays and lesbians within the group
37%	Quaker structure/lack of hierarchy
27%	Company and friendship
23%	Your own curiosity
34%	A feeling of coming home
11%	Quaker writings
27%	The idea of the inward light
17%	Born into Quaker family/ attended as a child
20%	Other (Please state below)

TABLE 6.3 Significant differences in Quaker belief in God, 1990–2013

'Do you believe in God?'	1990 %	2003 %	2013 %	Significant differences*
Yes	74.8	73.5	57.5	1990/2013, 2003/2013
No	3.4	7	14.5	All
Not Sure	21.8	19.5	28.1	1990/2013, 2003/2013

*Statistically significant.

TABLE 6.4 Significant differences in Quaker descriptions of Jesus, 1990–2013

'Which of the following best describes your view of Jesus?'	1990%	2003%	2013%	Significant differences*
Containing that of God within as we all do	63.3	49.1	50.2	1990/2003, 1990/2013
An ethical teacher	46.9	42.1	53.8	1990/2013, 2003/2013
God made human	19.2	17.1	13.9	1990/2003
* Statistically significant.				

TABLE 6.5 Significant differences in Quaker descriptions of prayer, 1990–2013

'Which of the following best describes what prayer is for you?'	1990%	2003%	2013%	Significantdifferences*
Talking to / listening to God	42.5	36.3	35	1990/2013, 1990/2013
Asking God to change things	12.6	8.0	7.4	1990/2003, 1990/2013
Seeking communion with the divine	32.2	25.5	30.2	1990/2003
Seeking enlightenment / guidance	60.6	50.4	52.2	1990/2003, 1990/2013
Still and silent waiting	51.1	49.5	63.2	1990/2013, 2003/2013
Praise	23.8	19.4	13.4	1990/2013, 2003/2013
Confession	22.9	14.8	10.2	All
Seeking healing	31.7	23.8	22.3	1990/2003, 1990/2013
Thanksgiving	60.6	50.4	52.2	1990/2003, 1990/2013
*Statistically significant.				

TABLE 6.6 Significant differences in Quaker self-definition, 1990–2013

'Do you consider yourself as a ...'	1990%	2003%	2013%	Significant differences*
Christian	51.5	45.5	36.5	All
Universalist	22.5	18.8	15.6	1990/2013
*Statistically significant.				

'universalism' has become normative amongst British Quakers and therefore less of a distinctive or particular identity apart from the term 'Quaker'.

As might be expected, given the analysis of the liberal belief culture above, we find a drop in stated belief in God, explicitly religious descriptions of Jesus, explicitly religious articulations of the meaning of prayer, and in Christian self-definition. It can be argued that 'belief in God' may no longer be an appropriate measure within Quaker spiritual pluralism, and that Quaker-ism is post-Christian in its understandings of prayer and of Jesus. In other words, the survey items may be the wrong questions to determine levels of religiosity.

However, given that people are drawn in by the 'Quaker way of life' and political values and commitment to peace and social justice, I also want to suggest that pluralism and the emphasis on silence and the lack of vocal confession of faith may have accommodated a degree of internal secularisa-tion. The 'lack of religious dogma' was the most popular reason participants gave for their attraction to the group.

In other words, people may be drawn in not only by the lack of religious dogma but by the lack of religion at all. The recent formation of the Non-Theist Friends Network (https://nontheist-quakers.org.uk/) and ongoing cor-respondence in *The Friend* confirms that the 'religious' nature of the Religious Society of Friends is being challenged or interrogated in the way that Chris-tianity within Quakerism was 40 years ago. Stewart Yarlett has talked about the 'communal and cultural resources' that attract non-theist Quakers (2018). A highly specific demographic largely consisting of highly educated and white professionals may have created a cultural affinity that has transcended a spiritual one.

It is also worth noting again that only one-third of those joining the group had an immediately prior faith-affiliation (Hampton 2014: 66). Thus, new Quakers are not 'saints' from elsewhere, part of the circulation of saints that typically accounts for the rise and fall of church membership statistics (Bibby and Brinkerhoff 1973) but seekers dipping their toes into collective spiri-tuality. In Kelley's terms, they are stepping up the seriousness ladder (1972), but as Mark Read suggests, on their own terms:

> Affiliates tend to make a rational choice to convert to the Quaker church rather than mainstream Christian churches. This Quaker conversion is pre-mised on an alternative conceptualisation of Christianity which privileges the individual perspective above that of the collective view. (2017: 275)

In her work on Quakerism as heterotopic, as described above, Pilgrim argues that as the 'world' caught up with the Quakers, e.g. dropping the use of titles and the use of you as a deferential term, the Quaker heterotopic impulse did not fade but rather became turned inward (2003: 152). There is plenty of anecdotal evidence of Quaker self-perception as a group full of idiosyncratic eccentrics.

In a study of two Methodist churches in Chicago, Robert Stauffer asked participants what they believed and how normative they imagined their beliefs to be (1973). Stauffer found 'substantial doctrinal pluralism' (1973: 346) but also that those interviewed believed their beliefs were shared by their fellow congregants. In other words, participants were ignorant of the extent of diversity within their congregations. In research I carried out amongst

Quakers in the 1990s, the opposite phenomenon was apparent whereby each interviewee expressed uncertainty about where they fitted into the general picture. In this state of collective anxiety about what was normative Quaker belief, accommodatory practice was high. Those who claimed a strong belief in God would translate the Quaker idea of 'that of God in everyone' into 'that of good in everyone' and those for whom the term God was difficult would nevertheless use the phrase 'that of God in everyone' as each participant tried to accommodate their perception of their listener's views (Dandelion 1996: 309).

Rhiannon Grant's work on British Quaker believing particularly explored the use of 'lists' when Quakers wished to describe the divine. She found a construction such as 'Inner Light, Holy Spirit, Divine Principle, The Light of Christ, and many more besides' (2018: 29) was common practice amongst British Quakers. This reflected the orthocredence of Quakers, but also acknowledged and accommodated diversity as normative. Accommodation of difference is normative for British Quakers.

Accommodation is not always the predominant motivation, and the combination of multiple strong identities creates tensions within the group and for Pilgrim had led to a schism in 1993 (when the 'Friends in Christ' broke away from the rest of British Quakers) and ongoing internal fragmentation (2003: 153). The debates between christocentric and universalist Quakers in the 1980s and between non-theist Friends and the wider Society in the early twenty-first century are also moments of explicit tension. However, these explicit tensions are rare and discomforting for Quakers who in both cases worked hard to reach places of mutual acceptance (Plüss 1995), preferring to accommodate diversity by broadening the parameters of Quaker belief culture rather than excluding those who in other ways followed the orthopraxis of Quakerism. Even non-belief is acceptable within orthopraxis. It may logically undermine some of the premises of praxis but the outward display or performance of Quakerism is what signifies Quaker identity. All else is now privatised and individualised. Indeed, to paraphrase Troeltsch, mystical religion may after all become the '*secret* religion' of the Quaker classes.

Chapter summary

British Quakerism can be characterised by its non-doctrinal nature and its reliance on orthopraxy and orthocredence to maintain cohesion. The high demands these mechanisms place on adherents tends to suggest an element of sectarianism but at a popular level, Quakerism represents a permissive spirituality. Numbers are falling as might be expected from our reading of Steve Bruce's analysis in Chapter 2. Chadkirk (2004) has suggested that there will be no viable group of Quakers left in Britain within the next 20 years if present trends continue. Unlike the reforms of the 1860s which abolished endogamy and the 'peculiarities' as compulsory, which halted falling numbers, there is little major structural reform open to British Quakerism to reverse the trend.

Quaker numbers are not falling because of disownment but because of a failure to attract enough new participants. However, recruitment remains high at 90% of all participants and one-third of the group have joined in the last decade. It might appear that the certainty and clarity around orthopraxy and orthocredence might be operating to stem the tides of secularisation.

However, explicit religiosity within British Quakerism is in decline and one of the main attractions to the group is the lack of religious dogma. It is suggested that, thus, the apparently curious case of continued recruitment within a non-doctrinal group does not necessarily militate against secularisation theory but may rather be hallmark of it. It is the very lack of explicit religion combined with freedom of expression and the affirmation of counter-cultural values that appear to be leading factors in recruitment.

Even if secularised, continued recruitment is fascinating in an age of 'bowling alone' (see Chapter 2) but we may see a parallel in the growth of the Sunday Service, and church for the atheists: whilst that group may still be underpinned by the charismatic authority of its founders (Bullock 2017), perhaps the subjective turn within Quakerism creates a charismatic authority of self and self-definition (back to what John Knox has labelled 'sacro-egoism': see Chapter 2) within Quakerism to the point that it appears (personally and privately) to the individual to be certain of itself (if changing) and authoritative to the degree that the Quaker space becomes an interesting place to self-locate. When and if it no longer fits, the very permissiveness of the group allows resignation or non-attendance in ways much more elastic than previous incarnations of Quaker sectarianism allowed.

The next chapter looks at how this potential for internal non-religion can lead to internal secularisation.

Notes

1 The first part of this chapter is based on Dandelion 2008.
2 By semi-realist, I refer to the idea that the experience is considered real but the articulation of the experience is considered interpretative rather than factual.

7

INTERNAL SECULARISATION: ELEMENTS AND AGENCY

Religious groups and participants are continually making choices about how they relate to wider culture and to state regulation, be it constraint or opportunity. These choices can be cast in terms of accommodation or resistance. In a secularising culture, these choices equate to secularisation or, as Mauss, suggests, retrenchment (1994). Given the difference between popular and organisational religion, we may find contrasting or differing responses from different aspects of religious life. Saba Mahmood has demonstrated that secularisation is never a complete process: by privatising religion the secular State embeds religion rather than creates a society freed from it (2016: 21). A more thorough secularisation then appears as privatised religion itself tends to either decline or internally secularise, losing its explicitly religious dimension. As Asad notes: '"the secular" obviously overlaps with "the religious" … changes in concepts articulate changes in practices' (2003: 25). Talcott Parsons saw secularisation as a 'dual process'. On the one hand, there is 'a one-way change' in which religion is sacrificed to secular interests. However, at the same time, the secular order changes in the direction of the norms provided by religion. Secularisation is a paradoxical process; it involves not only the loss of religious values but their institutionalisation as well (Parsons 1971: 216–218). This is the kind of process we see illustrated in the scholarship on secularism. As Asad states, history has been about the rearrangement of practices, not the triumph of the secular (2003: 25). Internal secularisation, secularisation within religion, then is about reconceptualising those practices, not foregoing them: 'We have to understand what people do with and to ideas and practices before we can understand what is involved in the secularization of theological concepts in different times and places' (Asad 2003: 194). This chapter charts aspects of this process of internal secularisation.

As outlined in Chapter 1, the global north, or the 'high income countries' of the world, are currently experiencing, in Charles Taylor's term, 'a secular age' (2007: 1).

> Belief in God is no longer axiomatic. There are alternatives. And this will also likely mean that at least in certain milieu, it may be hard to sustain one's faith … secularity in this sense is matter of the whole context of understanding in which our moral, spiritual or religious experience and search takes place. (Taylor 2007: 3)

For Taylor, and for Grace Davie (2015), religion is operating in terms of the secular market place, a differentiated element of modernist consumption. The Quaker commentator Sean O'Flynn talks of

> a market of ideas from which we pick and choose: philosophies, religions, and ethical theories are along there with cars, electronic goods and holidays, to be chosen from and consumed at will, a smorgasbord in which there are no absolute preferences. Without a transcendent dimension, relativism spreads everywhere: it is a quagmire within which we are sucked into the anti-spiritual terrain of the absurd. (2018)

Taylor states that certainty is diminished and that everyone is living:

> between two standpoints: an 'engaged' one in which we live as best we can the reality our standpoint opens to us; and a 'disengaged' one in which we are able to see ourselves as occupying one standpoint among a range of possible ones, with which we have in various ways to co-exist. (2007: 12)

Thus even the faithful see their faith from a worldly perspective, with faith prescribed as an option rather than a soteriological necessity. As Jose Casanova writes: 'Secularity becomes the default option, no longer in need of justification' (2010: 266).

Whilst Taylor suggests religion has moved from a set of practices to a set of (optional) beliefs to which one assents or not, Mahmood suggests that for those enmeshed in Christian culture, belief is not a cognitive stance but a subjective one, an 'almost unconscious enmeshment' (Mahmood 2010: 284). Thus, religious sensibility never completely disappears and secular society is not one in which religion has been subtracted (Mahmood 2016: 22); rather, explicit religion is marginalised and, for Taylor, 'the presumption of unbelief has become dominant' (2007: 13).

Religion is no longer the opium of the masses but the option of the masses. Religious freedom is not about organisational rights but freedom to privately interact or not with organised religion. Religion becomes subjectivised, and explicit religiosity moves from the transcendent to the immanent, 'the turn within'.

As Wade Clark Roof writes:

> Ernst Troeltsch, were he here today, might ... say that his prediction had come true that a mystical form of religion with its emphasis upon inner experience was now no longer 'the secret religion of the educated classes,' but was in fact gaining popular support as perhaps the dominant religious form in the latter years of the twentieth century. (1996: 153)

Colin Campbell, in 1978, suggested that Troeltsch's types of spiritual and mystic religion described the 'new religiosity' emerging in the midst of secularisation. Indeed, Campbell suggested that it was internal faith dynamics that creates a secularisation process through a critique of traditional church forms and beliefs. Campbell cited the *Honest to God* controversy and other aspects of 'new theology' that promoted mystical interpretations of faith over and against organised religion, literalism and dogma. Campbell talked of a 'purely personal, non-church' expression of faith (1978: 151). This fits with Grace Davie's analysis of 'believing without belonging' (1994) as well and more recent scholarship by Karen Leth-Nissen on 'churching alone' (2018) which offers a religious mirror to Robert Putnam's work on societal shifts towards lone and non-committal activity, 'bowling alone', more generally (2000). Cathedral attendance is currently popular because there are no requirements or pressures for ongoing commitments. People believe but don't necessarily belong. The indices of secularisation in these terms are underpinned by internal faith dynamics rather than say a growth in rationalist atheism and fit well with Troeltsch's description of the 'the secret religion of the educated classes' (1931: 749) and 'radical religious individualism' (1931: 735). Troeltsch may have been writing about Quakers when he said of mystical religion: 'the dichotomy between spirit and flesh disappears, and inwardness and individual aesthetic becomes developed allowing ... an artistic sensibility and a sense of harmony – everything having its place, mysticism embeddded in wider world' (1931: 793–794).

Nevertheless mainline religions continue to transmit explicit religion and to attempt to resist secularisation. For non-doctrinal groups with high levels of syncretism and interiorised spirituality, there is a high propensity to accommodate the subjective turn and personal religious radicalism. In this they potentially accommodate internal resistance to traditional religious premises within their corporate religious identity. In other words, non-doctrinal religious groups, such as the British Quakers, in their very celebration of liquidity and elasticity potentially accommodate internal secularisation, as was suggested in Chapter 6, as the explicit religious association of the stated aims and values of the group declines. We may find that groups such as these no longer fit the descriptions of either sect or denomination but rather represent an association of those performing their religiosity (Day 2011: 187–188) in their own way.

Jürgen Habermas has suggested that within post-secularity secular citizens need to engage with religious citizens at a level above that of tolerance in the way, he suggests, that religious citizens have already needed to transcend their religious viewpoints to engage with the secular. It is not an expectation or invitation to agreement but of a mutually rational discourse (Habermas 2006). In the analysis pursued in this chapter, contrary to Habermas, the secular and religious citizens are the same people. As Mahmood states, Habermas should not be surprised that religion endures in secular democracies when secularism and religion are so entwined, privatising and regulating (2016: 22). People are still believing but choosing what to believe and whether or not to belong. For those who do choose to belong, this heterodoxy and implicit heteropraxis (as traditional interpretations of liturgical form are reinterpreted privately) breaks down any sense of corporate or collective shared religious understandings. This highly individuated and privatised religiosity colludes with societal preferences to mask the religious in everyday life.

Internal secularisation

The sociology of internal secularisation is limited. Pfautz defined secularisation as 'the tendency of sectarian religious movements to become part of and like "the world"' (1956: 246). Peter Berger noted the development of a cultural religion, 'a religious affirmation of the same values held by the community at large' in which secular values ('an intense this-worldliness', 'success competitively achieved', 'activism', 'social adjustment', etc.) replace sacred values (Berger 1961: 39–50).

In 1966, Bryan Wilson claimed that whilst secularisation in Britain was reflected by declining church attendance and membership, on the other side of the Atlantic it was reflected in 'a growing vacuity of American religious belief and practice' (2016: 111). Wilson claimed that American churches had been absorbed by society and were 'ideationally … bankrupt'. In other words, American churches were self-secularising. This sentiment was mirrored by Berger a year later: 'in America … the churches still occupy a more central symbolic position, but it may be argued that they have succeeded in keeping this position only by becoming highly secularized themselves' (Berger 1967: 108).

Berger claimed disenchantment, the process internal to religion which has accommodated secularisation, started with Judaism and its emphasis on monotheism rather than the 'magic' of multiple deities (cf. Bruce 2011: 28), and was reaffirmed as part of the Protestant reformation. Thomas Luckmann also talked briefly of 'internal secularisation' (1967: 37) and the way in which doctrinal differences had become 'virtually irrelevant for members of the major denominations' (1967: 34). Luckmann argued that churches in the USA adopted a secular version of the Protestant ethos: 'whereas religious ideas originally played an important part in the shaping of the American dream, today the secular ideas of the American dream pervade church religion' (1967: 36). Contrasting European and North American religiosity, Luckmann claimed that 'religion was pushed to the periphery of "modern" life in Europe while it became more "modern" in America by undergoing a process of internal secularization' (1967: 37):

> If the churches maintain their institutional claim to represent and mediate the traditional religious universe of meaning, they survive primarily by association with social groups and social strata which continue to be oriented toward the value of past social order. If, on the other hand, the churches accommodate themselves to the dominant culture of modern industrial society they necessarily take on the function of legitimating the latter ... the universe of meaning traditionally represented by the churches becomes increasingly irrelevant. In short, the so-called process of secularization has decisively altered either the social location of church religion or its inner universe of meaning. (Luckmann 1967: 37)

As mentioned in Chapter 2, Karel Dobbelaere suggested there were three levels of secularisation: societal, meso (within religion) and micro (individual), and that these were interlinked and only together comprised secularisation (2002: 13). Inger Furseth and Pal Repstad talk of 'inner secularisation' (2006: 83, 96), or an organisational secularisation, following the last two levels of Karel Dobbelaere's version of secularisation.

Scholars have often linked internal secularisation to processes over centuries and unintended consequences of theological emphasis (e.g. Pfautz 1955–1956; Herberg 1967), to denominationalisation and the adjustment of sects to the values of wider society. Pfautz's case study of Christian Science revealed how testimonies of healings revealed a shift from an affective motive to a rationalist-purposive motive, i.e. from a religious to a rationalist premise (1955–1956).

Mark Chaves discussed internal secularisation in the light of his work on the dual nature of religious organisations and how they can be understood as comprising both religious authority structures and agency structures (1993). Religious authority structures are singular within any denomination and tend to rely on charismatic or traditional authority, in Weber's terms, whereas agencies tend to locate authority in rational-legal systems. Chaves claimed this dichotomous typology could be used to better define the nature of religious organisations, to think about power shifts within denominations, to better understand conflict and schism within denominations and, finally, to better explore internal secularisation (1993: 164). For Chaves, internal secularisation is 'the declining scope of religious authority's control over the organizational resources within the agency structure' (1993: 165). In other words, agency structures, such as publishing or fundraising, can become detached from the religious authority of the parent body and start to resemble secular equivalents.

Bruce charts the process of secularisation along the following axes:

a　A decline, generationally, in commitment to what were once orthodox Christian beliefs (e.g. that the Bible is literally true, in heaven and in hell) (2011: 160)

b　An increased psychologization and subjectivization of faith (epitomised by preachers such as Harry Fosdick Emerson and Norman Vincent Peale, for whom good was represented by the power of positive thinking and evil by a lack of self-confidence) (2011: 161).

c　An increase in a liberal attitude to morality and ethics even amongst evangelicals, e.g. in terms of dress, dancing, television, and divorce (2011: 163).

d　An increase in relativism amongst churchgoers with fewer people prepared to make universal claims for their faith, e.g. on whether Christianity is the one true religion to which everyone should convert, and more people prepared to admit that many religions could lead to eternal life. Sectarian certainty has diminished. (2011: 165)

We can mirror this process within religious organisations: belief become marginal, diffuse and plural, faith and ethics are subjectivised, and universal claims are replaced by personalised provisonality.

This scholarship on internal secularisation (a) masks the distinction made in this volume between organisational and popular religion and (b) also discounts the key role of linguistic culture. I address both here.

Organisational and popular religion

We have already seen how organisational and popular forms of religion can interact differently with non-religion and are in negotiation with each other. They can also forms differential parts of religious life. In the work of John Fulton et al. on Roman Catholicism (2000) and John Walliss' work on the Brahma Kumaris (2007), the phenomenon of different levels of identification and commitment amongst adherents was found to be crucial in determining the nature of organisational religiosity. There were those who were part of core and super-core elites who practised and believed their faith in very different ways from the wider laity. In Quakerism, we can find corporatists, congregationalists and individualists depending on where authority is located (Dandelion 1996: Foreword). In hierarchical groups, the super-core may determine the direction of the organisational expression, but at a popular level exist mutated forms within nominally traditional masks. In all groups the popular represents the majority and can determine the public perception of the group, also the necessary denominator that the super-core needs to take account of in order to sustain popular participation. John Knox's identification of sacro-egoism (2016, see

Chapter 2 of this volume and below), the authority of the self in determining religious choices is a form of modernist 'pleasure-driven' consumerism. It corresponds to Leth-Nissen's 'churching alone' (2018) but is centred more on authority structures than behavioural disposition.

Arjun Appadurai emphasises this concentration on pleasure as the arbiter of modern consumerism and in particular the pleasure to be found in ephemerality, the way in which the present is so quickly transformed into the past. The appeal of tradition is minimal compared to the attraction of a higher pace of change in the goods of consumerism and also the lifestyle framing of them. Appadurai argues that 'the dominant force, spreading through the consuming classes of the world, appears to be the ethic, aesthetic and material practice of the ephemeral' (2008: 84). In terms of religious life, it might appear that the seeker-emphasis on the journey would fit well, but the organisational domain of religion would need to be light on its feet to sustain interest. Failure to adopt an ephemeral stance separates the popular from the organisational or in the Quaker case study, the corporate from the congregational or the individual. Wade Clark Roof claims that 'the religious stance today is more internal than external, more individual than institutional, more experiential than cerebral, more private than public' (1996: 153).

As Robert Putnam has illustrated a decline in social capital (2000), so Roof claims that religious capital is elusive (1996: 157). This is especially true in liberal or progressive settings which may seek to befriend secularisation by adapting religious forms. Bryan Wilson's claims about American church content ('a vacuity of belief and practice') were in contrast to numerical decline in Britain, a more explicit form of secularisation. However, these 'American' signs of internal secularisation are now similarly evident in British church settings. The patterns within British Quakerism may be exaggerated by its non-doctrinal nature but similarly we might surmise that other groups will start to exhibit similar signs of self-secularisation. What is important to register, however, is that they may occur at different rates in organisational and popular settings. The second aspect of internal secularisation I want to highlight is linguistic culture. Rather than follow Chaves' analysis of the shifting power balance between structural authority and agency, I want to highlight the popular/organisational divide. I suggest Chaves' work points to symptoms of internal secularisation rather than the mechanics.

Linguistic culture

Oliver Tschannen claimed that 'When religion becomes generalized, it pervades secular institutions under disguise' (1991: 401). Warren Goldstein has also made the point that whilst religion becomes secularised, the secular realm contains religious elements (Goldstein 2009a:149). Robert Bellah's seminal work on civil religion was also about religious elements reappearing, even in fragmented and reinterpreted forms within the secular realm (1970). I suggest, given the discussion above, that the converse is also true: when secularity becomes generalised, it pervades religious institutions in disguise.

When secularity-pervaded religion is then re-expressed in the public sphere, we need to pay attention to the language of religious expression. I suggest that for the religious mask to remain intact, linguistic culture, or the way in which religious group identity is expressed in the public sphere, is key. It may be that actions such as public prayer or dress denote faith but typically it is ideas, expressed in language, which delineate religion from non-religion, which constitutes meaning and perception of meaning.

There are two elements to the internal secularisation of religion as expressed linguistically, (a) individualism and subjectivisation, and (b) rationalism or de-theologisation.

Individualism/subjectivisation

The paradox for the Quakers was that it was the peculiarity of outward forms which signified their beliefs in an inward spirituality. Outward materiality anchored interiorised spirituality. The end of outward forms, even if unintentionally, accommodated the rise of the potential for a private life outside the Meeting House, especially as the collective management of domestic life fell away. Also, the end of outward peculiarity created an anomaly of other aspects of Quaker differentiation. Privatised individualism, in such a permissive setting, was perhaps inevitable.

Diffuse interpretations of core aspects of Quaker religiosity such as peace coupled with decentralised congregational practices, such as membership procedures, has enhanced a shift towards the autonomisation of the congregational and individual away from the corporate. The option of un-tethering moral values from faith has led to a wider range of points of entry into the group, and a high rate of conversion without a strong faith transmission has encouraged individual interpretation of liturgy and practice. Quakers are eclectic in their beliefs and in their moral decision-making (Scully 2008). Religious identity becomes personalised, even bespoke, part of a commodified religious landscape or religious marketplace. One Quaker taking part in his Meeting's enquirer's programme related how he had been told that he was not to say what Quakers believed, only what he as an individual believed, should he be asked a theological question. Individualism was thus presented as normative. The sign at one Meeting House invites the outsider to 'come and join us and explore your inner values'. At this point, the subjectivisation of faith connects with its de-theologisation.

De-theologisation

The process of rationalisation or de-theologisation is about changing the linguistic assumptions and linguistic expression of faith, as is privatisation, hence my focus on it. It is about the decline in explicitly religious language within faith descriptions and explanations. It is about the portrayal of morality and ethics in rational rather than religious terms and of history in terms of human decision-making rather than providence. It is about locating cosmology in terms of historical time.

We can see this process in the decline of explicitly religious motivations and frames of understanding, e.g. the use of sin, salvation, God etc., and the concomitant decline in the traditional religious imperatives of soteriology and mission. It is visible in low and nominal membership criteria and particularly in the interpretation of religious symbols, beliefs and language in non-religious ways, e. g. within Quakerism the shifts from the phrase 'that of God' to the phrase 'that of good' (see 'On God' https://soundcloud.com/qwitness, for example), and from the shift in the description of Quaker decision-making from the idea of 'will of God' to the idea of 'sense of the Meeting'. It may be that these replacement terms still incorporate or encapsulate religious meaning for many, but their ambiguity potentially opens the way for the secular as equally valid. Values direct the everyday life, rather than faith experience and religious forms are given common-sense interpretations. For example, the vote-less Quaker way of conducting business is presented in terms of the psychological benefits of there being no winners or losers (rather than the seeking of God's will) and silent worship is presented as psychologically helpful or meditative rather than a way of directly encountering the divine. The Quaker involved in the enquirer's programme who had been told to answer questions not with 'Quakers believe' but 'I believe' was also told he was not to use the term 'God'. Within this rubric, the term 'will of 'God', the traditional Quaker rendering of divine guidance, becomes a contested site, complexified through individualised (a)theological interpretation: Penelope Cummins has applied Adam Kuper's typology of decision-making processes (1971) to the Quaker setting at its national level and has argued that some decision-making has become ceremonial, the Meeting 'rubber-stamping' a decision that has been made elsewhere (2017). She argues that Local Meeting practices follow the patterns set by Yearly Meeting. Quakers, in deciding to maintain their charitable status, have taken on the apparatus of trusteeship and in Cummins' analysis have lost sight of erstwhile processes of collective spiritual discernment (2018).

Mysticism is seen by some participants as a concept rather than a reality, with few British Quakers claiming a personal encounter with God, and even fewer writing about it. In this way, Quakerism becomes a rationalised ideal of a religious form, appreciated for its theo-logic rather than through its spiritual outcomes. The passage from *Brideshead Revisited* comes to mind where the sceptic Charles is talking to the Catholic Sebastian about his faith:

> But my dear Sebastian, you can't seriously believe it all.
> "Can't I?"
> I mean about Christmas and the star and the three kings and the ox and the ass.
> "Oh yes, I believe that. It's a lovely idea."
> But you can't believe things because they're a lovely idea.
> "But I do. That's how I believe."
>
> (Waugh 1997: 65)

Part of the internal secularisation of Quakers is that the ideas of Quakerism become the objects of reverence. One contribution in a Quaker Meeting talked of how the speaker's children and grandchildren were hardly Quaker or not Quaker at all, but how that didn't matter as what mattered above all was a moral life. Thus, faith becomes an option even within the life of the faith group. As mentioned above, Quaker Janet Scott commented in her lecture on Quaker theology and whether it was necessarily Christian, what matters 'is not the label but the life' (1980: 70).

Charles Taylor identifies the signs of the secular in 'excarnation' (2007: 746) and the way Christianity and Christian epistemology is distancing itself from the bodily, how worship is 'disenfleshed' (2007: 739) or disembodied. Religion is ordered rationally and worship becomes a rationalised activity. This is pertinent to the Quakers whose early experiences were highly embodied (Tarter 2001) and who sometimes still 'quake' (Lunn 2008). It is said that in the early twentieth century Quaker theologian Rufus Jones was admonished for beginning a contribution with the words 'I was thinking ...' as the Quakerism of the time was so set against such a worldly activity as part of the spiritual life. However, in the recent British Quaker Survey, 'thinking' was the highest ranked activity within Meeting for Worship (Hampton 2014: 97). In a thinking place, belief claims become the object of thought, a function of Taylor's disengaged self. The group becomes presented in increasingly secular terms and belief claims become optional. Whilst Quakers operate an orthocredence of absolute perhaps, other religious groups include those who operate 'perhaps-absolutes', choosing to pick and mix amongst their church's certainties as personal and collective beliefs become distinct. As Richard Fenn wrote: 'The more a religious group narrows the scope of the sacred and reduces its demands for integration between corporate and personal values and standards, the more adapted is such a group to a secular society' (1978: 65).

Secular and atheist viewpoints become accommodated and validated and the 'world' in its pejorative sense all but disappears except on single issues, e.g. war in the Quaker case. Religious identity is more difficult to maintain as distinct in such plural and diffuse modes. The *raison d'être* of organised religion becomes less obvious and participation falls away, or the collective identity is re-expressed in personalised terms. Understandings of religious authority and attribution of events become channelled in a rationalist direction and outreach or mission becomes redundant or values or issue-based. The propositional is replaced by the attitudinal. There is a disintegration of common faith that marks the end or orthodoxy to be replaced by a privatised heterodoxy.

Francois-Andre Isambert found in his study of the Catholic Church that it was no longer accepted as the final arbiter of every action but of general orientation alone. Individuals took on the role of deciding the best means to achieve the goals proposed by the church. The church was no longer perceived to be the competent body to deal with the detail (1976: 581–583). At the same time, he found that liturgy was increasingly understood in symbolic terms, with a preference being given to the teaching ministry over the expressive function of the Mass and the administration of the sacraments (1976).

Both Isambert and Berger point to the influence of secular thought on theology and the undermining of its credibility (Dobbelaere 2002: 125). In the Quaker setting, the Quaker business method becomes used for some settings or decisions but not for all. Heteropraxy then follows heterodoxy. Secular and spiritual practices sit side by side, equally acceptable. Identity is fractured and Lefebvre's understanding of creating coherent spaces, where space is a complex social construction of values and meanings, becomes apposite:

> Groups, classes or fractions of classes cannot constitute themselves, or recognise one another, as 'subjects' unless they generate (or produce) a space. Ideas, representations or values which do not succeed in making their mark on space, and thus generating (or producing) an appropriate morphology will lose all pith and become mere signs, resolve themselves into abstract descriptions, or mutate into fantasies (Lefebreve 1991: 416–417)

Warren Goldstein charts the consequences of religious rationalisation:

> Religion, by promoting rationalization, paradoxically weakens itself. There are three options for those who want to preserve the religious tradition: deduction, reduction, and induction. The deductive option embraces the authority of the religious tradition and defies the challenges posed to it by modern secularity ... The reductionist option attempts 'to secularize the tradition' ... Induction attempts to recall the experiences contained in the tradition. (2009b: 167)

Quakers, in this reading, have taken the reductionist approach. Charisma has become routinised (Goldstein 2009a: 146) and there is a consequence to internal changes in relation to external context.

In this secularising context, it might appear as if differentiated groups had lost sight of their hedge, of the distance they once claimed was necessary to separate the pure from the impure. Passages such as Romans 12:2 might be cast as anachronistic or can be seen to be forgotten. Yet, in this place of increasing congruity between religion and 'world', such coherent flow may also be seen as a sign of success in two ways: (a) that the religious ethic can be applied unhindered by State or popular interference (because the religious is no longer perceived or experienced as a threat) and that (b) the lack of dissimilarity between denomination and State and wider culture can be taken as a sign of sectarian victory over the corrupt world or at least of denominational stability. In the Quaker case, the originating desire to transform the world so that it became Quaker can be seen to be closer than ever before when Quaker sensibilities are so closely aligned with non-Quaker.

Agency and accommodation

Quakers have over time joined the coalition of systems of privilege and have benefited from that connection. As the hedge has been lowered, so mainstream culture has infused the movement partly through its high recruitment rate.

Conformity also allows freedom. I have a memory of the British politician Enoch Powell claiming in a television interview that he loved his years in the army because, as he said, if you followed the rules, you could do what you liked. Thus, the conformist religious group, accepted as harmless, and increasingly allied to dominant secularist cultural values, can proceed unpoliced by any external agency.

The above section has suggested two aspects to the role of linguistic culture in the process of internal secularisation: subjectivisation and individualism, and de-theologisation. It has tended to treat the religious group as single entity and so the next section differentiates religion again into organisational and popular, and suggests how the function of linguistic culture in internal secularisation gains agency and momentum in religious groups through, primarily, popular expression.

From the previous chapters, we can recast relations between religious adherents and their organisations and the State and wider popular culture in terms of competing agency, theorised in Chapter 5 as flows which may at one point cohere or produce patterns of incoherent motion or turbulence.

At any point in time coherent motion can be transformed to incoherent flow along any axis, as we have seen in the case of Quakers and their resistance to war and conscription, and the differing stances taken between Quakers as an organisation and Quakers themselves and the State and wider culture.

At the same time, the received sociological wisdom depicting denominationalisation as the fate of sectarian religion appears to be correct, even whilst the timing of transition and the completeness of the shift need to be cast in more dynamic terms.

We can also see from Chapter 6 that in the case of British Quakers it is not religious freedom that might appear desirable to converts but freedom from religion. It is the very absence of doctrine and the space that this provides to believe or not believe in anything beyond the material that may act as a draw to the 90% of Quakers who join the group as adults, two-thirds of whom had no prior religious affiliation. The pluralisation and marginalisation of explicit religious belief, and the fragile belief-basis of religious or liturgical form, suggest a process of internal secularisation.

Thus, we can suggest that sectarian groups ultimately move towards a greater conformity with their host culture even to the point of losing their own religiously based identity when that host culture is secularised. The rest of this chapter considers the mechanisms at play that cultivate conformity and looks at a mechanism within religious groups that can lead to internal secularisation, an ultimate marker of conformity short of disbanding the group altogether.

In the twenty-first century in a secular democracy, what are the agents of conformity? Obviously the State rewards conformity and equivalence with rights, as discussed above, but it is no longer interested in regulating the internal processes of religion. Instead, I suggest, the State regulates social dynamics across religious and non-religious populations. It is easily possible to imagine the equivalent of a Quaker Act of 1662 in 2022 (see the activities of the DRA in the case of the Alevis mentioned in Chapter 2) but it is also possible that behaviours and practices deemed undesirable would be contained by legislation introduced for the population at large. Indeed, a marker of secularist society is the feigned disinterest maintained by the State towards *internal* religious affairs. If religious groups and their participants obey the laws of the nation, the secular State will generally not interfere with belief content. There is nothing to be gained in terms of State affirmation in swapping religious identity motifs for non-religious ones within the group.

Popular pressure on religious groups at a nationwide level is limited. We might imagine an orchestrated media campaign against a group deemed harmful or ridiculous, but for a sect popular disapproval merely confirms the theology of differentiation. If anything, such a concerted campaign against a whole group might strengthen resistance rooted in a sense of distinctive rather than encourage adherents to desire conformity with the very culture which was attacking them.

Religious organisations themselves, I suggest, tend to be conservative. As above, John Fulton et al. in their study of Catholic religiosity (2000) and John Walliss in his study of the Brahma Kumaris (2007) both identified a core of committed, conformist and conservative adherents close to the centre of their respective organisational settings. Within Quakerism, the need for the group to at least agree to agree on any innovation (see Chapter 6) tends to an organisational conservatism. This structural element inherent in Quaker practice is further consolidated by the fact that most of those making the decisions tend to be those Quakers who still adhere to the theology and practice of Quaker business method, a group I have termed 'corporatists' as opposed to congregationalists or individualists (Dandelion 1996: Foreword) and who, thus, are more likely to favour traditional practice. Whilst the 1994 'book of discipline' (see Chapter 3) removed many of the references to Christ found in its predecessor volume, it was conservative in the way that the new book remained very clearly theo-centric. When national press coverage ahead of the 2018 Britain Yearly Meeting suggested Quakers might drop the term God, the language of the formal sessions was particularly theistic.

My conclusion then is that the cultivation of conformity is rooted in popular and local religious expression, in particular through the secularisation of popular religious linguistic culture. In other words, people are describing their religious participation in secular terms, either because their 'faith' is indeed secular, as per the suggestion of the last chapter, or in order to minimise dissimilarity with wider culture. This latter mechanism is known as 'accommodation theory' and has been attributed to the desire to maximise social integration and thus to maximise positive reception, evaluation and response (Giles et al. 1991: 18).

As outlined in the previous chapter, Quakers operate a 'culture of silence' in which silence, as the means to the divine, is valued, whilst speech is devalued and regulated. This is most noticeable in worship settings where the normative mode is silence. The organisational line is as follows:

> We highly prize silent waiting upon the Lord in humble dependence on him. We esteem it to be a precious part of spiritual worship, and trust that no vocal offering will ever exclude it from its true place in our religious meetings. (*Quaker Faith and Practice* 1995: 2.14)

Quakers understand spirituality as ineffable and beyond linguistic codification (see Chapter 6). Silence becomes the means to the divine and the response: 'Quakers, in my perception, have arrived at a novel position. The response to any direct, precise question on faith or morals has to be silence' (Cowie 1990: 7).

As mentioned in Chapter 6, Alan Davies found that whilst the concept of the 'free ministry' operates, vocal contributions were rare and followed particular patterns of expression (1988). However, contributions may or may not be explicitly 'religious' or theological. This aspect of ministry, coupled with a lack of opportunities and inclination outside worship to discuss the potentially sensitive mater of doctrine (within a non-doctrinal group), accommodates the possibility of covert changes of individual belief which are both never voices and thus never challenged (Dandelion 1996: 258). The emphasis on silence as the preferred liturgical mode thus accommodates and masks changes in popular religious belief. Thus unspoken tradition is reinterpreted and in due course collective organisational expressions of Quaker faith, the Quaker orthodoxy drawn from popular assent, can be recast in innovative terms. For instance the book of discipline adopted in 1994 contained only one-third of the material in the previous book and, as mentioned above, vastly reduced the number of references to Christ. Theological change, underpinned by a dynamic diversity of believing, is accommodated by the Quaker emphasis on silence and the devaluation and regulation of speech.

Davies also found that contributions were often linked by thematic association and how linguistic construction, as mentioned above, was often mirrored across contributions, evidence of speech accommodation theory as developed by Howard Giles and Peter Powesland. Drawing on work on 'accent mobility' and 'accent convergence' (Giles 1973), Giles and Powesland had argued that those involved in a conversation adopt each other's phraseology and mode of speaking to minimise dissimilarity (1975) and thus maximise ideational harmony, or coherent flow. The receiver becomes an active participant in formulation of the speech – indeed can be seen as the very cause of the message. Without the receiver of the message, the speaker would not formulate it.

Giles and colleagues also found in time that this pattern of accommodation was not limited to speech but included gestures and posture, the para-linguistic, and thus related to communication more widely. Traits they explored included utterance length, speech length, information density, vocal intensity, pausing frequency and lengths, response latency, self-disclosure, jokes expressing solidarity, orientations and opinions, gesture, head nodding and facial effect and posture (Giles et al. 1991: 7). National differences have been identified with Japan and Korea, collectivist cultures, showing even higher levels of receiver-centred communication (Yum 1988). Speech accommodation theory then became known as communication accommodation theory (Giles et al. 1991). The dominant strategy identified is one of convergence, although it should be noted that not all aspects of accommodation will necessarily be at play in any one exchange. In some cases accommodation is only minor, partial, asymmetric or temporally limited. There are also examples of 'over-accommodation' where the process is misjudged. There are also differences between explicit convergence and perceived convergence (Giles et al. 1991: 14). This last attribute also relates to people converging to where they believe the listener desires them to be: one study of expatriates found that they converged with their host's attempts to converge with them (Cohen and Cooper 1986). Even accurate convergence, as in the case of black immigrants accurately matching white working-class speech patterns, may be perceived as divergent, as their white neighbours were trying to move away from these patterns (Giles and Bourhis 1976).

Accommodation happens most when social integration is most desired. Studies show that convergence happens more between people at one level of society and those above them socially or technically (Giles et al. 1991: 20). One study of a travel agent revealed the art of skilful selling as the travel agent adroitly accommodated their mode and content of communication to each separate client (Coupland 1984).

This theory over the decades has been multiply tested and developed. Studies of particular linguistic or cultural groups showed strong evidence of consistent linguistic patterns that created coherence and conformity within sub-cultural groups, and in opposition to perceived outsiders. One study of Welsh speakers found they broadened their accents when faced with hostile questions about their language from an English speaker (Giles et al. 1991: 9) 'Speech maintenance', that is using particular patterns of speech, is a frequent way of maintaining group identity (Bourhis 1979), creating divergence with other speech-groups. Giles et al. claim: 'divergence can be a tactic of intergroup distinctiveness of individuals in search of a positive social identity' (1991: 28), even at the cost of wider social integration.

In the Quaker case, we can see that for 200 years Quakers maintained a distinctive linguistic culture inside and outside Meeting for Worship through the use of plain speech, the use of 'thee' and 'thou' instead of 'you' and the numbering of days of the week and months of the year. There were also distinctive patterns of nasal or sing-song ministry, often in disconnected fragments (Wood 1978: 57).

Through distinctive vocabulary and patterns of speech, alongside their other 'peculiarities', Quakers created a cultural identity that affirmed insider-status and excluded outsiders. Within the hedge, there was a way of speaking and being Quaker. They operated a communication model which delineated and identified its participants as Quaker, in the same way that members of other religious groups conducted themselves along the cultural markers of their own sub-cultures. There are still ways in which Quakers identify each other as Quakers, for example with the use of particular cultural references or insider jargon or technical terms. Within their own versions of the hedge, there is a way for Methodists to speak and be Methodist and for Anglicans to speak and be Anglican.

Today, Quakers do not practice expressing their faith in 'Quaker time', the time they are together as Quakers, but do get practised at mutual accommodation. Explicit theological terms like 'God', 'worship' and 'prayer' can get converted to 'good', 'silence' and 'holding people in the light'. In one location, 'Meeting for Worship' has been rebranded as 'Breathe'. As Grant shows (2018), list-making supports and accommodates internal religious pluralism and avoids the conflict within a non-doctrinal group inherent in doctrinal surety. Participation or attendance is increasingly voluntary and for many, sporadic (Dandelion, B. P. 2014: 31).

This may mean that the majority of any adherent's expression of their Quaker identity may take place outside the group setting. Thus, speaking to non-Quakers becomes the practical expression of practising talking about Quaker faith. Only outside the group might Quakers need to face questions about their spiritual identity.

What I want to suggest is that in the twenty-first century, freed of any other outward form of particularity or peculiarity, and now wishing to enjoy full citizenship (see Chapter 4), Quaker participants express their faith and practice to those outside the group in accommodatory terms in order to minimise dissimilarity with those they are speaking to. They aspire to social euphony and to minimise dissimilarity in a secular culture entails articulating Quaker faith and practice in secular terms. Already dressing like anyone else, present-day Quakers thus lose their own distinctive in-group linguistic culture when speaking outside 'Quaker-time' in order to be part of a larger and wider in-group, the general public. In other words, Quakers have moved from a situation in which they perceived that everyone else, including the way they spoke, was theologically wrong to one where they seek to be integrated with that society. The role of the hedge has moved from protection to impediment. Adherents cultivate coherent flow, they cultivate conformity.

Studies of Quaker experience outside Quaker settings are rare but recent work by Mark Read on Quakers in the workplace reveals some interesting patterns. As might be expected, most of Read's participants were converts into the group, and yet the conversion process was affirming of previously held, rather than revolutionary, positions. These Quakers tended to downplay their Quaker affiliation in the workplace to minimise discord or disharmony (2017: chapter 7), or be open about affiliation and private about their theological beliefs (mirroring the mode of operation within the group) whilst inwardly working to maintain congruence between their own beliefs and aspirations and those of their job (Read 2017: 105). Thus they might try to stand up against workplace injustice or try to arbitrate disputes. Where public Quaker affiliation created discord, affiliation was masked (Read 2017: 203). The dominant finding, however, was that the personal interpretation of Quakerism had precedence over any organisational prescription. Read quotes one interviewee: 'What comes first is my mode of being, what comes second is Quaker' (2017: 273).

Thus, Quakers can be overt about their Quaker affiliation in the workplace insofar as they choose their workplace and insofar as that affiliation is cast and presented in their own terms:

> Affiliation is, thus, not cast by these Quakers as inevitable, inspired or as necessary for the realisation of essential goals except insofar as it facil-
> itates the converts' highly individualised ends. These individualised terms are portrayed by affiliates as usefully accommodated within the liberal and permissive construction of the contemporary Quaker church. (Read 2017: 274)

Quaker participation is viewed as instrumental and of pragmatic use, according to Read. It fits pre-Quaker identities and values (Read 2017: 282). Quakers at work avoid transgression and disharmony using the Liberal Quaker tradition's aspirations of a harmonious world as support and con-firmation of their compliance (Read 2017: 285). In the workplace, Quakers conform even whilst they transgress orthodox Christianity and often convert as a critique of mainstream Christian orthodoxy and ecclesiology. The theo-logical essentialisation of the 'absolute perhaps' (Chapter 6) does not transfer to Quaker social practice. In social settings, Quakerism is individualised and privatised (Read 2017: 290). Quakers accommodate to the workplace.

Patterns of accommodation operate within the group as different types of believer translate their beliefs in order to accommodate the perception of the others and thus to minimise dissonance. Indeed at least as three decades ago, 'that of God in everyone' was being replaced by 'that of good in everyone' in some internal Quaker discourse as an accommodatory measure (Dandelion 1996: 309). Indeed, this practice and practise of internal accommodation may have modelled the out-turning of accommodatory narratives towards wider society.

This pattern of 'faith accommodation' is encouraged by the non-doctrinal form of Liberal Quakerism which enforces self-constructed articulations of what it is to be a Quaker. Because there is no organisational doctrine, or shared narrative, the explanation of Quakerism falls to the individual to make up. Further, there are no structured opportunities for Quakers to share their faith.

The pattern of accommodation is also encouraged by the high number of converts to the group. As nearly 90% of those in the group have entered as adult converts, with only one-third coming from an immediately prior religious affiliation, then faith transmission becomes crucial if a particular religious and linguistic culture is to be maintained. In the non-doctrinal and volunteer-run context of Liberal Quakerism, this transmission has been problematic. Falling numbers can encourage congregations to welcome even those with differing views and there is no systematic or required induction process for newer participants. Britain Yearly Meeting cut its adult education staffing in 1995 and Woodbrooke, the independent Quaker learning centre which runs continuing education courses for Quakers, reports that only about 14% of the Yearly Meeting take one of its courses (Dandelion, B. P. 2014: 59). Faith transmission is often localised and ad hoc. With 33% of participants in the British Quaker Survey 2013 attending for less than ten years, belief statements are continually recast within Quaker time: what is important is not when someone entered the Quaker fold but how recently they re-expressed their belief in innovative ways, or indeed whether they publicly expressed anything at all.

Thus, two mechanisms are at play. The first is the lack of transmission of a distinctive Quaker linguistic culture across the Quaker population. The second is related to the consequences of adult converts wishing to retain their pre-Quaker identity or positive evaluation with non-Quakers through minimising difference with societal peers. This is the perceived need that induces high levels of communication accommodation. In other words, when new identities threaten consolidated ones, the desire is to minimise dissonance. Laminar confluence is preferred to turbulent transfluviality. In previous times, conversion to Quakerism would have involved new patterns of speech and dress, a particularity that reflected the desire for spiritual renewal or the reality of spiritual transformation. It was deliberately and explicitly a course of incoherent motion. Old ties would have been subservient to the new life. Given that present-day British Quakerism is not offering a 'new life' but rather presents itself as an optional enhancement (see Chapter 6), the new adherent needs to find convergence between affiliation and the rest of life. Thus, the presentation of Quakerism in terms of values rather than supernatural beliefs, of silence instead of 'worship' and 'that of good' instead of 'that of God' are all hallmarks of the secularisation of Quaker expression, and of religious expression in a secularist society.

Other than for the Quaker 'core' who maintain 'peculiar' ways of speaking about Quaker faith and practice and who can manage an organisational conservatism, these articulations become the modus operandi, linguistically, within popular Quakerism as adherents seek consistency and coherence within their own narratives of Quaker participation. Thus popular Quakerism, whilst upholding the central value of diversity but also released from any need to adhere to universal claims, becomes prone to a process of internal secularisation through the blurring of Quaker/non-Quaker styles and content of 'religious' speech acts, as well as the blurring of 'Quaker time' into public time, the spaces in which people converse with others. The equal sacramentality of all places and times can become the equal secularity of all places and times. More and more individual Quaker witness takes place in non-Quaker groups (Montemaggi 2018: part 2) and we know that the increased permissiveness of Quakerism has made it easier to dip in and out of Quaker time, so that Quakerism is no longer necessarily adherents' primary identification (Dandelion, B. P. 2014: 31). Indeed, for many it is Quaker faith that needs to be integrated with the 'rest', or most, of life rather than the other way round. Seamlessness demands accommodation.

Accommodation is the logical outcome of denominationalisation, but its content depends on the mode of wider society. A highly religious society would require for accommodation purposes a different speech content from a secular one. Sectarianism, as we have seen, can emerge at any stage, but in a secular setting in which group members are accommodating to wider society, we could expect prophetic acts to be framed in secular or rationalist terms. Quaker anti-fracking is presented in terms of climate justice or water-awareness rather than the book of Isaiah. Yet in certain locations, such as a strongly Muslim neighbourhood, Quakers report making their religious identification explicit. Accommodation can work in either direction. When accommodation involves internal secularisation, we might see that process as the ultimate endpoint of denominationalisation and 'world-acceptance'.

This idea of secularised communication accommodation in secular Britain fits with Gay Pilgrim's idea of the internalisation of the heterotopic impulse she identified amongst early Quakers (see Chapter 4). Pilgrim argued that given the diminishing points of dissonance between Quaker thought and wider culture, the Quaker desire to cultivate difference and dis-location had become internalised so that participants created dissonant individual and sub-cultural identities within Quaker space and time. In both cases, the one presented here and in Pilgrim's work, the boundary line between Quaker culture and wider culture dissolves whilst within the group, individualism and the desire for linguistic and doctrinal freedom prevails. The idea of secularised communication affirms Aarek's concept of the heterotopic denomination (forthcoming): the form and theory is still counter-cultural but the reality is world-accepting and world-accommodating.

However, it is language that is crucial to potential internal secularisation as it is these moments of speech that make explicit narratives of faith transmission and normativity. Quakers mask theological diversity and change through their emphasis on silence and their marginalisation of speech so that moments of explicit language become crucial indicators and teachers of the latest parameters of acceptability/ normativity. Whilst the revision of the book of discipline becomes key in terms of explicit organisational theological disposition, the less formal and more regular speech acts govern the extent and shape of Quaker faith in the meantime. They also co-construct the context for the next revision process. They underpin the popular heterodoxy that informs the collective construction of new orthodoxy.

Thus in terms of Rhiannon Grant's work on Quaker theologising in terms of list-making, in which the supernatural is spoken of in terms of a list of options (see Chapter 6), the choice of terms within the list becomes crucial to the types of faith or non-faith transmission that can take place within the group. A list such as 'God, Christ, Holy Spirit, Inward light ...' frames the possibilities of Quaker theology in a very different way from a list such as 'Spirit, light, love, mystery, goodness ...'.

Obviously in a liquid or non-doctrinal group (Plüss 2007), these lists can change at any point. In the same way that nothing has constrained the twentieth-century departure from a purely Christian Quakerism amongst British Quakers to a more pluralistic diversity of doctrinal and non-doctrinal positions, there could be a return to Quaker Christian orthodoxy. One method of this conservatism is schism, as documented by Pilgrim (2003) following the formation of the Yearly Meeting of Friends in Christ in 1993. This kind of departure tends to strengthen the position of those left behind, freed as they are from any counter-vailing theological preferences, but, with a continuing high number of converts, British Quakerism could in theory revert to a less pluralistic theological disposition. However, the linguistic shift from Christian to theocentric within the book of discipline and from theocentric to plural at a popular level, coupled with the high number of recruits, threatens the long-term maintenance of particular readings of Quaker tradition.

Danièle Hervieu-Léger has written compellingly about the breakdown in the 'chain of memory' and chain of belief across generations and how it affects faith transmission and the maintenance of tradition (2000). Pioneering the location of the concept of 'memory' at the heart of discussion about secularisation, Hervieu-Léger claims that religion implies the mobilisation of collective memory:

> In the case of differentiated societies where established religions prevail and where distinctive communities of faith emerge, collective religious memory is subject to constantly recurring construction, so that the past which has its source in the historical events at its core can be grasped at any moment as being totally meaningful. (2000: 124)

However, Hervieu-Léger claims, two trends threaten the strength of collective memory. The first is the expansion of memory, partly through technological change, that allows humanity access to vast amounts of unsorted information in which traditional modes of production and interpretation become replaced by an incoherent and shallower fragmentation of selected memory attuned to particular cultures or settings. We all know bits of something from different 'somewheres' rather than the knowledge linked to our own heritage. This connects with the second trend, that of increased fragmentation of the

collective location and tradition into individual choices to connect and participate in a limitless range of settings. Thus collective memory is both homo-
genised and fragmented, whilst the interpretative cultural linkages become
marginalised and anachronistic. Social ties become pragmatic and realised in
the present-moment rather than embedded within a cultural lineage (Hervieu-
Léger 2000: 128–130).

Religious practice and culture start to break down within this shift of the
sphere of believing. In her case study of French Catholicism, the parish ceases to
be the source of memory and the cradle of community in which a connection to
the church at the centre of the village is assumed if not realised. Hervieu-Léger
reflects whether this is a new mode of religion centred on the subjective, and
without continuity, or the end of religion altogether. For Hervieu-Léger, secularisation is the product of rationalisation but also collective amnesia, 'by the
obliteration of all recall that is not immediate or functional' (2000: 140).

The pattern of individual theological creation within a religious organisation challenges the division between 'religion' and 'spirituality' made popular
by Robert Bellah et al. in their study of the individualised spiritual path or
'utilitarian individualism' (also termed 'Sheilaism' after the report of one
participant) (1985), and implicit in studies of 'seeker spirituality' by Wade
Clark Roof (1993, 1999). Roof writes:

> … personal autonomy has a double face, one that reflects the dislocations
> of institutional religious identities in the contemporary world, and a
> second that mirrors a deeply personal search for meaningful faith and
> spirituality. (Roof 2003: 146)

Paul Heelas and Linda Woodhead, in their study of Kendal and their theorisation of a 'spiritual revolution' mentioned above in Chapter 2, also made the
distinction between 'religion' and 'spirituality' (2005). Building on Charles
Taylor's idea of the 'subjective turn' they divided faith practice into religion,
defined by its transcendent reference point, and spirituality, defined by its
subjective reference point. They measured religious and spiritual participation
(e.g. Reiki, yoga, etc.) in the market town of Kendal and, as far as their data
allowed, claimed that religious participation was in decline, in line with
national statistics, whilst spiritual practice was on the rise. When the two
levels of participation met, they suggest a 'spiritual revolution' would have
taken place, a point they predicted might occur within 30 or 40 years.

As also mentioned in Chapter 2, John Knox then replicated the study in
McMinnville, a similar-sized town in Oregon, USA, using identical methods
(2016). Unsurprisingly, given the differing average national levels of church
attendance, Knox found that religion, as defined by Heelas and Woodhead,
was in a stronger place in McMinville than Kendal with 21% attending
church on the day he and his colleagues made their count (2016: 53): the
figure was less than 7% in Kendal.

Knox found very little 'spiritual' activity. Nevertheless he was able to identify a distinctive mode of church-going. Knox divided authority for belief into 'sacro-theism' (direct from God), sacro-clericalism (through the authority of the tradition), 'sacro-communalism' (the authority of the group) and 'sacro-egoism' (the authority of the individual). Knox found that sacro-egoism was the most common form of religious authority for churchgoers in McMinville (2016). People decided for themselves who or what to believe and then selected their congregations accordingly. In other words, the subjective turn was operating within communal settings. In sacro-egoist settings, the host culture determines religiosity in relation to individual 'faith' choices. For Hervieu-Léger, sectarian religion, with its emphasis on conversion and on particular demands made of participants may fare better in this hyper-modern world than denominations that place their tradition into a society whose individuals which can decide to pick and choose the parts that suit them best (2000: 168). For denominations, sacro-egoism displaces sacro-clericalism.

Richard Flory and Donald Miller found the same phenomenon in their study of post-boomer spirituality (2008). They found this group wishing to express their spirituality within collective settings, what they termed 'expressive communalism'. Whilst comprising types of adherent utilising different strategies and emphases, Flory and Miller argue that a new preference for embodied worship sits alongside a commitment to a particular faith community (2008: 185–193). It is a preference that bridges spirituality and service and that draws in those of an older generation. As Flory and Miller claim, the 'individual spiritual quest is mediated through the communities in which they are active and in which they seek member-ship and belonging' (2008: 188).

Recent studies of everyday religion by Courtney Bender (2003), Nancy Ammerman (2007), and Meredith Maguire (2008), have also identified the primacy of individual preference operating within religious settings. The lit-erature thus subverts the spirituality/religion divide from both ends. We see the subjective aspects of spirituality within religious settings and through the work of historians like Leigh Schmidt (2005) we find that individualistic spirituality often has a communal element of public involvement in securing political or social goals.

Grace Davie (2015) and Charles Taylor (2007) have both noted the shift from the assumption of religious participation to a mode of religious consumption, that faith allegiance can no longer be taken for granted. Taylor has suggested this reflects a change of attitude and Davie that society have moved from reli-gious obligation to religious market. Thus worshippers become consumers making choices, a sensibility that extends, it appears, to religious authority. However, unlike Steve Bruce's suggestion that such choice plays out in terms of non-participation (why should anyone take the church seriously if they don't need to listen to the minister anymore?), it seems that many churchgoers still want to exercise their choices within religious organisational settings. It is just that religious citizenship is now individualistic and, in general, accommodatory. At the same time, participation and attendance become optional and played down in terms of an individual sense of 'belonging'. Adherents can belong without feeling the need to attend, and their participation can then be reframed in secular value-based terms. Mission is reframed in terms of spiritual sensibility. The tipping point to internal secularisation then is not about the extent of the religious 'market' but about the attraction of assimilation. As above, once one element of peculiarity disappears, the others become incongruent and also disappear. Religion itself becomes the final element of particularity or difference within secularised cultures. Bryan Wilson, as we saw in Chapter 1, ended up defining sects in terms of their soteriology. However for twentieth-century British Quakers (and indeed Unitarians or Unitarian Universalists), salvation is no longer a part of the theological map. Wilson looked for the equivalent and talked about Quakers in terms of being a reformist sect, reforming peoples' consciences in order to save the world (1970) but this conscience-based value-led agenda can easily be presented in purely secular terms.

Thus, contrary to Heelas and Woodhead, it is not that the threat to transcendent religion is coming from without but from within religious organisations at a popular level. In Mandair and Dressler's terms (see Chapter 2), religion-making from below is transformed into religion-*unmaking* within religion within secularist cultures.

The Quaker case confirms that this pattern is not confined to a single generational cohort. The average age of a British Quaker is 64 but Jennifer Hampton found theological patterns that crossed age demographics (2014). As explained in Chapter 6, Hampton's latent class analysis of the 2013 British Quaker Survey, suggested the probability of three dominant types of believer within British Quakerism. Hampton termed these 'traditional', 'liberal' and 'non-theist'. These three types did not correlate to particular generational cohorts, but could be found equally across the age range.

It would be tempting to say that this pattern of internal secularisation is confined to non-doctrinal groups such as Liberal Quakers, and that we would not find this linguistic-cultural mechanism at work in groups with strong doctrinal foundations. However, Abby Day, in her recent study of nominal believers, suggested that these actors manifested 'performative Christianity' in that they constructed a Christian identity from their social belongings rather than through doctrinal assent: 'how otherwise non-religious people can bring into being a Christian identity related to social belongings' (2011: 192).

> Anthropocentric, performative Christian Nominalism may be understood partly as the practice of self-identifying as Christian when asked to do so in particular social and temporal contexts, while not necessarily sharing Christian beliefs such as a faith in God or participating in any Christin public acts of worship or ritual observance. (Day 2011: 189)

Religious identity, in Day's study, is not about belief or practice but about identifying with particular people as a reference group (Day 2011: 186). In a similar
way, we can characterise Quakerism as a performative or relational religion.

Day argues that sociologist and anthropologists have been too focused on
belief (2011: 192), a reflection shared in the work of Francesca Montemaggi who
confirms a Protestant bias towards belief-centred religion running throughout the
sociology of religion that no longer matches the reality of faith for many contemporary Christians (2018: part one). Belief, for Day, is created out of the social
need for belonging: the object of worship within 'performative belief' is 'not an
entity such as god or "society" but the experience of belonging' (2011: 194).

We know that however strong the doctrinal or liturgical core of an organisation is its popular expression can be at some remove. This pattern is almost
implicit in the denominational stance. We can think of the popularity of John
Robinson's *Honest to God* (1963) and the way in which the rephrasing of
tradition encouraged many to stay within the Anglican Church (Towler 1984).

Vincett et al., following Flory and Miller, argued that belief as doctrinal assent is
less compelling than belief as 'embodied action' or performance for characterising
young Christian belief in the UK (2012: 278). 'In the face of heterodoxy and hesi-
tancy of belief [responses to pluralism and competing truth claims], belief as a
propositional system loses authority to belief as religious action' (2012: 286): for
Vincett et al., 'performance Christianity' de-emphasises doctrine and highlights
religious expression related to the everyday. Whilst Vincett et al.'s participants had
a clear sense of faith, it was not wedded to doctrine. Thus, even doctrinally based
faith groups may become more and more non-doctrinal in their communal settings.

Lichterman's work on pragmatic religious expression (2013) locates religion in
terms of its expression and meaning rather than in a fictional universal doctrinal
model: 'The pragmatic approach bids us to ask how people create social space for
expressing religious views and identities and linking them to action' (2013: 13).

This pragmatic approach to traditional doctrinal belief is also evident in
Pal Repstad's work amongst conservative Christians in Agder, Norway
(2014). Repstad and his colleagues describe a 'softening' of dogmatic traditional views towards elements of popular culture and lifestyle amongst the
grass roots members of the local congregations (2014), reinforcing the idea of
dynamic flows within even conservative religious organisations.

Woodhead has argued that many religious participants are de-differentiating
between religion and the secular and that their faith identities are becoming less
rigid and more blurred (2016). They are not rejecting religion as such but religious authority, a similar finding to John Knox with his idea of 'sacro-egoism'.

> So on the one hand, modern religious authorities lose their ability to police
> their own boundaries and maintain control and purity, whilst on the other
> hand, ordinary people feel new entitlements in relation to religion, as in
> other areas of their lives, and wish to think and choose for themselves
> rather than merely obey and be dutiful. (Woodhead 2016: 44–45)

Thus, surveys of belief miss the point and over-emphasise group distinctives rather than seeing the way in which, say, religious pluralism is an arena of constant optional personal involvement and personal remapping of religious expression. Thus the non-doctrinal example of the Quakers may simply exaggerate the performative expression of religious adherents in all kinds of religious groups.

Thus, it is perfectly reasonable to suggest that all religious groups within secular host cultures can be prone to a mode of internal secularisation brought about by the de-theologisation of popular expressions of church or faith participation in an attempt to minimise dissimilarity between adherents and peers in wider society. In both settings, within and outside the group, Quakers and other denominational believers want to accommodate to their perception of their listeners' preferences in order to minimise dissimilarity.

Chapter summary

The cultivation of conformity, within this reading then, comes not from complex or forced relations between secular State and the religious organisation trying to secure rights but comes instead through popular expression. Popular religion drives organisational choices. Popular secularisation precedes the organisational. Coherent flow is cultivated by the choices that participants make in constructing their religious identities within and outside the group. Practice at framing spirituality in non-doctrinal terms within the group has led to the expression of 'faith' in non-religious or accommodatory terms outside the group, which then feeds back into organisational life through the rare moments of collective expression of Quaker spirituality. In the Quaker setting this takes place when the group produces leaflets, minutes, epistles and their 'book of discipline' which is revised every generation or so. Popular heterodoxy at these key moments becomes codified into expressions of orthodoxy (Dandelion 1996: chapter 7). In the last century, these expressions have tended to be innovative, minimising Christianity in the 1990s, or producing fresh thinking on social concerns such as equal marriage or climate justice.

This mode of popular internal secularisation undermines organisational attempts to present themselves as interesting and 'serious' to would-be converts, but, paradoxically, creates spaces of 'expressive communalism' that might buoy recruitment, as it seems to have done in the Quaker case. Indeed, without organisational doctrinal resistance to individualised spirituality, the Quakers fare better numerically in a secular culture than would have been expected of a liberal religious group because of that very permissiveness. Whether conformity or coherence creates a sustained attraction to sacro-egoist seekers remains to be seen, but in the meantime the internal and external nature of religious organisational life in its sectarian and denominational forms within secularist nation states remains highly dynamic.

REFERENCES

Aarek, H-E. (forthcoming). 'The Modernisation of the Religious Society of Friends (or the Quaker Society) in Norway 1880 to 1970'. Unpublished Phd thesis, University of Tromsø.

Acheson, D. (1997). *From Calculus to Chaos: an introduction to dynamics.* Oxford: Oxford University Press.

Advices and Queries. (1995). London: Britain Yearly Meeting.

Alexander, R. (2006). 'Democratic Quakers in the Age of Revolutions'. Unpublished MA thesis, University of Lancaster.

Allen, R. C. and Moore, R. A. (2018). *The Quakers 1656–1723: the evolution of an alternative community.* State Park, PA: Penn State University Press.

Ambler, R. (1989). *Creeds and the Search for Unity.* London: Quaker Home Service.

Ammerman, N. T. (ed.) (2007). *Everyday Religion: observing modern religious lives.* New York: Oxford University Press.

Appadurai, A. (2008 [1996]). *Modernity at Large: cultural dimensions of globalization.* Minneapolis, MN: University of Minnesota Press.

Asad, T. (2003). *Formations of the Secular: Christianity, Islam, modernity.* Stanford, CA: Stanford University Press.

Ashton, P. (2000). 'Divided ideals: the Religious Society of Friends and the Irish Home Rule controversy, 1885 to 1886'. *Woodbrooke Journal* 6, pp. 1–32.

Bailey, R. (1992). *New Light on George Fox and Early Quakerism: the making and unmaking of a God.* San Francisco, CA: Mellen Research University Press.

Barclay, R. (2002 [1678]). *An Apology for the True Christian Divinity.* Glenside, PA: Quaker Heritage Press.

Bauman, R. (1983). *Let Your Words be Few: symbolism of speaking and silence amongst seventeenth-century Quakers.* Cambridge: Cambridge University Press.

Bauman, Z. (2000). *Liquid Modernity.* Cambridge: Polity Press.

Becker, H. (1932). *Systematic Sociology.* New York: Wiley.

Beckford, J. A. (1975). *The Trumpet of Prophecy: a sociological study of Jehovah's Witnesses.* London: Basil Blackwell.

Bellah, R. N. (1970). 'Civil Religion in America', in Bellah, R. N. (ed.), *Beyond Belief: essays on religion in a post-traditional world*. New York: Harper & Row.

Bellah, R. N., Madsen, R., Sullivan, W. M., Swidler, A. and Tipton, S. M. (1985). *Habits of the Heart: individualism and commitment in American life*. Berkeley, CA: University of California Press.

Bender, C. (2003). *Heaven's Kitchen: living religion at God's Love We Deliver*. Chicago, IL: Chicago University Press.

Bender, C. (2013). 'Pluralism and Secularism', in Bender, C., Cadge, W., Levitt, P. and Smilde, D. (eds), *Religion on the Edge: de-centering and re-centering the sociology of religion*. New York: Oxford University Press, pp. 137–158.

Berger, P. L. (1961). *The Noise of Solemn Assemblies: Christian commitment and the religious establishment in America*. Garden City, NY: Doubleday.

Berger, P. L. (1967). *The Sacred Canopy: elements of a sociological theory of religion*. Garden City, NY: Doubleday.

Berger, P. L. (1971). *A Rumor of Angels: modern society and the rediscovery of the supernatural*. Harmondsworth: Penguin.

Best, S. (2008). 'Adolescent Quakers: a community of intimacy', in Dandelion, P. and Collins, P. J. (eds), *The Quaker Condition: the sociology of a liberal religion*. Newcastle: Cambridge Scholars Press, pp. 192–215.

Best, S. (2010). 'The Community of Intimacy: the spiritual beliefs and religious practices of adolescent Quakers'. Unpublished PhD thesis, University of Birmingham.

Bibby, R. W. and Brinkerhoff, M. B. (1973). 'The Circulation of the Saints: a study of people who join conservative churches'. *Journal for the Scientific Study of Religion* 12, pp. 273–283.

Birkel, M. and Angell, S. W. (2013).'Richard Farnworth: prophet of light and apostle of church order', in Angell, S. W. and Dandelion, P. (eds), *Early Quakers and their Theological Thought*. Cambridge: Cambridge University Press, pp. 83–101.

Bishop, E. and Jung, J. (2018). 'Seeking Peace: Quakers respond to war', in Angell, S. W. and Dandelion, P. (eds), *The Cambridge Companion to Quakerism*. Cambridge: Cambridge University Press, pp. 106–128.

Björkqvist, K. (1990). 'World-rejection, World-affirmation, and Goal Displacement: some aspects of change in three new religions movements of Hindu origin', in Holm, N. (ed.), *Encounter with India: studies in neohinduism*. Turku, Finland: Åbo Akademi University Press, pp. 79–99.

Bourhis, R. Y. (1979). 'Language in Ethnic Interaction: a social psychological approach', in Giles, H. and Saint-Jacques, B. (eds), *Language and Ethnic Relations*. Oxford: Pergamon, pp. 117–141.

Braithwaite, W. C. (1912). *The Beginnings of Quakerism*. London: Macmillan.

Braithwaite, W. C. (1919). *The Second Period of Quakerism*. London: Macmillan.

Brendlinger, I. A. (2007). *To Be Silent … Would be Criminal: the antislavery influence and writings of Anthony Benezet*. Lanham, MD: Scarecrow.

Brock, P. (1990). *The Quaker Peace Testimony 1660 to 1914*. York: William Sessions.

Brock, P. (2015). *Pioneers of a Peaceable Kingdom: the Quaker peace testimony from the colonial era to the First World War*. Princeton, NJ: Princeton University Press.

Brown, W. (2015). 'Religious Freedom's Oxymoronic Edge', in Sullivan, W. F., Hurd, E. S., Mahmood, S. and Danchin, P. G. (eds), *Politics of Religious Freedom*. Chicago, IL: University of Chicago Press, pp. 324–334.

Bruce, S. (2001). 'Christianity in Britain, RIP'. *Sociology of Religion* 62, pp. 191–203.

Bruce, S. (2002). *God is Dead: secularization in the West*. Oxford: Blackwell.

Bruce, S. (2003). 'The Demise of Christianity in Britain', in Davie, G., Heelas, P. and Woodhead, L. (eds), *Predicting Religion: Christian, secular and alternative futures*. Aldershot: Ashgate, pp. 53–63.

Bruce, S. (2011). *Secularization: in defence of an unfashionable theory*. Oxford: Oxford University Press.

Bullock, J. (2017). 'The Sociology of the Sunday Assembly: "belonging without believing" in a post-Christian context'. Unpublished PhD thesis, University of Kingston.

Burrough, E. (1656). *A Trumpet Sounded Forth out of Sion*. London: Calvert.

Burrough, E. (1657). *All ye Inhabitants of the Earth in all Nations through the World*. London: Thomas Simmons.

Burrough, E. (1658). *A Message for Instruction*. London: Thomas Simmons.

Burrough, E. (1659a). *To the Present Distracted and Broken Nation of England*. London.

Burrough, E. (1659b). *A Message Proclaimed by Divine Authority*. London.

Burrough, E. (1659c). *Queries to the Fryars*. London.

Burrough, E. (1661). *The Case of Free Liberty of Conscience*. London: Thomas Simmons.

Calvert, J. E. (2009). *Quaker Constitutionalism and the Political Thought of John Dickinson*. New York: Cambridge University Press.

Campbell, C. (1978). 'The Secret Religion of the Educated Classes'. *Sociology of Religion* 39, pp. 146–156.

Carey, B. (2016). 'Anthony Benezet, Antislavery Rhetoric, and the Age of Sensibility'. *Quaker Studies* 21, pp. 141–158.

Casanova, J. (1994). *Public Religions in the Modern World*. Chicago, IL: Chicago University Press.

Casanova, J. (2010). 'A Secular Age: dawn or twilight?' in Warner, M., Vanantwerpen, J. and Calhoun, C. (eds), *Varieties of Secularism in a Secular Age*. Cambridge, MA: Harvard University Press, pp. 265–281.

Chadkirk, J. W. C. (2004). 'Will the Last (Woman) Friend to Leave Please Ensure that the Light Remains Shining?'. *Quaker Studies* 9, pp. 114–119.

Chadkirk, J. W. C. (2015). 'Patterns of Membership and Participation among British Quakers, 1823–2012'. Unpublished MPhil thesis, University of Birmingham.

Chambers, H. V. (2006). 'An Investigation into the Relationships between Quaker Engagement and Substance Using and Gambling Behaviours'. Unpublished PhD Thesis, University of Birmingham.

Chaves, M. (1993). 'Denominations as Dual Structures: an organizational analysis'. *Sociology of Religion* 54, pp. 147–169.

Clarkson, T. (1806). *Portraiture of Quakerism*. London: Samuel Stansbury.

Cohen, E. and Cooper, R. L. (1986). 'Language and Tourism'. *Annals of Tourism Research* 13, pp. 535–563.

Collins, P. J. (1996). '"Plaining": The social and cognitive process of symbolization in the Religious Society of Friends (Quakers)'. *Journal of Contemporary Religion* 11, pp. 277–288.

Collins, P. J. (2001). 'Quaker plaining as critical aesthetic'. *Quaker Studies*, 5, pp. 121–139.

Collins, P. J. and Dandelion, P. (2006). 'Wrapped Attention: revelation and concealment in non-conformity', in Arweck, E., and Keenan, W. (eds), *Materializing Religion: expression, performance, and ritual*. Aldershot: Ashgate, pp. 45–61.

Collins, P. J. and Dandelion, P. (2014). 'Transition as Normative: British Quakerism as liquid religion'. *Journal of Contemporary Religion* 29, pp. 287–301.

Coupland, N. (1984). 'Accommodation at Work: some phonological data and their implications'. *International Journal of the Sociology of Language* 46, pp. 49–70.

Cowie, I. (1990). 'On Not Having a Creed'. *The Staffordshire Quaker*, September, p. 7.

Crabtree, S. (2015). *Holy Nation: the transatlantic Quaker ministry in an age of revolution*. Chicago, IL:University of Chicago Press.

Crowther-Hunt, N. (1979 [1961]). *Two Early Political Associations: the Quakers and the dissenting deputies in the age of Sir Robert Walpole*. Westport, CN: Greenwood Press.

Crump, C. G. (ed.) (1900). *History of the Life of Thomas Ellwood*. London: Methuen.

Cummins, P. (2017). 'Quaker Decision-making: the insider's and the outsider's perspectives. Who is the culprit? Why, the audience of course! A Quaker narrative of authority, agency and blame'. Paper presented at the British Sociological Association Sociology of Religion Study Group Conference, Leeds.

Cummins, P. (2018). 'After the Charities' Act: governance and decision-making in Britain Yearly Meeting'. Paper presented at the Quaker Studies Research Association Conference, Birmingham.

Damiano, K. A. (1988). 'On Earth as it is in Heaven: eighteenth century Quakerism as realized eschatology'. Unpublished PhD thesis, Union of Experimenting Colleges and Universities, Cincinnati, Ohio.

Dandelion, B. P. (2014). *Open for Transformation: being Quaker*. London: Quakerbooks.

Dandelion, B. P., Gwyn, D. and Peat, T. (1998). *Heaven on Earth: Quakers and the second coming*. Birmingham and Kelso: Woodbrooke and Curlew.

Dandelion, P. (1996). *A Sociological Analysis of the Theology of Quakers: the silent revolution*. Lampeter: Edwin Mellen Press.

Dandelion, P. (2002). 'Those Who Leave and Those Who Feel Left: the complexity of Quaker disaffiliation'. *Journal of Contemporary Religion* 17, pp. 213–228.

Dandelion, P. (2004). 'Implicit Conservatism in Liberal Religion: British Quakers as an "uncertain sect"'. *Journal of Contemporary Religion* 19, pp. 219–229.

Dandelion, P. (2005). *The Liturgies of Quakerism*. Aldershot: Ashgate.

Dandelion, P. (2007). *Introduction to Quakerism*. Cambridge: Cambridge University Press.

Dandelion, P. (2008). 'The Creation of Coherence: the Quaker "double-culture" and the "absolute perhaps"', in Dandelion, P. and Collins, P. J. (eds), *The Quaker Condition: the sociology of a liberal religion*. Newcastle: Cambridge Scholars Press, pp. 22–37.

Dandelion, P. (2014). *Making our Connections: the spirituality of travel*. London: SCM Press.

Dandelion, P. (2017). 'The Layered Theoscape of Philadelphia: the Quaker experiment as a religious crucible', in Nelson, E. and Wright, J. (eds), *Layered Landscapes: early modern religious space across faith and cultures*. London: Routledge, pp. 150–166.

Dandelion, P. and Cooksey, E. (2010). 'Transitioning or Not? Why some groups accommodate to the world and others do not: a case study of Amish and Quaker trajectories'. Paper presented at the British Sociological Association Sociology of Religion Study Group Conference, University of Edinburgh.

Dandelion, P. and Martin, F. (2013). '"Outcasts of Israel": the apocalyptic theology of Edward Burrough and Francis Howgill', in Angell, S. W. and Dandelion, P. (eds), *Early Quakers and their Theological Thought*. Cambridge: Cambridge University Press, pp. 118–136.

Davie, G. (1994). *Religion in Britain since 1945: believing without belonging*. Oxford: Blackwell.

Davie, G. (2007). 'Vicarious religion: a methodological challenge', in Ammerman, N. (ed.), *Everyday Religion: observing modern religious lives*. Oxford: Oxford University Press, pp. 21–36.

Davie, G. (2015). *Religion in Britain: a persistent paradox*. London: Wiley-Blackwell.

Davie, M. (1997). *British Quaker theology since 1895*. Lampeter: Edwin Mellen.

Davies, A. (1988). 'Talking in Silence: ministry in Quaker Meetings', in Coupland, N. (ed.), *Styles of Discourse*. London: Croom-Helm, pp. 105–137.

Davies, A. (2000). *The Quakers in English Society, 1655–1725*. Oxford: Clarendon Press.

Day, A. (2011). *Believing in Belonging: belief and social identity in the modern world*. Oxford: Oxford University Press.

De Certeau, M. (1984). *The Practice of Everyday Life* (trans. S. Rendell). Berkeley: University of California Press.

De Vries, H. (2006). 'Introduction: before, around and beyond the theologico-political', in de Vries, H. and Sullivan, L. E. (eds), *Political Theologies: public religions in a post-secular world*. New York: Fordham University Press, pp. 1–90.

Dewsbury, W. (1655). *A True Prophecy of the Mighty Day of the Lord*. London: Giles Calvert.

Dixon, S. (2007). 'Quakers and the London Parish 1670–1720'. *The London Journal* 32, pp. 229–249.

Dobbelaere, K. (2002). *Secularization: an analysis at three levels*. Brussels: P. I. E.-Peter Lang.

Dressler, M. (2011). 'Making Religion through Secularist Legal Discourse: the case of Turkish Alevism', in Dressler, M. and Mandair, A-P. S. (eds), *Secularism and Religion-Making*. New York: Oxford University Press, 187–208.

Eisenstadt, P. R. (2005). *The Encyclopedia of New York State*. Syracuse, NY: University of Syracuse Press.

Endelman, T. M. (2015). *Leaving the Fold: conversion and radical assimilation in modern Jewish history*. Princeton, NJ: Princeton University Press.

Erbery, W. (1658). *The Testimony of William Erbery*. London: Giles Calvert.

Fell, M. (1655). *An Epistle to Friends*. London.

Fenn, R. (1978). *Towards a Theory of Secularization*. Storrs, CT: Society for the Scientific Study of Religion.

Finke, R. (1997). 'The Consequences of Religious Competition: supply-side explanations for religious change', in Young, L. A. (ed.), *Rational Choice Theory and Religion*. London: Routledge, pp. 45–65.

Flory, R. and Miller, D. (2008). *Finding faith: the spiritual quest of the post-boomer generation*. New Brunswick, NJ: Rutgers University Press.

Foucault, M. (1986). 'Of Other Spaces'. *Diacritics. A Review of Contemporary Criticism* 16, pp. 22–27.

Fox, G. (1653). *To All That Would Know the Way to the Kingdom*, n.p.

Fox, G. (1831a [1676]). 'Concerning the First Spreading of the Truth, and How that Many were Imprisoned, &c', in Whitehead, George (ed.), *A Collection of Many Select and Christian Epistles, Letters and Testimonies, Written on Sundry Occasions, by that Ancient, Eminent, Faithful Friend and Minister of Christ Jesus, George Fox*, 2 vols. Philadelphia andNew York: Marcus Gould and Isaac Hopper, pp. 10–16.

Fox, G. (1831b [1676]). 'To Friends at Dantzic'. Epistle 336 in Whitehead, G. (ed.), *A Collection of Many Select and Christian Epistles, Letters and Testimonies, Written on Sundry Occasions, by that Ancient, Eminent, Faithful Friend and Minister of Christ Jesus, George Fox*, 2 vols. Philadelphia andNew York: Marcus Gould and Isaac Hopper, pp. 127–128.

Frost, J. W. (1973). *The Quaker Family in Colonial America: a portrait of the Society of Friends*. New York: St Martin's Press.

Frost, J. W. (1990). *A Perfect Freedom: religious liberty in Pennsylvania*. Cambridge: Cambridge University Press.

Fulton, J., Abela, A. M., Borowik, I., Dowling, T., Marler, P. L. and Tomasi, L. (eds) (2000). *Young Catholics at the New Millennium: the religion and morality of young adults in western countries*. Dublin: University College Dublin Press.

Furseth, I. and Repstad, P. (2006). *An Introduction to the Sociology of Religion*. Aldershot: Ashgate.

Gerth, H. H. and Mills, C. W. (eds and trans.) (1946). *From Max Weber: essays in sociology*. New York: Oxford University Press.

Giles, H. (1973). 'Accent Mobility: a model and some data'. *Anthropological Linguistics* 15, pp. 87–105.

Giles, H. and Bourhis, R. Y. (1976). 'Black speakers with White Speech – a real problem?' in Nickel, G. (ed.), *The Proceedings of the 4th International Congress on Applied Linguistics*, Vol. 1. Stuttgart: Hochshul Verlag, pp. 575–584.

Giles, H. and Powesland, P. F. (1975). *Speech Style and Social Evaluation*. London: Academic Press.

Giles, H., Coupland, J. and Coupland, N. (1991). 'Accommodation Theory: communication, context and consequence', in Giles, H., Coupland, J. and Coupland, N. (eds), *Contexts of Accommodation: developments in applied sociolinguistics*. Cambridge: Cambridge University Press, pp. 1–68.

Gleick, J. (1988). *Chaos*. London: Penguin.

Goldstein, W. S. (2009a). 'Patterns of Secularization and Religious Rationalization in Emile Durkheim and Max Weber'. *Implicit Religion* 12, pp. 135–163.

Goldstein, W. S. (2009b). 'Secularization Patterns in the Old Paradigm'. *Sociology of Religion* 70, pp. 157–178.

Grant, R. (2018). *British Quakers and Religious Language*. Leiden: Brill.

Gross, E. and Etzioni, A. (1985). *Organizations in Society*. Englewood Cliffs, NJ: Prentice-Hall.

Gwyn, D. (1995). *The Covenant Crucified: Quakers and the rise of capitalism*. Wallingford, PA: Pendle Hill Publications.

Gwyn, D. (2000). *Seekers Found: atonement in early Quaker experience*. Wallingford, PA: Pendle Hill Publications.

Gwyn, D. (2016). *The Anti-War: peace finds the purpose of a peculiar people*. San Francisco, CA: Inner Light Books.

Habermas, J. (2006). 'Religion in the Public Sphere'. *European Journal of Philosophy* 14, pp. 1–25.

Hamm, T. D. (1988). *The transformation of American Quakerism: Orthodox Friends, 1800–1907*. Bloomington, IN: Indiana University Press.

Hampton, J. M. (2014). 'British Quaker Survey: examining religious beliefs and practices in the twenty-first century'. *Quaker Studies* 19, pp. 7–136.

Handrick, F. (2016). 'Using Bauman's Theory of Liquid Modernity to Understand Changes in the Lives of Amish Women'. Paper presented at the Conference of the International Association for the Study of Religion and Gender, Turin, November.

Handrick, F. (2017). 'The Amish in Transition: how old edges become new centres'. Paper presented at the British Sociological Association Sociology of Religion Study Group Conference, Leeds, June.

Healey, R. R. (2006). *From Quaker to Upper Canadian: faith and community among Yonge Street Friends, 1801–1850*. Montreal andKingston: McGill-Queen's University Press.

Heelas, P. and Woodhead, L. (2005). *The Spiritual Revolution: why religion is giving way to spirituality*. Oxford: Blackwell.

Helier, A. L. (2017). 'Publishing Persecution: How the early Quakers chose to challenge the authorities in the public arena'. Paper presented at the 'Jews and Quakers: on the borders of acceptability' Conference, Brighton, December.

Herberg, W. (1967). 'Religion in a Secularized Society', in Brothers, J. (ed.), *Readings in the Sociology of Religion*. Oxford: Pergamon, pp. 201–216.

Heron, A. (1992). *Caring, Conviction, Commitment: dilemmas of Quaker membership today*. London: Quaker Home Service.

Hervieu-Léger, D. (2000). *Religion as a Chain of Memory*. Cambridge: Polity Press.

Hetherington, K. (1996). *Expressions of Identity: space, performance, politics*. London: Sage.

Hetherington, K. (1997). *The Badlands of Modernity: heterotopia and social ordering*. London and New York: Routledge.

Homan, R. (2006a). *The Art of the Sublime*. Aldershot: Ashgate.

Homan, R. (2006b). 'The Aesthetics of Friends' Meeting Houses'. *Quaker Studies* 11, pp. 115–128.

Howgill, F. (1676 [1659]). 'How all Men upon the Earth, in the Degeneration, and in the Fall, and in the Transgression, Have Corrupted Themselves, & Have Been idolaters in Every Administration; (being gone from the Power) in which man had the ability, power, and wisdom to worship God aright, and honour the living God of heaven and earth', in Hooks, E. (ed.), *The Dawnings of the Gospel-day and Its Light and Glory Discover(ed.) (A True Relation of the Tryals, Sufferings and Death of F. H., Etc.)*, pp. 196–211.

Howgill, F. (1676 [1665]). 'The Glory of the True Church of God Discovered', in Hooks, E. (ed.), *The Dawnings of the Gospel-day and Its Light and Glory Discover(ed.) (A True Relation of the Tryals, Sufferings and Death of F. H., Etc.)*, pp. 401–497.

Huber, K. (2001). 'The Spirituality of Buddhist Quakers in Britain'. Unpublished MPhil thesis, University of Sunderland.

Hughes, W. F. and Brighton, J. A. (1999). *Fluid Dynamics*. Third edition. New York: McGraw-Hill.

Hunt, J. C. R., Wray A. A. and Moin, P. (1988). 'Eddies, Streams and Convergence Zones in Turbulent Flows'. https://ntrs.nasa.gov/archive/nasa/casi.ntrs.nasa.gov/19890015184.pdf, accessed 16/10/16.

Hussain, A. K. M. F. (1986). 'Coherent Structures and Turbulence'. *Journal of Fluid Mechanics* 173, pp. 303–356.

Isambert, F-A. (1976). 'La sécularisation interne du christianisme'. *Revue Française de Sociologie* 17, pp. 573–589.

Isichei, E. (1967). 'From Sect to Denomination among English Quakers', in Wilson, B. R. (ed.), *Patterns of Sectarianism: organisation and ideology in social and religious movements*, London: Heinemann, pp. 161–181.

Isichei, E. (1970). *Victorian Quakers*. Oxford: Oxford University Press.

Johnson, B. (1971). 'Church and Sect Revisited'. *Journal for the Scientific Study of Religion* 10, pp. 124–137.

Jones, R. M. (1921). *The Later Periods of Quakerism*, 2 Vols. London: Macmillan.

Kanter, R. M. (1972). *Commitment & Community: communes and utopias in sociological perspective*. Cambridge, MA: Harvard University Press.

Kashatus, W. C.III (1990). *Conflict of conviction: a reappraisal of Quaker involvement in the American revolution*. Lanham MD: University Press of America.

Kelley, D. M. (1972). *Why Conservative Churches are Growing*. New York: Harper & Row.

Kelley, D. M. (1978). 'Why Conservative Churches Are Still Growing'. *Journal for the Scientific Study of Religion* 17, pp. 165–172.

Kelly, T. (1944). *The Gathered Meeting*. London: Friends Home Service Committee.

Kennedy, T. C. (1989). '"Why did Friends Resist?" The war, the peace testimony and the All-Friends Conference of 1920'. *Peace and Change* 14, pp. 355–371.

Kennedy, T. C. (2001). *British Quakerism 1860–1920: the transformation of a religious community*. Oxford: Oxford University Press.

Kershner, J. R. (2018). *John Woolman and the Government of Christ: a colonial Quaker's vision for the British Atlantic world*. Oxford: Oxford University Press.

Knott, K. (2005). *The Location of Religion: a spatial analysis*. London: Equinox Publishing.

Knox, J. S. (2016). *Sacro-Egoism: the rise of religious individualism in the west*. Eugene, OR: Wipf and Stock.

Kuper, A. (1971). 'Council Structure and Decision-making' in Richards, A. and Kuper, A. (eds), *Councils in Action*. Cambridge: Cambridge University Press, pp. 13–28.

Laud, W. (1839 [1639]). *A Relation of the Conference between William Laud, Late Lord Archbishop of Canterbury and Mr. Fisher the Jesuit; by the command of King James of ever blessed memory; with an answer to such exceptions as A. C. takes against it*. Oxford: Oxford University.

Lefebvre, H. (1991). *The Production of Space*. Oxford: Blackwell.

Leigh-Schmidt, E. (2005). *Restless Souls: the making of American spirituality*. San Francisco, CA: HarperSanFrancisco.

Leth-Nissen, K. M. (2018). *Churching Alone: a study of the Danish Folk Church at organisational, individual, and societal levels*. First edition. Copenhagen: Det teologiske Fakultet. Publikationer fra Det Teologiske Fakultet, No. 79.

Levine, D. (ed.) (1971). *Georg Simmel on Individuality and Social Forms*. Chicago, IL: University of Chicago Press.

Levy, B. (1988). *Quakers and the American Family: British settlement in the Delaware Valley*. New York: Oxford University Press.

Lichterman, P. (2013). 'Studying Public Religion: beyond the beliefs-driven actor', in Bender, C., Cadge, W., Levitt, P. and Smilde, D. (eds), *Religion on the Edge: de-centering and re-centering the sociology of religion*. New York: Oxford University Press, pp. 115–136.

London Yearly Meeting (1883). *Book of Christian Discipline of the Religious Society of Friends in Great Britain; consisting of extracts on doctrine, practice and church government, from the epistles and other documents issued under the sanction of the yearly meeting held in London from its first institution in 1672 to the year 1883*. London: Samuel Harris.

London Yearly Meeting (1911). *Christian Discipline of the Society of Friends, Part II: Christian Practice*. London: Headley.

Luckmann, T. (1967). *The Invisible Religion: the problem of religion in modern society*. London: Macmillan.

Lunn, P. (1997). '"You Have Lost Your Opportunity": British Quakers and the militant phase of the women's suffrage campaign: 1906–1914'. *Quaker Studies* 2, pp. 30–55.

Lunn, P. (2008). '"Do We Still Quake?": an ethnographic and historical enquiry'. *Quaker Studies* 12, pp. 216–229.

Maguire, M. (2008). *Lived Religion: faith and practice in everyday life*. Oxford: Oxford University Press.

Mahmood, S. (2006). 'Secularism, Hermeneutics, and Empire: the politics of Islamic reformation'. *Public Culture* 18: pp. 323–348.

Mahmood, S. (2010). 'Can Secularism be Other-wise?', in Warner, M., Vanantwerpen, J. and Calhoun, C. (eds). *Varieties of Secularism in a Secular Age.* Cambridge, MA: Harvard University Press, pp. 282–299.

Mahmood, S. (2012). 'Religious Freedom, the Minority Question, and Geopolitics in the Middle East'. *Comparative Studies in Society and History,* 54, pp. 418–446.

Mahmood, S. (2016). *Religious Difference in a Secular Age.* Princeton, NJ: Princeton University Press.

Mandair, A-P. S. and Dressler, M. (2011). 'Introduction: Modernity, Religion-Making and the Postsecular', in Dressler, M. and Mandair, A-P. S. (eds), *Secularism and Religion-Making.* New York: Oxford University Press, pp. 3–36.

Marietta, J. D. (1984). *The Reformation of American Quakerism, 1748–1783.* Philadelphia, PA: University of Pennsylvania Press.

Martin, D. (1962). 'The Denomination'. *British Journal of Sociology* 13, pp. 1-14.

Martin, D. (1978). *A General Theory of Secularization.* Oxford: Basil Blackwell.

Massey, D. (2005). *For Space.* London: Sage.

Mauss, A. L. (1994). *The Angel and the Beehive: the Mormon struggle with assimilation.* Urbana, IL: University of Illinois Press.

Meads, H. C. (2011). '"Experiment with Light" in Britain: the heterotopian nature of contemporary Quaker spiritual practice'. Unpublished PhD thesis, University of Birmingham.

Mendl, W. (1974). *Prophets and Reconcilers: reflections on the Quaker peace testimony.* London: Friends Home Service Committee.

Montemaggi, F. E. S. (2018). *The Changing Face of Faith: how should Quakers respond?* London: Quaker Committee on Christian and Interfaith Relations.

Moore, R. (2000). *The Light in their Consciences: the early Quakers in Britain 1646–1666.* University Park, PA: Penn State University Press.

Muers, R. (2015). *Testimony: Quakerism and theological ethics.* London: SCM.

Mullett, M. (1984). 'From Sect to Denomination: social developments in eighteenth century English Quakers'. *Journal of Religious History* 13, pp. 168–191.

Mytton, J. (2008). 'On Being Raised in and Leaving the Exclusive Brethren: resonances in adulthood'. Paper presented at the Centre for Studies on New Religions (CESNUR) Conference, London.

Nickalls, J. L. (ed.) (1952). *The Journal of George Fox.* Cambridge: Cambridge University Press.

Niebuhr, H. R. (1975 [1929]). *The Social Sources of Denominationalism.* New York: New American Library.

O'Flynn, S. (2018). 'What Cans't Friends say in Ireland in the Twenty-first Century'. Paper delivered at Ireland Yearly Meeting, Limerick, July.

Parsons, T. (1971). 'Belief, Unbelief and Disbelief', in Caporale, R. and Grumelli, A. (eds), *The Culture of Unbelief: studies and proceedings from the First International Symposium on Unbelief held at Rome, March 22–17, 1969.* Berkeley, CA: University of California Press, pp. 207–245.

Patterns of Membership. (2018). London: Britain Yearly Meeting.

Penn, W. (1825). *Complete Works in Three Volumes.* London: William Phillips.

Pfautz, H. (1955–56). 'The Sociology of Secularization: religious groups'. *The American Journal of Sociology* 61, pp. 121–128.

Pfautz, H. (1956). 'Christian Science: a case study of the social psychological aspect of secularization'. *Social Forces* 34, pp. 246–251.

Phillips, B. (1989). 'Friendly patriotism: British Quakerism and the imperial nation 1890–1910'. Unpublished PhD thesis, University of Cambridge.

Phillips, B. (2004). 'Apocalypse without Tears: hybris and folly among late Victorian and Edwardian British Friends', in Dandelion, P., Gwyn, D., Muers, R. E., Phillips, B. D. and Sturm, R. E. (eds), *Towards Tragedy/Reclaiming Hope: literature, theology, and sociology in conversation*. Aldershot: Ashgate, pp. 57–76.

Pickard, D. (1864). *An Expostulation on Behalf of the Truth, against Departures in Doctrine, Practice, and Discipline: in which the revised queries, rules, and advices of London Yearly Meeting of Friends, are examined and compared with former editions.* London: A. W. Bennett.

Pilgrim, G. (2003). 'The Quakers: towards an alternate ordering', in Davie, G., Heelas, P. and Woodhead, L. (eds), *Predicting Religion: Christian, secular and alternative futures.* Aldershot: Ashgate, pp. 147–158.

Pilgrim, G. (2008). 'British Quakers as Heterotopic', in Dandelion, P and Collins, P. (eds), *The Quaker Condition: the sociology of a liberal religion.* Newcastle: Cambridge Scholars Publishing, pp. 53–69.

Plüss, C. (1995). 'A Sociological Analysis of the Modern Quaker Movement'. Unpublished DPhil thesis, University of Oxford.

Plüss, C. (2007). 'Analysing Non-doctrinal Socialization: re-assessing the role of cognition to account for social cohesion in the Religious Society of Friends'. *British Journal of Sociology* 58, pp. 253–278.

Plymouth Brethren (2015). http://theplymouthbrethren.org.uk/beliefs/faith-in-practice//, accessed 25/9/18.

Pointon, M. (1997). 'Quakerism and Visual Culture 1650–1800'. *Art History* 20, pp. 397–431.

Polder, K. (2015). *Matrimony in the True Church: the seventeenth-century marriage approbation discipline.* Farnham: Ashgate.

Pope, L. (1942). *Millhands and Preachers.* New Haven, CT: Yale University Press.

Punshon, J. (1989). *Letter to a Universalist.* Pendle Hill Pamphlet 285. Wallingford, PA: Pendle Hill Publications.

Punshon, J. (1990). *Testimony and Tradition: some aspects of Quaker spirituality.* London: Quaker Home Service.

PutnamR. D. (2000). *Bowling Alone: the collapse and revival of American community.* New York: Simon & Schuster.

Quaker Faith and Practice: the book of Christian discipline (1995). London: Britain Yearly Meeting.

Read, M. J. (2017). 'Quakers in the Contemporary Workplace: a critical analysis'. Unpublished PhD thesis, University of Birmingham.

Reay, B. (1985). *The Quakers and the English Revolution.* London: Temple Smith.

Repstad, P. (2014). 'When Religions of Difference Grow Softer', in Vincett, G., Obinna, E., Olson, E. and Adogame, A. (eds), *Christianity in the Modern World: changes and controversies.* Farnham: Ashgate, pp. 157–174.

Rickles, D., Hawe, P. and Shiell, A. (2007). 'A Simple Guide to Chaos and Complexity'. *Journal of Epidemiology and Community Health* 61, pp. 933–937.

Robertson, R. (1967). 'The Salvation Army: the persistence of sectarianism', in Wilson, B. R. (ed.), *Patterns of Sectarianism: organisation and ideology in social and religious movements.* London: Heinemann, pp. 49–105.

Robinson, J. A. T. (1963). *Honest to God.* London: SCM Press.

Roof, W. C. (1993). *A Generation of Seekers: the spiritual journeys of the baby-boom generation.* San Francisco, CA: HarperCollins.

Roof, W. C. (1996). 'God is in the Details: reflections on religion's public presence in the United States in the mid-1990s'. *Sociology of Religion* 57, pp. 149–162.

Roof, W. C. (1999). *Spiritual Marketplace: baby boomers and the remaking of American religion*. Princeton, NJ: Princeton University Press.

Roof, W. C. (2003). 'Religion and Spirituality: towards an integrated analysis', in Dillon, M. (ed.), *Handbook of the Sociology of Religion*. Cambridge: Cambridge University Press, pp. 137–150.

Rumball, H. F. (2016). 'The Relinquishment of Plain Dress: British Quaker women's abandonment of plain Quaker attire, 1860–1914'. Unpublished PhD thesis, University of Brighton.

Rush, D. (2002). 'They too are Quakers: a survey of 199 nontheist Friends'. *Woodbrooke Journal* 10, pp. 1–28.

Russell, J. M. (2015). 'Negotiating the Flow: an ethnographic study of the way two URC congregations shape and are shaped by members'. Unpublished PhD thesis, University of Birmingham.

Scott, J. (1980). *What canst thou say? Towards a Quaker theology*. London: Quaker Home Service.

Scully, J. L. (2008). 'Virtuous Friends: morality and Quaker identity', in Dandelion, P. and Collins, P. (eds), *The Quaker condition: the sociology of a liberal religion*. Newcastle: Cambridge Scholars Publishing, pp. 107–123.

Stanek, L. (2011). *Henri Lefebvre on Space: architecture, urban research, and the production of theory*. Minneapolis, MN: University of Minnesota Press.

Stark, R. and Iannaccone, L. (1994). 'A Supply-Side Explanation for the Secularisation of Europe'. *Journal for the Scientific Study of Religion* 33, pp. 230–252.

Stauffer, R. E. (1973). 'Church Members' Ignorance of Doctrinal Pluralism: a probable source of church cohesion'. *Journal for the Scientific Study of Religion* 12, pp. 345–348.

Swatos, W. H.Jr. (1975). 'Monopolism, Pluralism, Acceptance, and Rejection: an integrated model for church-sect theory'. *Review of Religious Research* 16, pp. 174–185.

Swatos, W. H.Jr. (1981). 'Church-Sect and Cult'. *Sociological Analysis* 42, pp. 17–26.

Taber, F. I. (1992). 'Paradoxical Understandings to hold in Creative Tension'. *Friends Journal* 38/7, p. 15.

Tarter, M. L. (2001). 'Quaking in the Light: the politics of Quaker women's corporeal prophecy in the seventeenth-century transatlantic world', in Lindman, J. M. and Tarter, M. L. (eds), *A Centre of Wonders: the body in early America*. Ithaca, NY: Cornell University Press, pp. 145–162.

Taylor, C. (2007). *A Secular Age*. Cambridge, MA: Harvard University Press.

Toennies, F., Simmel, G., Troeltsch, E. and Weber, M. (1973). 'Max Weber on Church, Sect, and Mysticism'. *Sociological Analysis* 34, pp. 140–149.

Tolles, F. B. (1948). *Meeting House and Counting House: the Quaker merchants of colonial Philadelphia 1682–1763*. Chapel Hill, NC: University of North Carolina Press.

Tousley, N. C. (2008). 'The Experience of Regeneration and Erosion of Certainty in the Theology of Second-generation Quakers: no place for doubt?'. *Quaker Studies* 13, pp. 6–88.

Towler, R. (1984). *The Need for Certainty*. London: Routledge & Kegan Paul.

Troeltsch, E. (1931 [1911]). *The Social Teaching of the Christian Church* (trans. O. Wyon), 2 Vols. London: George Allen & Unwin.

Tschannen, O. (1991). 'The Secularization Paradigm: a systematization'. *Journal for the Scientific Study of Religion* 30, pp. 395–415.

Turner, R. and Killian, L. (1957). *Collective Behavior*. Englewood Cliffs, NJ: Prentice-Hall.

Tweed, T. (2006). *Crossing and Dwelling: a theory of religion*. Cambridge, MA: Harvard University Press.

Tweed, T. (2011). 'Theory and Method in the Study of Buddhism: toward "transloca-tive" analysis'. *Journal of Global Buddhism* 12, pp. 17–32.

Vann, R. T. (1969). *The Social Development of English Quakerism, 1655–1755*. Cambridge, MA: Harvard University Press.

Vincett, G. (2008). 'Quagans: fusing Quakerism with contemporary Paganism', in Dandelion, P. and Collins, P. (eds), *The Quaker condition: the sociology of a liberal religion*. Newcastle: Cambridge Scholars Publishing, pp. 174–191.

Vincett, G., Olson, E., Hopkins, P. and Pain, R. (2012). 'Young People and Performance Christianity in Scotland'. *Journal of Contemporary Religion* 27, pp. 275–290.

Voas, D. (2003). 'Intermarriage and the Demography of Secularization'. *British Journal of Sociology* 54, pp. 83–108.

Voas, D. (2009). 'The Rise and Fall of Fuzzy Fidelity in Europe'. *European Sociological Review* 25, pp. 155–168.

Voas, D. and Chaves, M. (2016). 'Is the United States a Counterexample to the Secularization Thesis?'. *American Journal of Sociology* 121, pp. 1517–1556.

Voas, D. and Crockett, A. (2005). 'Religion in Britain: neither believing nor belonging'. *Sociology* 39, pp. 11–28.

Wallis, R. (1984). *The Elementary Forms of the New Religious Life*. London: Routledge & Kegan Paul.

Walliss, J. (2007). *The Brahma Kumaris as a 'Reflexive Tradition': responding to late modernity*. Delhi: Motilal Banarsidass.

Walvin, J. (1997). *Quakers: money and morals*. London: John Murray.

Waugh, E. (1997[1945]). *Brideshead Revisited: the sacred and profane memories of Captain Charles Ryder*. London: The Folio Society.

Weber, M. (2011 [1904–1905]). *The Protestant Ethic and the Spirit of Capitalism* (trans., with commentary, S. Kalberg). Oxford: Oxford University Press.

Weddle, M. B. (2001). *Walking in the Way of Peace: Quaker pacifism in the seventeenth century*. New York and Oxford: Oxford University Press.

Welsh, A. M. with Holiday, J. (2008). *Held in the Light: Norman Morrison's sacrifice for peace and his family's journey of healing*. Maryknoll, NY: Orbis.

Wilson, B. R. (1959). 'An Analysis of Sect Development'. *American Sociological Review* 24, pp. 3–15.

Wilson, B. R. (ed.) (1967a). *Patterns of Sectarianism: organisation and ideology in social and religious movements*. London: Heinemann.

Wilson, B. R. (1967b). 'The Exclusive Brethren', in Wilson, B. R. (ed.), *Patterns of Sectarianism: organisation and ideology in social and religious movements*. London: Heinemann, pp. 287–342.

Wilson, B. R. (1970). *Religious Sects*. London: Weidenfeld & Nicolson.

Wilson, B. R. (2016 [1966]) *Religion in Secular Society: fifty years on*. Oxford: Oxford University Press.

Wood, H. G. (1927). 'The Functions of the Society of Friends with Regard to Social and Industrial Questions'. *Friends Quarterly Examiner* 244, pp. 265–291.

Wood, R. E. (1978). 'The Rise of Semi-Structured Worship and Paid Pastoral Leadership among "Gurneyite" Friends 1850–1900', in Hall, F. B. (ed.), *Quaker Worship in North America*. Richmond, IN: Friends United Press, pp. 53–74.

Woodhead, L. (2013). 'Tactical and Strategic Religion', in Dessing, N., Jeldtoft, N., Nielsen, J. S. and Woodhead, L. (eds), *Everyday Lived Islam in Europe*. Farnham: Ashgate, pp. 9–22.

Woodhead, L. (2016). 'Intensified Religious Pluralism and De-differentiation: the British example'. *Society* 53, pp. 41–46.

Yarlett, S. (2018). 'The Reopening of the Liberal Quaker Theological Discourse: views emerging from the theism-nontheism debate'. Paper presented at the Society for the Study of Theology Conference.

Yinger, J. M. (1970). *The Scientific Study of Religion*. New York: Macmillan.

Yum, J. O. (1988). 'The Impact of Confucianism on Interpersonal Relationships and Communication Patterns in East Asia'. *Communication Monographs* 55, 374–388.

Zemaitis, D. S. (2012). 'Convergent paths: the correspondence between Wycliffe, Hus and the early Quakers'. Unpublished PhD thesis, University of Birmingham.

Zielinski, S. (1975). *Psychology and Silence*. Pendle Hill Pamphlet 210. Wallingford, PA: Pendle Hill Publications.

INDEX

absolute perhaps 82, 128, 130, 153
accent convergence 150
accent mobility 150
acceptance 26
accommodation 135, 151, 155;
    communication 155; faith 153;
    mutual 152; patterns of 151, 153;
    theory 149–50
accurate convergence 151
activism 140
'activist' groups 27
Act of Toleration in 1689 3
affiliation 153
Affirmation Act in 1694 3
Amish religiosity 113
anti-war 90
Apology (Barclay) 61
Appadurai, A. 105, 143
Asad, T. 38, 42, 137
assimilation 95–6, 111; levels of 98;
    'official response' to 97; patterns of 98;
    resistance and 76
autonomisation 32–3, 144
avoidance sects 17, 79

backflow, model of 111
Barclay, R. 59, 61–2
Barnard, H. 87
Bauman, R. 80
Bauman, Z. 105–6, 129–30
Beaconites 4
Becker, H. 17
Beckford, J. 27

behavioural creed 117, **123**, 128; concept
    of 82; conformity and 121–2;
    individual and 124
behaviours, and practices 55
belief-centred religion 160
beliefs 5, 153, 158; and aspirations 153;
    central core of 127; Christian 142;
    claims 117; clusters 130; collective
    affirmation of 121; content 123–4, 128;
    diversity of 120; forms and 139; in
    God 138; individual 126; in innovative
    ways 154; and language 145;
    marginalisation of 120; non-doctrinal
    religion as 129; normative mode of
    128; patterns of 117; permissive
    approach to 122; personal and
    collective 146; pluralisation of 124–5;
    religious 125; statements 154; surveys
    of 161; traditional doctrinal 160;
    transmission 130
belief stories 128; privatisation of 129–30
believers 124
Bellah, R. 143, 157
Benezet, A. 65–6
Berger, P. 26, 46, 140
Berger, P. L. 147
Bibby, R. W. 44
biblical criticism, enthusiasm for 118
Birkel, M. 74
Bright, J. 88
Brighton, J. A. 100
Brinkerhoff, M. B. 44
Britain Yearly Meeting 149, 153